CANADA

Fraser R.

Victoria
Puget Sound
Olympic Penin.
Seattle
WASH.
Mt. Rainier 14,410
Columbia River
Mt. Hood 11,245
Portland
Willamette River
OREGON
Crater Lake

MONTANA

IDAHO

Snake River

WYOMING

Great Salt Lake

UTAH

COLORADO

NEW MEXICO

Coos Bay
CAPE BLANCO

COAST
CASCADES

Mt. Shasta 14,162

Eel River
CAPE MENDOCINO

SIERRA NEVADA

NEVADA

Lake Tahoe

Mt. Whitney 14,495

Colorado R.

ARIZONA

Sacramento
POINT REYES
San Francisco
Santa Cruz
Carmel

RANGE

CALIFORNIA

San Jacinto 10,831
Transverse Ranges

MEXICO

POINT CONCEPTION
Santa Barbara
Los Angeles
CHANNEL ISLANDS
San Diego
Tijuana

SIERRA SAN PEDRO MÁRTIR

Gulf of California

OCEAN

I. GUADALUPE
Bahía de Sebastián Vizcaíno
I. CEDROS
PUNTA EUGENIA

CABO SAN LUCAS

NF

0	200	400	600

SCALE IN MILES

EDGE OF A CONTINENT

The Pacific Coast from Alaska to Baja

EDGE OF A

CONTINENT

The Pacific Coast from Alaska to Baja

By DON GREAME KELLEY

With a foreword by Robert C. Miller

AMERICAN WEST PUBLISHING COMPANY

PALO ALTO, CALIFORNIA

THE EDGE OF THE CONTINENT, this Pacific edge, is just an irregular line on a map — until one sees it himself and discovers that it is color and motion and form, now one, now another, now all combined — varied, changing, infinite.

. . . Form of mountains, clouds, and shoreline: snow-clad ranges of Vancouver Island (PRECEDING PAGE, TOP) *and the gentle seaward sloping of California's San Luis Range* (BOTTOM).

. . . Motion of surf and powerful swimmers: Steller sea lions on the Northern California coast (AT LEFT).

. . . Color of flame at sunset: sea-fig with red leaves in spring, on the Monterey Peninsula (FOLLOWING PAGES).

5

THE LONG CURVING SHORE

. . . from the snow-capped mountains of the north to the warm Pacific seascapes of the south.

Shore birds alighting at the edge of the surf.

This book is lovingly dedicated to

M A R K   T R A C Y   K E L L E Y

Airman, United States Navy

[1945-1967]

who loved the sea, the shore, the mountains,

and all wild places

Library of Congress Card Number 78-119004

ISBN 0-910118-19-1

CONTENTS

PASSAGES from the following books have been reprinted by permission: *Bent's Life Histories of North American Birds* edited by Henry Hill Collins, Jr., vol. 1 (New York: Harper & Brothers, 1960). *Black Robes in Lower California* by Peter Masten Dunne (Berkeley & Los Angeles: University of California Press, 1952; permission granted by The Regents of the University of California). *The California Coast: A Bilingual Edition of Documents from the Sutro Collection* reedited by Donald C. Cutter (Norman: University of Oklahoma Press, new edition copyright 1969). *Edge of the Sea* by Rachel Carson (Boston: Houghton Mifflin Company, 1955). *The Evolution of North America* by Philip B. King (Princeton, N.J.: Princeton University Press, 1959). *Font's Complete Diary of the Second Anza Expedition*, translated and edited by Herbert Eugene Bolton. Anza's California Expeditions, vol. 4. (Berkeley & Los Angeles: University of California Press, 1931; permission granted by The Regents of the University of California). *The Forgotten Peninsula: A Naturalist in Baja California* by Joseph Wood Krutch (New York: William Sloane Associates, 1961). *Historical Memoirs of New California* by Fray Francisco Palóu, edited by Herbert Eugene Bolton (Berkeley & Los Angeles: University of California Press, 1926; permission granted by The Regents of the University of California). *Journey of the Flame* by Antonio de Fierro Blanco (New York: Brandt & Brandt, 1933). *The Last of the Conquistadors: Junípero Serra (1713–1784)* by Omer Englebert (New York: Harcourt Brace & Co., 1956). *The North American Deserts* by Edmund C. Jaeger (Stanford, Calif.: Stanford University Press, 1957). *Travels in Alaska* by John Muir (Boston: Houghton Mifflin Company, 1915).

FOREWORD

THERE ARE MEN who love the desert, men who love well-watered lands; men who love the mountains, men who love the sea. There are those who wish to explore the world as it is today, and those who wish to study the evidence of ages past, to learn of how the present came to be. This is a book that deals with all of these; it has an interest for every possible reader.

The author has achieved something that all authors aspire to but which few attain — to have found a new subject and to have treated it in a distinguished way. There have been scores, perhaps even hundreds, of books on the Pacific Coast of North America. It remained for one author to write *Edge of a Continent*, and to write it in a way that every reader will appreciate and enjoy.

Don Kelley not only has found a unique subject, but has approached it in a highly original way — first with a sweeping overview of four thousand miles of coastline, from the Aleutian Islands to Baja California, as one might see it from the air; then a closer view, as if one were to retrace his journey in the leisurely way of a naturalist-explorer to obtain a more intimate knowledge of the sea and shore. The book deals with almost every conceivable facet of its subject — geography, geology, oceanography, meteorology; forests, deserts, islands and inlets, tidepools; shore birds, marine birds and mammals, fishes of particular interest; the coming of early man, then the Conquistadores, and at last ourselves — the impact of civilization on the delicate balance of the environment.

This immense amount and variety of subject matter is well organized and ably presented. It is written with the enthusiasm of an author thoroughly in love with the area of which he writes, eager to impart to others the interest and beauty he has found on the shore of our western sea.

Don Greame Kelley was born and raised on the Pacific Coast. A lifelong student of the out-of-doors, he began writing for publication while still in his teens. As the first editor of *Pacific Discovery* (magazine of the California Academy of Sciences), he launched it on its continuing career. In fourteen years at that post, he matured a style of writing that came naturally to him; and surely one cannot critically read hundreds of manuscripts by scores of authors without broadening the scope of his own information.

This is a book to be read, to be enjoyed, to be treasured, to be referred to again and again, because the wealth of information it provides cannot be absorbed in a single reading. It is a book of reference that reads like a novel. It is an unparalleled handbook of the Pacific Coast.

ROBERT C. MILLER, *Senior Scientist*
California Academy of Sciences

PREFACE

SKY AND SEA are universal over the earth. As one watched the clouds on a long flight or voyage, their repertoire seems to change very little; as one walks beaches in Australia and Bermuda and Washington state, one senses that surf is surf everywhere.

But land is different. The edge of any land mass is a collection of very particular objects, from landscapes to seashells. Thus the western coast of North America is a unique piece of geography and at the same time a magnificent example of coastlands in general. Two, three, four books this size would only begin to tell its full story. Yet, I hope that this one is enough to open for many readers the doors to personal discovery. The writing has opened new doors for me, even though I have lived most of my years along the Pacific shore.

A further and very earnest hope is that the book may inspire more people—whether they live on this coast or come to it as visitors—to occupy it with love and respect, and to help protect it from ever increasing threats to its integrity and beauty.

MORE MINDS AND HANDS go into the making of such a book as this than can ever be counted. My first and in some ways greatest debt is to Peter Farb, who suggested this book and shared in the early planning. More recently, Robert C. Miller has taken much time from his own writing to read every word of mine, giving it the critical benefit of his awesomely wide knowledge of the natural world, as well as a generous Foreword. His own recent book, *The Sea*, has both informed and inspired me. I am deeply indebted to him on many counts over more than twenty years.

Enthusiastically and patiently, Elna and Gerhard Bakker have shared knowledge, insight, experience, and source material without stint. The host of other friends who have contributed in countless large and equally needed small ways includes Marjorie and Heath Angelo, Eleanor and the late Charles Borden, Howard Cogswell, George L. Collins, Maud and Erving Easton, William Garnett, Lanphere B. Graff, Joel W. Hedgpeth, the late Robert F. Hoover, Eileen and George Ingram, Kathy Jackson, Estelle and Douglas Kelley, Doris F. Leonard, A. Starker Leopold, George E. Lindsay, Martin Litton, John Macrae, Robert T. Orr, Margaret and Nathaniel Owings, James R. Rideout, Carl Ortwin Sauer, Margery and Arthur Sell, Ward C. Smith, Edwin Way Teale, Ira L. Wiggins, and Samuel A. Wright. And my wife Marion has more than devotedly fulfilled the role of the author's long-suffering spouse; she has quite literally made it possible for me to complete my task.

A great deal of what has gone into this book, especially about the Pacific Ocean, reflects many months of travel and study under a grant (1957–58) from the John Simon Guggenheim Memorial Foundation, to the trustees of which I am also deeply grateful.

Space does not permit listing all the numerous technical sources I have drawn upon: textbooks, journals, reports, manuals. However, many of them are included in the guide to further reading in the back of this book, and I acknowledge indebtedness to every author mentioned. I trust the reader will find these books as rewarding as they have been to me.

PART ONE:

THE LONG CURVING SHORE

The shoreline, as here at Vancouver Island, British Columbia, is an endless succession of curves — great sweeps of coast, small arcs of coves, overlapping fringes of white foam, and the arch of the sky.

CHAPTER 1

A FOUR-THOUSAND-MILE VIEW

*Panorama of the long Pacific shore
from the glaciers of Alaska to the deserts of Baja.*

ASTRONAUTS have seen the whole earth as the rest of us see a globe. When the atmosphere is right over the Western Hemisphere, a great line is visible extending nearly from pole to pole, crooked as a dog's hind leg but unbroken. It is the Pacific coastline of the two Americas. The only solid edge of the largest ocean basin (which itself covers almost a hemisphere), this is the longest, most prominent demarcation line on earth. And it is sharpened by the shadow of adjacent mountains. Our story concerns a little more than a third of this great two-continent coast.

To orient ourselves to the geography of its mountains, rivers, capes, large islands and inlets, and even submarine features indicated by ocean color change, let us imagine ourselves at jet altitude—forty thousand feet—above the sweeping arc of the Pacific Coast. Being airborne is itself a reminder of the atmospheric part of the picture; and clouds drifting across the shoreline or shading the summits of snow peaks far below us signify ocean's gift of water to an always thirsty land.

Take-off is from Dutch Harbor, Unalaska Island, out on the Aleutian chain. Now crossing Unimak Pass, we gain altitude above Unimak Island's symmetrical, fuming Shishaldin volcano, reminder that we are upon an active part of the great "Ring of Fire" around the Pacific, where earth's internal forces frequently show their power to build and to destroy landscape features. Beyond a narrow channel lies the Alaska Peninsula and the North American mainland. Bearing northeastward along the 4,000- to 8,000-foot

Aleutian Range, bleak backbone of the peninsula, we look to our left toward Bristol Bay, a large arm of the Bering Sea. On our right, in the Pacific beyond wide Shelikof Strait, lies Kodiak Island.

As we near the Alaskan mainland there appears on our left the first of many coastal areas set aside as unique scenic or scientific preserves. This is Katmai National Monument, largest unit of the National Park System, where in 1912 a spectacular volcanic display created the Valley of Ten Thousand Smokes. Soon we are flying up Cook Inlet, named for Captain James Cook, who in 1778 turned back here from his search for the Northwest Passage. On this inlet in 1915 was founded the Alaskan railroad town that grew to be the forty-ninth state's largest city. Then no one could have predicted that half a century later thriving Anchorage would be shaken to pieces by the severest earthquake to strike the Pacific Coast in historic times. But today's geological maps show major faults in the broken crust rimming the scenic Alaskan Gulf coast. From Anchorage, daring ribbons of road lead crookedly northward over icy passes of the Chugach and Talkeetna ranges, over the Alaska Range with its continental summit, Mt. McKinley, and down to the Tanana River valley to reach Fairbanks, the Alaska Highway, the Yukon drainage, and now the oil fields beyond the Brooks Range.

From our height, man's settlements, roads, farm clearings, and other efforts show scarcely at all upon the great sweeping wilderness of peaks and glaciers, fiords, islands, and plunging broken seacoast which forms the huge rim of the Gulf of Alaska. Civiliza-

The active volcanic area of Mount Katmai on the Alaska Peninsula: view southeastward across Shelikof Strait to Kodiak Island.

19

tion fades from view altogether before we sight that mighty geographical hingepin of the Alaskan Panhandle, Mount St. Elias. Standing with it is a massive group at the juncture of the St. Elias, Chugach, and Wrangell ranges, and born of all their perpetual snows are some of the world's grandest glaciers.

On a southeast bearing now, we cross the peninsular Fairweather Range and enjoy the sense of discovery that came, in 1879, to John Muir, the first white man to see that awesome wilderness of mountain and ice, Glacier Bay.

Southeastern Alaska's Alexander Archipelago, two hundred and fifty miles long, is part of this glacial world although the rivers of ice that carved its islands and channels retreated long ago to the mainland. The old Russian capital, Sitka, faces seaward while the modern capital, Juneau, and other island towns sit on shores of the Inside Passage. Flying southward along that renowned scenic waterway we see spread below a bewildering labyrinth of blue-water channels criss-crossing a green forest belt more than one hundred miles wide and creating some eleven thousand islands. All these islands were Indian country once, and to a degree still are. Waters teeming with salmon and forests tall with hemlock, spruce, and cedar provide an abundant life.

Now, after fifteen hundred air miles, Alaska is behind us but not yet the far-flung Northwest Coast island world. Another, more closely knit archipelago, Queen Charlotte Islands, lies off the British Columbia coast. This group, with but little white settlement, is the home of the Haida, maritime Indians who hunted fur seal straggling into Hecate Strait; and it was a haven of all life in this region in that time when ice took over.

Between the seaport cities of Prince Rupert and Vancouver, British Columbia meets the Pacific with four hundred miles of deeply fiorded, island-studded coast. We see a green tide of rain forest washing the feet of the Coast Range, here a continental rampart of icy peaks. Queen Charlotte Sound funnels into a series of straits that form the Inside Passage splitting Vancouver Island off from the mainland.

Here, as around the Alaskan Gulf and Panhandle, the landscape below us reflects the shaping power of ice. Cirqued Coast Range summits, rounded lower slopes, deep-cleft winding valleys partly drowned as

inlets of the sea, channeled island groups that look like jigsaw puzzles — all are witness to the ice caps which covered and carved this mountain coast several times, the last not more than ten or twelve thousand years ago. On our coast, Puget Sound is the southernmost major work of that vast glaciation, although many small glaciers are active today on nearby Coast Range and Cascade peaks.

Vancouver Island is far the largest island of the entire Pacific Coast. Its wild northwestern cape juts into wilder ocean waters; its civilized southeast rests in calmer Puget Sound. There Victoria, provincial capital, stands in sharp white contrast to her dark green hinterland. Like most cities and towns from the Alaskan Gulf to Puget Sound, she has her back to the forest and her feet in salt water. Opposite the great island, on the mainland side of Georgian Strait, the solid geometry of metropolitan Vancouver gives sudden notice that we are passing from the watery wilderness of the Northwest Coast.

Leaving the southern tip of Vancouver Island, we cross the Strait of Juan de Fuca, midway marker on our coastal journey and a major dividing line in Pacific Coast topography. The mighty medley of islands, fiords, and channels to the north seems to deny any proper separation of land and sea. But with Juan de Fuca and Cape Flattery begins the longest stretch of virtually unbroken coastline on earth. Except for the Gulf of California, it is not again entered deeply by the sea until the break-up of southern Chile into its islanded fiordland. South of Puget Sound and the Olympic Peninsula, ocean is ocean and land is land. Their eternal battle line is now more sharply drawn.

Even from our aerial viewpoint, the disappearance of glaciers and their work is not the only sign that water has lessened its grip on land. Another is the change in the character of the forest cover. Around the northern rim of the Alaskan Gulf this growth is sparse and stunted, a scatter of spruce and hemlock hanging on through the long cold and the short growing seasons. Then on the milder maritime lowlands between the gulf and Puget Sound, and climactically on the Olympic Peninsula, the continent's heaviest precipitation sustains the densest growth of coniferous trees on earth. But south of the Olympic rain forest, the coastlands become progressively drier on their way to Baja California's Vizcaíno Des-

*Great Central Lake, Vancouver Island, British Columbia. The view is west-by-north to the
seven-thousand-foot peaks of Strathcona Provincial Park. All of the island's many lakes
and inlets are similar glacier-carved troughs, as are those of the nearby mainland.*

ert. While the forest belt rolls southward to produce
a second climax in the coast redwoods, it never again
achieves the sheer vegetable luxuriance of the Pacific
Northwest, and indeed it yields almost entirely to
coastal scrub and chaparral south of the Golden Gate.

Winging south over Washington and Oregon along
the low, barely defined crest of the Coast Range, we
see the east and west boundaries of our coastal "province" stretching ahead like sides of a straight road.
The Puget Trough, extending to the Willamette
Valley on our left, and the coastline following the
124th meridian on our right, guide us compass-true

for more than two hundred and fifty miles. The gentle highland from the Chehalis River on the north
to the winding Umpqua on the south is a restful
change from the rugged grandeur we have left behind. At the broad Columbia estuary, the range is
severed cleanly; elsewhere it is being quietly reduced
to a series of rounded blocks by the many small rivers
running eastward to the Puget-Willamette trough
and westward to the sea.

This coastland once wore a nearly unbroken carpet
of forest fifty miles wide but it is now a tattered patch-
work of burns, logged-off sections, and farm clear-

ings. Nevertheless, the stand of Douglas-fir is still awesome, its darker green fingering down the eastward spurs of the range to meet the verdant fields and orchards of the interior valleys.

Along the shore, cliffs and headlands cap every view from tide's edge. The edge itself, as expressed in elongated fingers of sand, strikes a silvery line to the farthest reach of even our aerial view. Washington has the longest such strand on the entire Pacific Coast, the twenty-mile strip guarding Willapa Bay. There is nothing comparable until the Bahía de la Magdalena area of Baja California.

With the Umpqua River and Coos Bay behind us, and Oregon's most westerly headland, Cape Blanco, in sight, we soon confront the most confusing jumble of highlands on our course. Here the Klamath Mountains close the long corridor between the Coast Range and the Sierra Nevada–Cascade System. Where is our coast region's eastern boundary now? Certainly not at Mount Shasta, or even the Salmon–Trinity Divide. Taking a cue from the land itself, our "province" will stop where the coast redwood belt reaches its farthest up the drainage of the Klamath, Eel and other coastal streams. This is sea fog country, redwood country, and cannot be mistaken for any other.

The rugged out-bulge of California's Cape Mendocino and Punta Gorda, where the King Range rises four thousand feet sheer from the beach, stands like a shield raised against the sea. Offshore lie the routes of centuries of seafarers—whales and men.

If it were late fall and we were flying lower, we might see the long straggling lines of the California gray whales move down the coast, close enough inshore to be sighted from bluffs by tallying watchers. Out of the Bering Sea, through the gates of the Aleutians they come, plowing the swells. Their goal is Scammons and other quiet lagoons of the desert coast; their purpose, to breed in the southern spring. Along the same lanes for two centuries and a half to 1815, the creaking Manila Galleons drove before the westerlies near the 40th parallel, hopefully beating the season's first storms. Acapulco bound, they favored Cape Mendocino or Kings Peak as their California landfall, but more than two hundred years' probing of the coastal fogs failed to discover a badly needed haven for repair and refreshment in Alta California after that arduous easting.

However, San Francisco Bay and its narrow outlet to the sea, the Golden Gate, had long figured in the story of nature on the continent's edge. This great bay is a drowned valley; near its broad upper lobe, we see the confluence of the rivers that flooded it: the Sacramento–San Joaquin Delta. The Golden Gate is the last major river mouth we shall see as we fly southward, the last large waterway to mountain streams once crowded bank to bank with salmon going home to spawn.

Another story comes dramatically into view south of Cape Mendocino, in the Bay Area—the uneasy one of the San Andreas Fault. We see—in sharp relief from the air—its long shear across the base of the Point Reyes Peninsula just north of the Golden Gate and its slash inland on a tangent to San Francisco's Ocean Beach. The rift runs the length of the Inner Coast Range, through the desert mountains to the Gulf of California—our final eastward boundary. Our course follows the southeasterly direction of this long fault all the way from Cape Mendocino to the end of the coast region.

Past San Francisco Bay now, we look for significant changes in landforms and life. Certain differences become apparent south of the region of Monterey Bay. In general, signs of aridity begin to strike us although here and there dark patches of Monterey pine around Pacific Grove and Carmel recall similar stands of the closely related Bishop pine north of the Golden Gate. Instead of the many flashing rivers of the north there is only one in this area—the Salinas, flowing northwestward to Monterey Bay between the coast and the San Andreas rift. The steep ridges of the Santa Lucias west of the Salinas Valley are stark, and not often softened by forest cover.

People enjoy the beaches and tidepools along the shoreline around Santa Cruz and the Monterey Peninsula; but farther south, where the Santa Lucia Range springs straight up from the surf line, the rocks and coves are reserved, by their sheer inaccessibility, for sea lions, sea otters, and birds. Even with a highway clinging to the cliffs high above the tide, this is a wild coast.

The upsurging mountains gradually diminish to gentler slopes which, from San Simeon southward, provide a shoreline which lends itself more readily to human use—and misuse. A rash of unattractive seaside resorts spreads across pastoral acres; and the three huge power-plant stacks at Morro Bay do not enhance the beauty of Morro Rock's parabolic dome.

We now shift our focus to an area of important new directions and changes in geological structure, living communities, and even climate. After Point Buchon, Pismo Beach, and Nipomo Dunes—California's largest coastal sand dune area—the shore runs due south for fifty miles and then makes a great double-elbow bend to the east around two points. The first, Arguello, faces west. Point Conception, facing south, is the nub of this transition area. The

The Monterey coast of central California. Along this rugged shore, State Highway 1 follows the curve of Garrapata Beach northward to Point Lobos and eventually the Monterey Peninsula. The Santa Lucia Range rises sharply from the coast.

23

*The arid landscape of Baja California is in stark contrast to the glacier-carved troughs
and snowy peaks of Vancouver Island. Instead of forest, the only vegetation is a sparse
scattering of desert plants which can exist for years on the periodic moistening of coastal fog.
The aerial view is southward across Bahía Tortugas on the peninsula's Pacific Coast.*

latter is often mentioned in accounts of Pacific Coast animal and plant life.

The coast arcs in a long bow from here to San Diego, more to the east than to the south. Conversely, the edge of the submarine platform now widens in the opposite direction, carrying California's offshore islands like a giant tray. These islands are different in many respects from those of the Northwest Coast, and we shall find them important in coastal geology, ecology, and history. The northernmost of them are a partly drowned western prong of the Transverse Range, that remarkable interruption in the northwest-southeast trend of California's Coast Range, which reaches two hundred and forty miles east into the Mojave Desert, in addition to its westward prong at Point Arguello. This great cross-thrust of mountains has not only cut through the outer and inner Coast Ranges, but has also tied them together in a tectonic knot into which the southern Sierra Nevada has also been pulled, via its terminal extension, the Tehachapi range. So once more the great interior corridor is closed. Viewing this jumbled nexus of ranges from the air, one experiences an exciting sense of great earth-things having happened here—things that could happen again. And if one's excitement comes from the contemplation of life, evolution, and the intriguing patterns of plant and animal distribution, he will find this coastal-bend region a great meeting and mixing place. Here many temperate and sub-tropical species reach one limit of their range, whether in tidepools off Point Conception or on the brushy slopes of nearby mountains.

Cruising high over Los Angeles International Airport, our sight encompasses all aspects of a vast sea-land basin. Seaward it tilts to the rim of the platform supporting the offshore islands; landward it slopes gently to the foot of a suddenly rising rim of mountains. Between that and the cross-line of the scarcely elevated shore sprawls one vast tide of humanity. If the air is windswept clear over the Los Angeles Basin—it is, some days—we might think it is a marvelous place for so many millions to live. If it is smog filled, we turn from thoughts of man's unbalanced ecology to the more pleasant contemplation of the long, high ridges of the Peninsular Ranges, rising like islands from a miasmic sea and sweeping southward to a clearer horizon.

Beyond them is the deep trough of the Salton Sink and Colorado Desert, in the rain shadow of lofty San Jacinto. Progressing southward, we pass San Diego and Coronado's strand. The ranges dip near the border, then rise again, conjoined as Baja California's backbone massif. First the Sierra Juarez come into view; then loom the pine-clad summits of the Sierra San Pedro Mártir, where the 900-mile-long granite batholith of the peninsula lifts to the surface in weathered grandeur.

Baja is a long march of ranges, canyons, mesas, deserts, and beaches, and an astonishing wealth of things living under hot sun and scant rain—all the way down to Cabo San Lucas, land's end for our coastal "province" and our story.

THERE IS, of course, neither an end nor a beginning, in space or in time. A part of earth there was, the day the crust began to form; but only in the last few minutes could we have known its shape. Life is continuous; only individuals start and stop, begin to live and cease living.

Our 4,600-mile non-stop orientation trip began not far below the Arctic Circle and ended within the Tropic of Cancer. There was neither magic nor logic in the direction; it could just as well have been reversed. The gray whales migrate from the Bering Sea to the breeding lagoons of Baja California and the Sea of Cortés; they also go back again. If there is a start, it is of the life of each newborn whale, and, in that sense, of a journey.

On our journey, conceivably of one very long day's duration, we have only scanned earth's most magnificent coast. We have ranged from the remnant edge of a once vast polar ice cap, around the Gulf of Alaska, to the mouth of a nearly tropical cauldron, the Gulf of California. We climbed up over a bleak, fogbound northern peninsula and came down upon a sun-parched southern one—a thirsty tongue of desert between two salt seas. Land's edge has been covered by glacier and forest, by grass, chaparral, and sand. Mountains have skirted it always. Life in great abundance and myriad kinds comes, stays, goes, begins and ends, in every part of it. Man has discovered, explored, settled, and exploited it, and now looks anxiously ahead, uneasy about the terms of his tenure. The terms, he knows now, are chiefly nature's.

CHAPTER 2

SHAPING OF A SHORE

Portrait of the ever-changing edge of the North American continent—its geological past and present.

HERE IS A STILLNESS at the altitude of our flight. The sea stands as motionless as a painted ocean on a giant map. Clouds rest, with no hint of wind. The continent's hard edge looks as immutable as the face on the moon. Only the gradually shifting scene evinces movement—that of the aircraft. But change is ceaseless on our planet; reason tells us that were we to cover the same ground in, say, fifty years or even less, some signs of change would be visible. The thin edge of a continent, appearing so firm when seen in the distance or drawn on maps, is not fixed for all time as we have just seen it. Despite its look of ageless endurance, small changes which add up to major ones—cliff retreat, fault-line movement, the building, destruction, and reshaping of beaches and bars by ocean waves—are often measurable within a human life span.

Occasionally, profound changes are wrought in a single day. Volcanic eruptions are the most sudden and dramatic landform changers. In 1912 Mount Katmai on the Alaska Peninsula collapsed explosively, while six miles away a new volcano, Novarupta, broke ground and spewed out enough ash to cover several thousand square miles a foot deep.

Earthquakes are another restless force in the shaping of our Pacific Coast. On the night of July 9, 1958, a severe quake—7.75–8 on the Richter scale—shook the Fairweather Range along the Alaskan Gulf. Great avalanches and ice falls from two glacial sea-cliffs plunged into Lituya Bay, a six-mile inlet with a narrow entrance, slamming huge waves two hundred feet up the timbered mountainsides. A wide section was stripped completely bare to 1,800 feet above the sea, presumably by the combined force of wave and avalanche. Conspicuous as the gash was then, it grows wider and deeper as storms tear yearly at the naked earth. The same quake hit nearby Yakutat Bay, where some people in a boat saw a tongue of land rise twenty feet into the air and sink, taking three unfortunate souls down with it.

Advancing and retreating glaciers may also alter the landscape on a large scale in a few years. The Johns Hopkins Glacier, flowing from Mount Crillon in the Fairweather Range, has occupied a long, deep, and narrow inlet. Between 1916 and 1937 this glacier's retreat opened six miles of salt water formerly iced wall to wall. Some ice fields have melted down rapidly at the surface, exposing *nunataks*—small rock peaks—that have not been visible for centuries.

Waves are powerful and rapid in shaping land's edge, wiping out broad beaches in a single violent storm, leaving rocks and gravel, threatening cliff feet long protected by yards of dune-dry sand. The sand thus thrown back into the boiling sea may soon reappear as an offshore bar, high enough to make breakers where only swells rose before. Pounding surf and soaking rain can together plunge large cliff sections down to wave level; continuing stormy seas may wash the mass quickly away. Wherever storms hit hard and often, from the right direction, and opposing land faces are structurally weak, the landscape may change noticeably from year to year.

From the air, as on a navigation chart, short-term shoreline changes are most evident at river mouths,

A fraction of a second on the geological time clock is expressed by the natural arch and sea stack at Sunset Cliffs Park, San Diego, California. In another second on that scale of time it will be gone, just a passing moment in the process of shaping a shoreline.

bay and harbor entrances, estuaries and channels—places where stream sediments pile up around rocks, reefs, and other elevations on the sea bottom, and are then taken in tow by waves and currents.

Volcanoes, earthquakes, glaciers, storms, waves, currents—these are the chief natural agents of rapid change in local shoreline configuration. Their effects, small and short-term compared to the works of great earth-shaping forces, range from mudbanks and rockslides to cinder cones and altered inlets, from the violent happenings of a day to the slow developments of a number of years. They are convincing evidence of unceasing activity by the forces of change. The next step of mind and imagination is to grasp the fact of *long*-term change in the larger design of an ocean shore or a continent. Taking that step might lead us from a brief glance inside the planet to a more leisurely exploring of some elements of its surface design: waves, wind, rock, sand, soil, rain, sunlight, and life, seen as the fabric of this coast.

THE EARTH'S CRUST is a very thin eggshell on which we walk. As scientists probe the inside of the egg, they can at least tell us it is more like a partially hard-boiled than a fresh one. It has, presumably, a solid metallic inner core and a liquid outer one; around them a solid rock mantle nearly two thousand miles thick; and finally the rock crust, averaging twenty to thirty miles in depth from the surface. Between mantle and crust an abrupt change in density occurs; "floating" on the mantle, the lighter crust is twofold. The overall layer is basalt; it forms the floor of the oceans and the base of the continents and larger islands. These are plates or blocks of granitic rock resting upon the basalt and, where they are thickest, as beneath mountain ranges, pushing it down into the mantle. This accords with the principle of *isostatic equilibrium*, which accounts for the tendency of the earth to equalize the weight shifting about its center; when crustal material thickens and sags of its weight in one area, what lies beneath it is displaced to the side, contributing to a thickening and uplift in an adjacent area. (This working theory is useful to keep in mind as we talk about such things as rising coasts or sinking lands.)

By whatever geological processes and events the continents were formed (authorities are still debat-

ing that question), the story of our continent's progress through time tells of alternate rise and fall of land, invasion and retreat of the sea. Mountains are built by crustal uplift, folding, faulting, volcanic outpouring; they are eroded away to hills and plains, and rise again. Molten rock seeps between layers of sediment to raise plateaus, like blisters, which are block-faulted and water-carved into ridges and valleys. Long-term climatic changes, too, play their part in landform evolution, as through glaciation. And always there is the struggle between land and sea for possession of parts of the global surface. Always there is change, as one force or another gains the upper hand for a long or brief geological moment. This edge of North America, lying on one of the major earthquake and volcano belts of the earth, is one of the most active, and rapidly changing.

Moon studies suggest the earth is at least four and a half billion years old. Roughly two-thirds of that span may represent the age of continents. Somewhere along the edge of one, in a "warm and shallow sea" as the story is usually told, life somehow began, perhaps two billion years ago. The first billion years may have produced only such minimal living matter as the blue-green algae; in the next half billion only the simplest of animal forms evolved. The significant part of life's fossil record originated about 500 million years ago, with the Paleozoic era.

During this era's 300 million years, life rose from primitive marine invertebrates and algae to land dwellers—insects, reptiles, and such plants as cycads and pines. In the next era, the Mesozoic, dinosaurs had their day; near its close birds took wing, flowering trees and small primitive mammals appeared. Sixty to seventy million years ago, when the Cenozoic era began, the last great shallow seas had receded from our continent's heart. The major mountain systems rose, mammals became dominant, and North America at last took essentially the shape we know today, a shape that may last a long geological moment—say a hundred million years.

Each thing we see is a link in a chain of events. A coastal terrace is cut flat by waves. Giant kelp grows a hundred feet long. Sea lions bark to the surf from a rock ledge. Redwoods march down fog-filled valleys to the sea. A V-shaped lagoon curves behind a sandspit. Plant tissue adapts to salt in a marsh. Gulls fly

The sequence of ancient wave-cut benches or marine terraces on the Palos Verdes Hills near San Pedro, California, is an example of the changing relationship between sea level and land level through a relatively short period of coastline building. Between the present beach and the 1,480-foot summit, there are thirteen terraces (not all shown in this aerial view). Fossil shells at the oldest and highest level belong to late Pleistocene time, roughly a million years ago.

seaward at dusk to ancient roosts on offshore islets. Each is neither a first nor a last link. Our minds reach for the whole chain.

For example, knowing a little of land-building, then of climate change leading to glaciation, we may understand the presence in our time of the Northwest's beautiful Inside Passage. We can picture the many-channeled waterway on a backdrop of snowy peaks. Knowing how life comes, we can visualize its island and inlet shores crowded with giant red cedar and Sitka spruce, then peopled with red men who found there an abundance of things for their living—water and wood, furs and salmon. And we are prepared for the carved paddles giving way to sail and steam; for the cutting of forests, not single trees; for the taking of salmon by the millions to canneries, not by the thousands to drying racks. We understand that all things of earth and life partake in the evolution of a landscape and in the growth, functioning, alteration, and eventual decay and replacement of those

ecological associations it carries successively through time. And we are there, somewhere.

To know, however slightly, the story of its shaping is to see the whole picture of the Pacific Coast more clearly. As we take a brief glance back in time, we are aware that moving forces work ceaselessly, that time and geological periods are human inventions.

If the pre-Cambrian era is represented on this coast it awaits future discovery. There is a hazy glimpse of the Archeozoic era, however, in some of the oldest known rocks of the western edge, found in Southern California's Transverse Ranges. Over a billion years old, they are a product of the weathering of yet older rocks, reaching back a possible two billion years.

A long jump forward into the Paleozoic era—into the last 15 percent of known geological time—takes us to the Alaskan end of the coast for landmarks. Some slates and limestones in the Chugach–St. Elias mountains contain fossils of marine invertebrates,

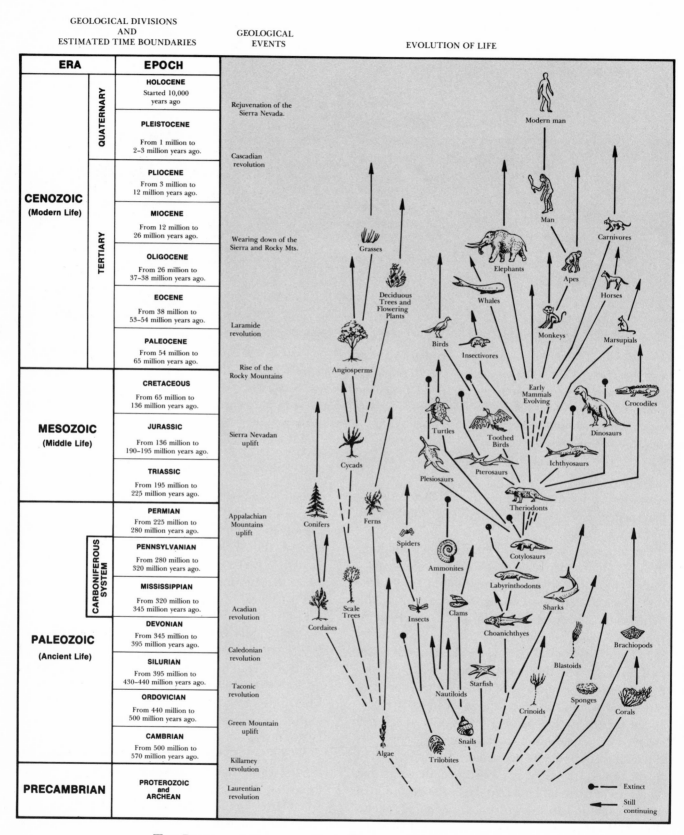

GEOLOGICAL DIVISIONS AND ESTIMATED TIME BOUNDARIES

GEOLOGICAL EVENTS

EVOLUTION OF LIFE

ERA		EPOCH
	QUATERNARY	**HOLOCENE** Started 10,000 years ago
		PLEISTOCENE From 1 million to 2–3 million years ago.
CENOZOIC (Modern Life)	TERTIARY	**PLIOCENE** From 3 million to 12 million years ago.
		MIOCENE From 12 million to 26 million years ago.
		OLIGOCENE From 26 million to 37–38 million years ago.
		EOCENE From 38 million to 53–54 million years ago.
		PALEOCENE From 54 million to 65 million years ago.
MESOZOIC (Middle Life)		**CRETACEOUS** From 65 million to 136 million years ago.
		JURASSIC From 136 million to 190–195 million years ago.
		TRIASSIC From 195 million to 225 million years ago.
PALEOZOIC (Ancient Life)	CARBONIFEROUS SYSTEM	**PERMIAN** From 225 million to 280 million years ago.
		PENNSYLVANIAN From 280 million to 320 million years ago.
		MISSISSIPPIAN From 320 million to 345 million years ago.
		DEVONIAN From 345 million to 395 million years ago.
		SILURIAN From 395 million to 430–440 million years ago.
		ORDOVICIAN From 440 million to 500 million years ago.
		CAMBRIAN From 500 million to 570 million years ago.
PRECAMBRIAN		**PROTEROZOIC and ARCHEAN**

Geological events:
Rejuvenation of the Sierra Nevada.
Cascadian revolution
Wearing down of the Sierra and Rocky Mts.
Laramide revolution
Rise of the Rocky Mountains
Sierra Nevadan uplift
Appalachian Mountains uplift
Acadian revolution
Caledonian revolution
Taconic revolution
Green Mountain uplift
Killarney revolution
Laurentian revolution

THE PERIODS OF GEOLOGIC TIME, SHOWING MAJOR GEOLOGICAL EVENTS AND LANDMARKS IN THE EVOLUTION OF LIFE

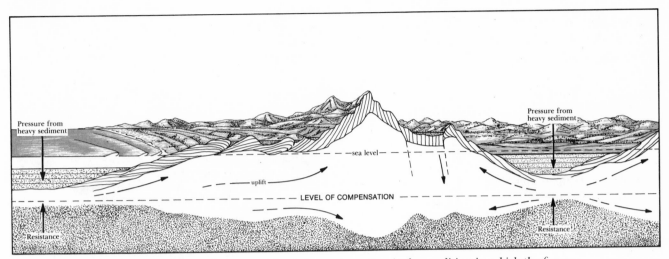

THE PRINCIPLE OF ISOSTASY: *Isostatic compensation is the condition in which the forces tending to elevate the earth's crust balance those tending to depress the crust.*

high-and-dry evidence of an ancient Pacific shoreline. Paleozoic marine sediments alternate with volcanic rocks in several areas. In general, the picture of the continent's western edge 300 million years ago is that of an elongated volcanic archipelago. Islands rose, were leveled and washed over, and erupted again.

This struggle between crustal and oceanic forces went on into the Mesozoic era, which early shows tremendous volcanic activity. Later in that era, strong folding and igneous intrusion began building Canada's Coast Range, the Klamaths, Sierra Nevada, and the backbone of Baja California. Another period of sinking and sedimentation followed in the southern section; then coast ranges rose, and perhaps a new volcanic archipelago offshore. So it went: great beds of material were laid down in the sea, compressed, and uplifted as dry land. The gist of this story told in the rocks is that the ocean has repeatedly breached this western rim, overrun interior regions, and withdrawn, leaving the salt-crust of old shorelines and deposits of rock for the building of new landscapes. Who can say what will be land a million years hence, and what will be sea?

The past million years of flexing to and fro shaped the shoreline of this moment. And the last epochal change of the Great Ice Age brought man to the scene, as well as many new plants and other animals. The rigorous late Pleistocene epoch, during which northern climates fluctuated four times between gla-

cially cold-dry and temperately warm-rainy, was a restless time for living things. Animals and plants migrated back and forth between Asia and North America, mostly eastward, over the Bering land bridge. Though land uplift alone could build it, and has probably done so at one time or another, that intercontinental highway emerged periodically when a vast amount of water shifted from ocean to ice cap.

Sea level change has been an important factor in the shaping and reshaping of the shoreline in glacial periods and others as well. We'll see some of its effects in greater detail when we look more closely at glaciers and coastal islands.

Such change is relative; when coastlands rise or sink, the effects are the same as when the level of the sea actually changes. A crustal shift may be imperceptible in progress while affecting a large area, or rapid and localized as it was along the Gulf of Alaska during the 1964 earthquake. A slow shift is caused by the layering of sediments, at or offshore from the mouths of rivers, such as the Columbia, the Colorado, or those discharging through the Golden Gate. Undersea volcanism also builds up shoals, causing local waterline changes. Sea level is altered by change in sea-water temperature, as when the glacial and interglacial climate fluctuations caused overall contraction and expansion of world sea water. In whatever way it is manifest, there is a mutual relationship between *sea* level and *land* level.

31

THE LONG CURVING SHORE

THE SEA is the most constant and uniformly behaving part of the earth's surface. Shorelines differ greatly in character, place to place, because the land varies so much in composition and structure. The sea's contrary goal seems to be the shaping of all shores in a few common molds and it succeeds to a perhaps surprising degree. Its offensive weapons— waves, tides, currents—impose a relentless strategy: attack. Land loses battle after battle, but its flexible and ultimately unconquerable defenses keep the war a stalemate. Crumbling here, it rises there. Engulfed on a front, it breaks water behind enemy lines.

The eternal give-and-take has to balance out. Geologists speak of a "marine profile of equilibrium." Studies show the ideal profile of a shoreline cross section as a smooth, sweeping curve, increasingly concave as it moves from below to above tidewater, from nearly flat seaward to steep at the berm of the beach. Local conditions modify the ideal. The average profile at Baja's high Punta Banda is doubtless different from that off the spit at Grays Harbor, Washington. And the profile of any beach must respond to long-term changes of every kind.

Doing the same old things in the same old way— that is the way of the sea, or more broadly the way of the earth in shaping and reshaping the features of its own face. The minor profile of the beach is reflected in a larger basic profile of all seashores, the form of the wave-cut terrace. Wherever this appears —it may be hundreds of feet above sea level, hundreds of miles inland—it proclaims the boundary of some former province of the sea or an earlier state of a present shoreline. Offshore soundings locate such terraces of an old, drowned coastline.

The edge of the sea, where it tapers to meet the shore, is a cutting edge. In this shallow zone, from

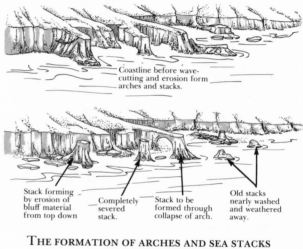

Coastline before wave-cutting and erosion form arches and stacks.

Stack forming by erosion of bluff material from top down

Completely severed stack.

Stack to be formed through collapse of arch.

Old stacks nearly washed and weathered away.

THE FORMATION OF ARCHES AND SEA STACKS
BY WAVE-CUTTING AND WEATHERING

thirty feet to zero in depth, water loaded with sand and rock particles whipsaws across the plane of the terrace. Corrasion is rapid or slow depending on the resistance of the opposing material, but all kinds of rock eventually yield to sea power. And as land rises or sinks, waves simply go to work on the new level.

Wave-cut terraces reveal that much vigorous uplifting has occurred along our coast quite recently. In the Palos Verdes Hills, a prominent landmark near Long Beach, California, thirteen giant steps rise from a hundred feet above the beach to the 1,480-foot summit; each terrace is paved with marine sediments containing shells of still existent types. The age of the most recent terrace has been put at merely thirty thousand years. This is indeed a youthful coast on the way up, defying the ancient ocean.

Sea stacks are remnants of terraces, striking holdouts of coastal land. Standing with feet in the surf, or high and dry upon levels uplifted long ago, these picturesque formations appear at many points but are the special hallmark of Northern California, Oregon, and Washington. Often they loom as dark, gaunt ghosts partly shrouded in offshore haze or fog, their loneliness heightened by the cries of sea birds

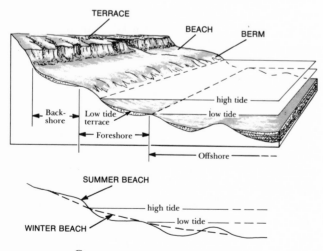

TERRACE

BEACH   BERM

high tide

Back-
shore   Low tide
terrace   low tide

Foreshore

Offshore

SUMMER BEACH

high tide
low tide

WINTER BEACH

CROSS SECTION OF A SHORELINE

The 930-foot cone of Isla Coronados in the Gulf of California shows how volcanoes, as shoreline builders, can cause rapid change. Onshore or insular, outpouring lava can quickly extend a coastland into the sea. This two-mile-long island lies north of Loreto, and is waterless and quite barren.

roosting on juts and ledges, and by the thunder of surf against their bases—sounds muffled in the mist. Ashore, they sit dry like beached old mariners, silent reminders of former shores. Having outlived the battering of past seas, they wait a slower, quieter death by weathering alone.

Sometimes a single stack becomes the object of local pride or concern, especially when it comes and goes within the span of human life. Such a stack was Jump-Off Joe, near Newport, Oregon. Around 1890 it was firmly attached to the mainland. A small arch appeared, grew large, fell in—and Joe became a proper seagoing stack. But within fifty years the entire structure was all but gone to the waves. Newport had seen how fast the sea can work.

IN THE SHAPING OF SHORELINES, as in many other things natural or human, destructive processes and their results are readily noticed. A portion of undercut cliff slides into the surf. An arch falls or a stack topples. A fine beach is gutted by a single storm.

Isolated "strikes" of erosive force—especially the here today–gone tomorrow kind of thing—are marked as they happen or soon after. There are also, however, quiet building processes continuously at work, whose less sudden effects are recorded only geologically or, in the shorter range of our own experience, through periodic observation and measurement. They range from slow crustal uplift to the often rapid shifting of erosion detritus—from large stones and gravels to fine sands and silts—by waves and longshore currents. This last is the process, or complex of processes, by which beaches and the whole "movable feast" of related shoreline features are built: bars, spits, tombolos, triangular headlands of sand—all the classic forms of coastland accumulation. These more or less mercurial structures are so intimately connected with the physics and mechanics of waves, the flow of currents, the patterns of winds and tides, and the changes of the seasons, that we can understand them only if we understand the ocean itself and the air that helps generate its power.

CHAPTER 3

CURRENTS AND SEA WINDS

*The Pacific Ocean as a breeder of winds, waves,
and tides shaping land and life on the shore.*

THE OCEAN distinguishes Earth from all other members of our solar system. This unique watery envelope, together with the outer one of breathable atmosphere, had to exist before the planet could have rain, rivers, sculptured landscapes, or higher forms of life. The ocean system is the great thermostat: it changes temperature slowly within a limited range between the freezing and boiling points of water, a range tolerable to life as a whole. Water—running, raining, or solid—is moreover the chief architect of landscapes, both in large form and in detail. Nowhere is this more evident than upon a coastline, and it is powerfully evident upon the Pacific Coast of North America, which has been profoundly affected by water from land, sea, and sky.

Salt water covers 70.8 percent of the planet, almost half of it in the Pacific Ocean. Flooding virtually a third of the global surface, the Pacific is both the largest and the deepest of the four oceans. In it lies the greatest known deep, the 35,800-foot Mariana Trench; and from its floor rises the earth's highest peak measured from true base to summit, Hawaii's 32,024-foot Mauna Kea. If the earth were the size of an apple it would be just as smooth; all the ocean basins and deeps and all the land elevations could be formed in the wax on the skin. The real wonders are the infinitude of components, the intricacy of organization, the ceaseless motion and throbbing vitality, the absolute indispensability to a living earth of that slight wetness on its surface, the enveloping ocean.

Where did all this water come from—*340 million cubic miles* of it? After the fiery young earth cooled,

a popular theory suggests, vapor condensed, and it then rained nonstop for centuries until all the oceans were filled—and that was that. However, one contemporary authority has called the origin of water an unsolved puzzle, and chemists have found it extremely difficult to synthesize.

Oceans, the Archean rocks tell us, were here during earliest geologic times. Wherever and however it formed, water early took its place as part of the planet's envelope, just as the crustal rocks did. There it has remained, in intimate relationship with these rocks, dissecting and transporting them, sifting and sorting them, reassembling their materials into new rock, and reshaping their surfaces into new sculptural forms. In one of its forms, water *is* rock: glacial ice is a geological material as well as a rock-carving, land-shaping tool. The ice caps covering Antarctica and Greenland are as much a "permanent" ground as the country rock is in more temperate zones.

The seeming permanence and—in the global sense—regional stability of liquid water has surely aided the development of certain oceanic "systems" which affect the land: tides, currents, temperature zones, atmospheric pressure systems, and winds. The last, though part of the atmosphere and free to roam, to a large extent are generated over the sea. Of land masses, only Antarctica and Asia, as reservoirs of dry, cold air, are major climate producers. Other continents are more on the receiving end of the final product, weather. The great expanses of level ocean surface enable winds to prevail in definite paths and patterns, in response to the earth's rotation. Crossing

*The ocean speaks to the land in the ceaseless rhythm of waves, the unending
flow of currents, and the roar and the whisper of winds. This moment under
the sun was caught at Mukkaw Bay, south of Cape Flattery, Washington.*

water, they make waves rise. On reaching land, they are more or less impeded by all projections above the level, from mountain ranges to trees, shrubs, or structures on coastal plains. The edge of the land presents baffles to the winds, as it does to the tides.

Is THE TIDE coming in or going out? Newcomers to the beach often ask this question. If they are going swimming, tidepool watching, fishing, or just over the rocks to the quiet little cove around the point, they are wise to learn the state of the tide—coming in or going out, how high and how low.

Suppose the earth's surface were all ocean, uniform in depth, with giant gauging poles at every major latitude-longitude intersection. It would be quite simple then to calculate and predict the exact tide level at each marker at any time, for the magnitude and direction of each of the forces causing tides are precisely known. But the earth being as it is, what actually happens? Everything under the sun—and moon! Land barriers create basins in which oceans and seas, gulfs and bays, slosh their waters back and forth, confused by winds, currents, and the inflow of rivers. Widely varying depth is an important factor; and such things as offshore islands, channels, inlets, breakwaters and other man-made structures, throw local monkey wrenches into the gears of the massive tide machine.

On our Atlantic Coast and elsewhere, the two daily tides run about equally high and low. A few of the world's shores, including some of the South Pacific islands, have only one tide a day. Our Pacific with its *mixed tides*—two unequal highs and lows per day—has its share of widely differing shoreline configurations and other conditions which work for higher or lower, faster or slower tides.

Although they rise and fall well within the world's extremes (no tide at the North Pole; fifty feet or more in Canada's Bay of Fundy), Pacific Coast tides in certain places have achieved long-standing notoriety. Two areas with exceptional tides once figured in man's search for nonexistent sea passages. In late May of 1778, Captain Cook rounded the Alaskan cape which he named Elizabeth. Was this, at last, the Northwest Passage? Sailing in on high tide between converging shores, he faced an estuary, not a passage —Cook Inlet. He knew that with this tide rising to

thirty feet in a tight inlet, he had to wait to sail out again. Turnagain Arm it was named—the closing of the funnel and of hope. And at Anchorage, high and low springs can differ by 36 feet. Alaska's terrible earthquake of 1964 struck Anchorage at 5:36 P.M. on March 27. At 6:12, a 30-foot spring tide flooded the shattered harbor. That night a full moon stared at the wrecked cities of the inlets and islands.

The Gulf of California is one of the earth's greatest tidal funnels, the range running from a few feet at the entrance to twenty-three feet at the Colorado River delta, where the bore has been described as a six-foot "crumbling wall between two levels" of water, the incoming on top of the outgoing. Disappointed in his search for an open sea passage to the north, in 1722, the homebound Juan de Ugarte barely made it through the maze of islands confusing the mid-gulf tides. The tidal currents there, the exploring padre wrote, "are not like the others of the gulf which can hardly be detected, but they form running streams as if the water were sweeping forth from a dam . . . and they growl as water running over rocks." Sailors still respect and fear the tides and currents of the upper Sea of Cortés, grave of many an unlucky vessel.

Tides of the outer coast are normally moderate, ranging from lower in the south to higher in the north—for example: from four to five feet off San Diego; from eight to ten feet on Vancouver Island's outer shores. Each extensive inlet—San Francisco Bay, Puget Sound, the multichanneled Inside Passage—has its own peculiar tidal pattern. The latter is noted for 15- to 20-foot tides racing in and out of its narrow passes. Deep troughs like that of the Golden Gate are scoured clean by tidal currents carrying tidal basin debris out to sea.

The sea is forever moving. There is the small orbiting of individual water particles set in motion by the passage of waves; the surging of streams in constricted tidal channels; the onrush and backwash of the seas' thinned edges upon the world's strands. Everything they touch feels the impact of these swifter movements of water.

Ocean currents are vast, slow-moving flows within and upon the body of the sea. Probably the best known of the great currents is the Gulf Stream, that huge "ocean river" of deep blue cutting through the colder gray-green of the North Atlantic to bring to northwestern Europe a touch of tropical mildness from the Caribbean. Earth's sea gates are open. Any bit or particle passing through one could return, in time, to its starting point, after a progress around the world by one route or another. The unfettered mobility of ocean waters is not random but organized, like a kind of global circulatory system operating through increasingly better understood surface and subsurface currents and drifts. The prime movers are prevailing winds, the spin of the earth, and sundry modifiers of sea-water density. Winds, in concert with the earth's rotation, chiefly govern the set and speed of drifts and surface currents on the open sea. Density has to do with subsurface currents.

The northeast and southeast trades of the tropics and the prevailing westerlies of the higher latitudes, north and south, are the continuously but oppositely blowing chief components of the planetary wind system. Through friction these winds drag surface water along beneath them, until it is deflected by the north-south barriers of the continents. Thus—the spin of the earth playing a part—the North and South Pacific and the North and South Atlantic each has its circuit of wind drift, like a giant wheel. These rotate clockwise in the Northern Hemisphere, counter-clockwise in the Southern. Actually they are not closed circuits, since each sends off and receives tangential currents. Despite many irregularities and differences, however, these major ocean drift systems clearly follow a plan under geophysical law. (The accompanying chart of the North Pacific shows the winds and currents relating to our coast.)

There is a fascination in these slow, silent rivers of the world-wide sea, with such names as Gulf Stream and West Wind Drift bespeaking the restless ocean. The beachcomber in us responds to things wafted from shore to distant shore—green glass floats from Japanese fishing nets, for instance, beached on our coast from Alaska to Baja by the Kuroshio–North Pacific Drift–California Current.

Climate, in league with winds and atmosphere, is a more vital if less tangible gift of ocean currents. Moderation between extremes marks coastal climates: they are the most strongly influenced by the sea as regulator of global temperatures.

Currents play a part in climate, too: those drifting from low to high latitudes tend to be warmer than adjacent waters, those moving oppositely, cooler. Thus the Kuroshio, up from the tropics, warms Japan in passing, cools as it becomes the North Pacific Drift, and tempers our coast as the California Current augmented by arctic water. Surface water temperature in the Pacific Ocean is revealing: warm in the west, and on the same latitude in the east, cool. Upwellings, or the rising of cold water from the depths, are quite important in keeping water along western coasts cool in temperate latitudes. These occur particularly off Baja and Southern California, and enrich the upper layers of water by bringing up fresh supplies of nutrient salts for the plankton.

The ocean's winds and air pressure systems in concert with its currents bring this long Pacific Coast a climate of remarkable consistency, conducive to comfortable living. They also have played a part in history.

In november, 1564, a fleet of five Spanish ships sailed from Navidad, on Mexico's west coast, across the Pacific to conquer the Philippines. They went westward with ease under the trades, as others had some years before. While his mission was to found colonies in the islands, the commander Legaspi also had royal orders to seek a return route to New Spain without delay. Legaspi dispatched the *San Pablo* from Cebu in 1565, under the command of Salcedo with the veteran Urdaneta as senior pilot. Using the monsoon on the Philippine Sea, the *San Pablo* rose northeastward until, below the 40th parallel, she picked up the westerlies. Sloping down to latitude 27° or 28°, the navigators made a Baja California landfall and, after 129 days at sea, dropped anchor off Acapulco.

This sailing marked the first official west-to-east Pacific crossing; but, for the record, Salcedo and Urdaneta found they had been scooped by two daring and competent knaves, Martín and Arellano. Somewhere in Micronesia on the westward voyage, these renegades had slipped the fleet with a tiny tender *San Lucas*, probably fired by the royal promise of a reward for discovery of an eastward route. After rounding Mindanao and the whole Philippine archipelago, they had made for the open North Pacific. The *San Lucas* had climbed to 43°, made her easting along the 40th parallel—first European sail ever in those waters—and fetched California about where

In Turnagain Arm of Cook Inlet, in 1778, Captain Cook was caught between tides where the daily range between high and low is thirty-three feet, and had to wait for slack water because he could not sail out against so great an incoming tidal current. The water retreats over half a mile to bare these mudflats, then returns to cover them with some of the world's highest tides.

the *San Pablo* did, but two months before the galleon.

History awards to Andrés de Urdaneta, an experienced and for his time scientific navigator, the palm for masterminding a great "first" of world seamanship. And the *San Pablo* was indeed the first of the fabulous Manila Galleons, which for two and a half centuries—1565 to 1815—annually braved the extreme hardship of a North Pacific crossing under sail. It was the longest in duration of all shipping lines the world has yet known.

Although the passages became routine in year-in, year-out persistence (Cavite to Acapulco with jade and china, silk and spice; Acapulco to Cavite with silver pesos), their adventures and misadventures created a lively extravaganza of Pacific history. Out of it all, two things fall into place in our story. One is the operation's spurring of the search for a suitable California port of refuge and refreshment after the stormy, scurvy-ridden eastward passage. The other is its absolute, round-trip dependence upon reliable easterly and westerly winds. Like farming and commercial fishing, it was a human enterprise that required an unfailing natural phenomenon.

It was more than two centuries after the first cross-

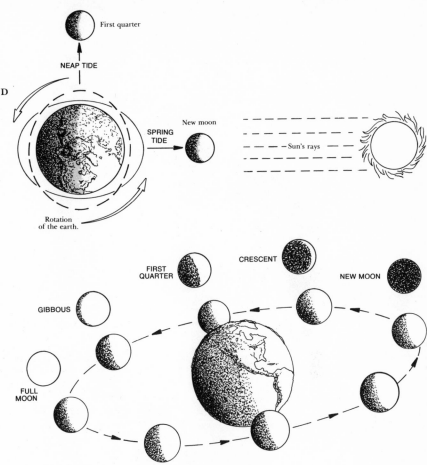

HOW THE GRAVITATIONAL PULL OF THE MOON AND SUN CAUSES THE EARTH'S TIDES (UPPER DIAGRAM)

Spring tides (large tides) occur at all times of the year when the new moon and the sun are aligned on the same side of the earth, and when the full moon and the sun are aligned on opposite sides; whether in concert or opposed, the pull of both bodies is exerted on the same circumferential band around the earth. Neap tides (small tides) occur when the sun and moon are pulling at right angles to each other, as during the moon's first and last quarters; then the pull of the sun weakens that of the moon by 40 percent of its force.

THE PHASES OF THE MOON (LOWER DIAGRAM)

ing before the ports of San Francisco, Monterey, and San Diego were established. Paradoxically, while the variable and stormy westerlies contributed to the need for such ports, they undoubtedly helped delay the search for them by sea.

As decades and generations went by, pilots accumulated a vast store of knowledge born of hard experience—knowledge of that sea, its currents, its shores, the design of its winds and weather. They performed everything humanly possible to keep basically ill-suited and often ill-found vessels harping true on the chords of the resonant winds—the well-tempered trades and the *fortissimo* westerlies.

No task of the wind is more essential to us and to all life than the carrying of water vapor from sea to land. Wind brings us fresh water distilled from the global reservoir of brine. Some aspects of climate and weather are by-products of the process. The ingredients are concentrated in the bottom layer of the atmosphere, the troposphere, where are found the necessities for making the whole thing go—radiant heat, atmospheric pressure, and water vapor.

Consider the simplest wind. Everyone who spends some time at the seashore is familiar with the classic sea breeze blowing onshore in late morning or early afternoon, as the faster-heating land becomes warmer under the sun than the nearby ocean. If land gets colder than ocean surface during the night as heat radiates outward, the reverse, or an offshore wind, may be expected. Such small local winds may blow in any direction, in accord with air pressure differences—they blow straight from high to low. Not quite so simple, but also pressure controlled, are the big winds of the large global systems, such as the prevailing westerlies that shape the climate on this edge of the continent. These bring from the ocean the cool, fresh weather of our summer dry season, and from the same ocean surface the rain, snow, and storms of our wet fall-winter-spring.

Pressure centers are pivots in the revolving doorway of the westerlies. Blowing straightest in the unbroken sea latitudes (called the Roaring Forties) of the Southern Hemisphere, these winds are variable in the Northern, between 30° and 60°, their global path interrupted by the great land masses.

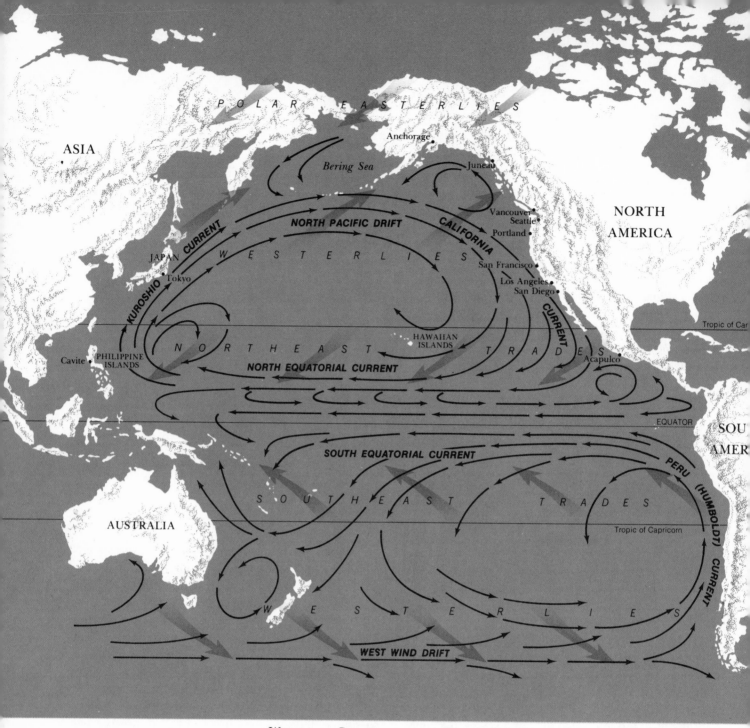

WINDS AND CURRENTS OF THE PACIFIC OCEAN

What are pressure belts over long reaches of the open sea become pressure centers in the atmosphere above the North Pacific.

Confrontations between dissimilar air masses, which may spread over large areas, give the coast its winter storms. They are exciting, and can be terrible. Powerful winds lash the ocean, drumming shoreward the highest, swiftest, most crowded waves of the year. Combers barrage beach and cliff like heavy artillery. Backwash drags huge quantities of sand into the sea to pile up in double lines of offshore bars. In spring and summer, the lighter, steadier winds, forever driving the waves—eight thousand may hit the beach every twenty-four hours—help them rebuild storm-ravaged strands as the gentler water inches the sand back to the widening berm.

It is time now to leave the wide face of Balboa's Great South Sea, and come ashore. After the larger view of an ocean and a glance at the elemental forces it brings to bear on its rim of land, we will take a closer look at tideland, beach, and cliff, at animals and plants that live on this many-faceted edge.

When the waves which wash the shore at high tide
recede and uncover a maze of rocky pools and channels,
a rich realm of life is exposed to our wondering exploration—the realm of intertidal life, and the true shoreline.

Overleaf: Diablo Canyon stretches to the sea from the
foot of California's exquisite, miniature San Luis Range.
At the right is the beginning of another of man's
encroachments: an atomic power plant.

CHAPTER 4

WHERE LAND AND OCEAN MEET

*The living world of land's edge and sea's fringe
from sandspit and sea stack to the hidden ocean floor.*

*The shore is an ancient world, for as long as there has been
an earth and a sea there has been this place of the meeting
of land and water. . . . Today a little more land may belong to the sea, tomorrow a little less. Always the edge of the
sea remains an elusive and indefinable boundary.*

—Rachel Carson, THE EDGE OF THE SEA

SURF SOUND and salt smell are in the air. At the
edge of the tide, our eyes scan beyond the
breakers to the great curve of the horizon,
sweeping to meet some near or distant headland.
The line is sharp or mist-blurred, according to the
kind of day it is, and perhaps broken by tall offshore
rocks or sea stacks. Landward, the edge of the view
is likely to be close and high, a blufftop above the
strand; or it may be at distant eye level, the far shore
of a bay beyond an enclosing spit. In its thousands
of miles the Pacific shore is variously edged—by the
treetops of a Panhandle islet, the low terrace front
of a California coastal prairie, grass plumes cresting
the dunes in many places from the Olympic Peninsula to Baja. Whatever the view, we see it, now, not
from the air or the ocean but from the shoreline itself, looking outward to its visible bounds, or down
to the immediate detail of it, the living detail of some
special kinds of environment.

In the forming and the life of these environments,
the sea appears in the active role, the land in the pas-
sive. The flexing of the earth's crust and activity
within and beneath it determine the general shape of
the land mass and configuration of the ocean shore,
and the sea adapts to the land's action. But the sea

and its spun-off cohorts, wind and rain, are the master craftsmen of coastline landforms. Land submits
its edge to the cutting, fraying, crumbling force of
the waves; its coastal hills and mountains to the erosion of weather. Even the patterns of maritime vegetation were set by the parent climate. Further proof
of the sea's dominance is found in the animals and
plants of that ultimate edge of both land and sea,
the tide zone. Intertidal algae and invertebrates are
sea forms adapted to part-time aeration, not land
forms submitting to periodic immersion.

Our focus is now upon this living world of land's
edge and sea's fringe, from kelp anchorages below
the surf to spindrift's airiest reaches, from ocean
bottom under lowest low tide to spray-moistened
rocks above highest high. Along the Pacific shore
exist some of the more numerous and varied communities of life on earth. Many marine vertebrates—
fishes, birds, mammals—found along or near the
shore, although given character by this pulsing margin
of the sea, are not in total bondage to it. The plant
and animal communities of upper beach, dune, and
seacliff are modified either adversely or favorably by
sea-shaped terrain or maritime climate. The concept
of a living shoreline is not complete without their
inclusion. With them, the continent's flora and fauna
must halt their march to the sea.

WHAT IS a *shoreline*, let us ask, and what are some
significant particulars of this shore? The *Century Dictionary* says that a shoreline is simply "the line
where shore and water meet." From the Middle En-

*A view to the south along one of the most celebrated portions of
the Pacific shore, California's magnificent Monterey coast.*

glish *schore* (meaning "to cut" or "to shear"), our modern *shore* is etymologically related to both *shear* and *score*. The word *coast* comes to us from the Latin *costa* ("a rib, a side"), which by medieval times had taken on the added meaning of "seacoast."

The connotation of something "sheared" or "cut" and the idea of a "shorn cliff" fit our Pacific shore perfectly. The western coast of North America is the earth's most cliff-bound, as though indeed cut with giant shears. As to *coast,* the definition "side, edge, or margin of the land next to the sea" implies something broader than the shore. The root meaning "rib" falls in place: if the Rockies are the backbone, the Coast Ranges are the continent's outer ribs.

The shoreline is literally a line only on maps. To be truthful the drawn line should vary in width, for the actual tidal zone varies enormously. Cartographically this would be impractical, of course; the important thing is to note the shoreline basis or *datum* of the chart in hand. Usually this is "mean sea level," the average of mean high and low waters of the coastline covered. On navigational charts, however, soundings (in feet or fathoms) are depths below "mean lower low water." The larger scale coast charts, when understood, reveal graphically the contrast between

steep, plunging shorelines and those with broad, virtually level intertidal zones. At one extreme—as on the Point Reyes headland where at some points the sea rises and falls literally on a vertical shoreline —the intertidal zone has no horizontal width to speak of. South San Francisco Bay exemplifies the opposite: an intertidal zone measured in hundreds of square miles of mudflats, alternately exposed and covered by a creeping sheet of water.

How long is the Pacific Coast? The question is harder to answer than one might think. We called our hypothetical jet survey a four-thousand-mile view. Its irreducible minimum is a great circle flight from Dutch Harbor to Puerto Vallarta, picking up the coast off the Golden Gate—4,000 statute miles. Doglegging it between the same two points via Anchorage, Juneau, Seattle, San Francisco, Los Angeles, and La Paz, along the coastline, gives 4,600 miles.

But what is the true length of our *shore*line? Much, much greater. To measure the actual length of, say, the California coast, must we walk the beach, climb the rocks, and calculate it with a yardstick? Almost! Fortunately it can be done, accurately enough for all practical purposes, on charts and topographic maps —small sections of coast drawn in large scale. The

This view of Dungeness Spit (the thin white line near the horizon, some five miles in length), on the Olympic Peninsula coast opposite Victoria, British Columbia, shows several effects of natural forces. Longshore currents coming through Juan de Fuca Strait from the ocean build eastward-growing spits such as this. The flagging of the trees shows the strong, prevailing northwest winds that blow unopposed through the strait. The broad little peninsula jutting from the main Olympic mass lies in the rain shadow of the Olympics and the ranges of Vancouver Island across the strait.

U.S. Coast and Geodetic Survey has already done it, in fact, and has official "Detailed Tidal Shoreline" (DTS) figures for our coasts. The survey explains how they are measured: "On the largest scale maps and charts available the shoreline of bays, sounds, and other bodies of water is included to the head of tidewater or to the point where they narrow to a width of 100 feet." Thus, California's DTS is 3,427 miles long, or more than four times the air distance. Add to this Oregon's 1,141 and Washington's 3,026 and you have a subtotal of 7,863 miles. Alaska—islands, inlets, and all—fronts the Pacific with a 31,383-mile DTS. This makes the U.S. total 39,246 miles. For British Columbia an authoritative estimate is 16,900 miles, for peninsular Baja California 3,500 miles. Grand total: 59,646 miles of shoreline! Because the smallest bits and pieces get left out, it is fair to round this off to 60,000 miles.

Sixty thousand miles of Pacific shoreline: stretched out, it would extend almost two and a half times around the earth. That is a lot of beach, tidepool, rock, cliff, mudflat, salt marsh, and other habitat for plants and animals. It runs the gamut of variations on the "meeting of land and water" theme. Picture, at one extreme, Baja's Salina Ojo de Liebre, absolutely level salt pans surrounded by low Vizcaíno Desert land, trapped under shimmering heat. Then imagine Guyot Glacier in Alaska's Icy Bay: sheer walls of ice plunging into the sea, with Mount St. Elias towering eighteen thousand feet above.

Hot, dry, flat; frigid, watery, mountainous—extremes dramatize the spectrum of variability. But the important thing is what governs the range of life within it, and that is nothing less than the sum of all factors and conditions. The configuration of a bit of land has much to do with local variations—microclimates—in regional climate patterns. These help determine what lives there. A southwest-facing headland such as Point Reyes makes a sheltered embayment to southeast. The windward side of that point is open or *exposed* outer coast; the lee or bay side is *protected* outer coast. Each, in this case, has both sand beach and rocky shore habitats. Each exposure has its distinctive assemblage of intertidal and upper shoreline animals and plants—or lack of them. In this and like situations the critical factor for living things is wave-shock, which is geared in turn to the

force of the wind. Exposure to wind affects the distribution of shore life adversely. The well-known association of starfish, mussel, and barnacle found clinging or anchored to the most wave-battered rocks and reefs of the outer coast is not there because conditions are good. This trio has, best of all intertidal animals, adapted to a bad deal for survival.

Of all influences on the distribution of life between the tides and in the sea, water temperature is most important. The sameness of some snails, barnacles, and algae on the rocks at many places between Sitka, Alaska, and Point Conception, California, is evidence of a narrow range in surface water temperature within a wide range of latitude. Conception has already been mentioned as a major ecological turning point. From here to Cabo San Lucas, our farthest point south, the latitude change is only half as much as from here north to Sitka, yet the surface water temperature difference almost doubles. Actually, the gradient does not rise sharply until the vicinity of San Lucas, and Mazatlán, across the Sea of Cortés on the mainland. There a northern temperate and transitional belt of seashore life ends, and a tropical one begins, in a latitude of significant change. The reason for coolness persisting offshore to that point lies in ocean currents and the related phenomenon of upwelling.

The North Pacific Current or Drift is the great surface water temperature equalizer of the eastern North Pacific. We have seen its start in the warm Kuroshio ("Black Current" or commonly Japan Current). Between the Kurile and Aleutian chains it meshes into and pulls along the cold Okhotsk Current; south of the Aleutians the Subarctic Current merges into it, and the whole vast flotage of surface water drifts slowly toward our continent. In these high latitudes it is still relatively warmer than the most northerly Pacific waters, and has in fact been termed the North Pacific Warm Current.

What happens then has tremendous import for the life of the whole Pacific Coast from the Gulf of Alaska to the tip of Baja. Somewhere off the Canadian border region the broad drift divides, the left branch bending sharply northward to become the Alaska Current, which warms the gulf. The right branch, some four hundred miles wide, drifts southward at a leisurely 0.2 to 0.6 miles an hour. This is the California Current, famous for the year-round coolness it brings to the coasts of Washington, Oregon, and the Californias.

In its sluggish drift over deep layers of colder, saltier ocean water, the California Current, while warming under a more and more direct sun, remains *relatively* cooler than adjacent surface waters. The influence of the cold Subarctic Current stays with it to a degree, moreover, until at the Tropic of Cancer off Cabo San Lucas it veers away to sea once more toward Hawaii. Warm now, its waters merge into the North Equatorial Current.

One of the major areas of upwelling occurs off southernmost Baja, as the warm northeast trade winds pull the surface waters—tail end of the California Current—away from land. Occurring along the coast in lessening degree as far as Oregon, this frequent replacement of warming surface water by colder, denser bottom water has a most vital, positive effect on both offshore and shoreline life, for the lower layers contain more of the nutrient salts which phytoplankton organisms near the surface must have to maintain their role as the sea's basic food. These minute, free-floating, one-celled plants are the pasturage that feeds zooplankton and, ultimately, all other marine animals.

Sometimes an imbalance occurs at this lower end of the food chain, which leads to overproduction of certain plankton forms. Partly owing to extra enrichment of the upper layer by winter upwelling, every few years a veritable population explosion occurs among various species of dinoflagellates along some shores. These are organisms having both plant and animal characteristics—chlorophyll-bearing, they photosynthesize; and they ingest food. One of them, *Gonyaulax*, has achieved notoriety on the Pacific Coast, where it is known to the general public by the ominous-sounding term "red tide." Other shores have their "poisonous" dinoflagellates which periodically kill untold millions of fishes and invertebrates, porpoises and sea turtles. By quantity alone, the natural content in the minute organisms of an apparently nitrogenous substance—one of the most toxic to the human system yet known—becomes deadly. It accumulates in the livers of many shellfish of unprotected outer shores, especially the California mussel. The time of year for avoiding such seafood varies from place to place; local regulations

should be carefully checked. Fortunately, the vast majority of species in this second-largest phytoplankton group appear to be quite harmless.

IN SUMMER, great lazy eddies of ocean water revolve counterclockwise near the coast. One, a large and enduring surface-water wheel, has its hub somewhere among the outer Channel Islands off Southern California; its radius is fifty miles or more at times. The rim of the wheel brushes the shore as far north as Point Conception and as far south as Los Coronados —rock islets off northern Baja. The center is an area of surface water enriched by upwelling and phytoplankton. Conversely, where some of the California water swings around the southern rim toward Ensenada, it sinks from the surface impoverished. There is here a virtual summertime desert in the ocean off Baja California. Such sea-surface changes greatly interest marine biologists, especially those charged with solving mysteries like that of the plankton-feeding California sardine, which in recent years has disappeared from most of its more northerly range, ending there a flourishing industry.

The constant movement of waters along the shore has its various and considerable effects on near-shore, intertidal, and shoreline life as well as upon shore-line configurations and formations. There is a continual overturn of bottom water to the top, replenishing nutrients; ceaseless onshore and longshore transport of food particles for the host of intertidal organisms; and a degree of temperature equalization, conducive to the wide distribution of many forms.

OUR FLIGHT along the Pacific Coast encompassed in one sweep a vast reach from north to south and a narrow coastal zone from west to east, both ever-changing. In the big view the particular place loses its identity and the nature of the shoreline its clarity. It is time to shorten the range and sharpen the focus, associating nature with place through examples, from Alaska's gulf to Baja's cape.

Around Glacier Bay and northwestward along the gulf where ice meets ocean, old glacial shores are brokenly timbered, although when glaciers melt back they sometimes reveal stumps of anciently crushed forests. In retreat, the ice gives us more shoreline and an inshore frequently cluttered with bergs.

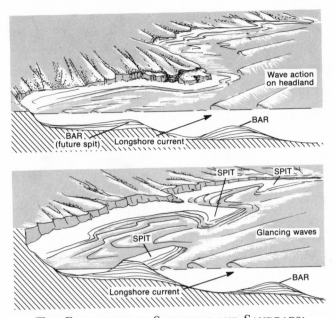

THE FORMATION OF SANDSPITS AND SANDBARS: *Wave action cuts headlands back, while longshore currents deposit material to build sandspits and sandbars, and enclose bays between the headlands.*

The coast from southeastern Alaska to Puget Sound has a shoreline in depth. Breaking the main force of ocean winds and waves, the outer islands of the Alexander Archipelago and the Queen Charlottes stand against the Pacific a hundred miles from the continental mainland—horizontal "depth" creating its own shoreline contrasts, from crashing surf to quiet tidewater. The Inside Passage and its many channels and arms have a shoreline world of their own, one familiar to a resident of Puget Sound but strange to a Californian. Forgetting the tides, there is often the feeling of sailing a river or standing on its bank—many of the waterways are extremely narrow, and often the forest crowds the shoreline, which is not usual for a seacoast. Or, when channel bends cut off all view of open water, one seems to be on a lake.

So much of the Puget shoreline that once marked the clean, sharp edge of forest is now a botch of modern human implements and constructions that it is more and more difficult to trace the old ecological patterns of nature and man. The same is true of San Francisco Bay. Settlers cut redwood groves, down to the wet of tidal creeks and marshes, and stripped bayside savannas of their oaks. Today, a few bay people are trying to awaken the rest to the value of the re-

maining natural shoreline—there is very little left.

Our wildest shores now are the rockiest, with here and there a stretch of beach where one may walk a wild way still. Rare foresight saved fifty-two miles of Washington's ocean shore when the Pacific Coast Area of Olympic National Park was secured in 1953. This islanded and rock-studded strip, with its forest edge and abundant animal life, is one of the most primitive sections of seacoast we have left.

Oregon's coast is a classic battleground of the ancient land-sea war. Scarcely another thousand miles of shore can boast so many "textbook examples" of various formations—river mouths, bay-mouth spits, sheared-off headlands, beaches, dunes, rock islets and stacks, arches and caverns, alternating in endless succession far down the Northern California coast.

The ocean seems determined to straighten every indented coastline. It batters bulging headlands down, grinds their rock into sand, and uses it to fill the gaps between. First it builds crescent beaches in small coves, then bay-head beaches; last, it throws bay-mouth spits and bars across deeper and wider embayments. The normal conclusion of the latter effort is completely closed lagoons, where a stream is too small or sluggish to keep a sea channel open. The battle goes to the sea when the river fails to offset losses due to evaporation, percolation, silting, or other curtailment of flow, and thwart the bay-to-lagoon process. Our coast is replete with examples.

There are many miles of very long and broad beaches on the Pacific Coast, and there are places where coastland merges gently with ocean horizon, although coastal plains are few. The most typical picture, however, representing all but a few uncharacteristic scenes of this coast—the familiar view in thousands of postcards, slides, movie frames—is an L of ocean, beach or rock, and cliff. If the uprise is enhanced by straight and tall conifers, the scene is from Northern California northward. If the trees are somewhat contorted pines or cypresses, it may be as far south as the Monterey coast, or near La Jolla in Southern California. Where cliffs are stark, sprouting grasses and scrub on abutting slopes, most likely the view is from central California southward. Regardless of detail the cliffs are there, hallmark of the Pacific Coast. Our western edge almost never slides quietly down to the sea. It thrusts boldly to the battleground.

CHAPTER 5

LIFE BEYOND THE BREAKERS

*Offshore and longshore birds and mammals—
the life cycle of the free swimmers and far fliers.*

WHERE WEATHERING ROCKS, kelp-skirted ledges, cliffs, and sundered islets hold the outer shore against the first wave-shock; where swells charge upon these bastions and explore in thundering cascades of foam—there are the most dramatic scenes of this western coast. Shoreline strongpoints, such places feel the forces of land and sea where they are most relentlessly pitched in battle. Yet, with all this going on—this unremitting inanimate action—here too is life, life with the resilient strength of flesh and blood, fur and feathers, bone and shell and plant tissue.

The several forms of life, quite at home in this seemingly most inhospitable environment, are fittingly bold, vigorous, mobile, or equipped to hold fast to bottom or rock face while riding out the heaviest seas at the surface. Birds, mammals, even the kelp heads tossing like flotillas of small craft at anchor in an open roadstead have the look of living things which possess and use the freedom won through mastery of uncompromising habitats.

By far the best way to fully savor the tang of wildness is, first, to get beyond the sight and sound of human constructions and implements; second, to do it alone. One or two congenial companions may enrich the experience, but a crowd of strangers will most surely destroy the mood of personal adventure. An illusion, at least, of remoteness is still to be found, and with it—if one is lucky—the shining edge of discovery. It may be an extremely small wedge of shoreline, no more than can be encompassed within the field of vision; and it may show a face that has changed through countless millennia only at the imperceptible rate of geological and evolutionary processes. Wildness and timelessness are part of each other. No human ear heard the first sea lion roar or the first gull cry on the shore. No sea lion heard the first surf thunder. With thoughts of this kind, in such a place, one may discover something of the time and tide that govern affairs of the natural world.

Even before the feet have found a suitable outlook point, the scouting eyes may have caught a kind of giant raft rising and falling, as though at anchor, on the swells beyond the breaker line. From some points on the highway—from, say, the Monterey coast to Oregon and Washington—perhaps two hundred feet or more above the shore, binoculars may be needed to recognize the material of the raft. There, shining in the water, are the same ripe-olive bulbs, often eight inches in diameter, with long, rubbery ribbons twelve feet long or more multibranching from the large end, the other end tapering into a considerable length of tubing (often seen stranded, inert, on the beach). It is familiar kelp—ribbon, or bull kelp—and from the behavior of the raft it is evident that its organized integration is more vertical than horizontal: each unseen small end of a tube must be a kind of holdfast anchoring one bulb or head to the bottom, and so it is. Thus the whole group or "forest" of these brown algae surfaces as a floating dock, not a raft, and is in fact often called a "kelp dock."

Kelp may appear anywhere from Alaska to Point Conception (another kind, the giant kelp, takes over in Southern California waters), offshore on the open

The rocky open coast and unprotected outer shores receive the full force of winds and waves. Their rugged beauty is the product of these forces, and everything that lives there must be hardy to adapt to them. These are turbulent places.

coast or in the larger bays and inlets. There must be a fair current, a rocky bottom, and depth not greatly exceeding fifty feet. And it must be summer in these northern waters. Then the huge algae, fastest growing of all plants, are seen in their annual glory. Early coast explorers sometimes mistook their dense, dark masses for islands. For the docks may extend for several acres, and support a transient surface population of resting sea birds, and occasional migrants from land. Below decks a kelp dock becomes, in its growing and flourishing period, a true biological island. It is tenanted at the various economic, or ecological, levels from the topsides, betweensides, and undersides of the ten- to twelve-foot ribbons intertwined like noodles on a platter, all the way down the stipes or stems, to the rootlike holdfast clinging to the rocks twenty to fifty feet below.

Summer boarders of the kelp beds range from salmon—often shoaling in such numbers around the docks that trawlermen do likewise, to their profit—to jellyfish, snails and limpets, nudibranchs, bryozoans, and dainty little red and green algae, plant on plant like moss on trees. There are many others, some attaching themselves at favorable levels to snatch passing food from the water, some free swimming, all taking advantage of the situation or of each other. They must live to the hilt while they can because, like all summer colonists, when the establishment closes down at the end of the season they must go elsewhere until next summer's crop appears.

The kelp plant has been called the redwood of the seaweed forest, and like the tree has great commercial attractiveness. None who greatly enjoy our wild shore and offshore waters and their dependent life, however, will condone a too extensive industrial appropriation of the kelp forest, especially since the docks are once again harboring on this coast their most fabulous summer guests—the sea otters.

On rare moments as one watches a kelp bed floating in the sunlight, a shiny head may seem to detach itself from its anchored stem, and move at a different beat through or away from the bobbing kelp mass. Seal, or sea lion, most likely. But since this midcentury, between the Monterey Peninsula and Morro Bay and around the Channel Islands, the chances are better year by year for that erratic head to belong to an animal making a quiet comeback from oblivion.

IT IS NOT hard to tell. A sea lion or seal head in the water calls to mind a short-haired dog swimming with ears flattened. But a sea otter is more like a cherubic little old man with grizzly whiskers. And it is likely to be swimming, or just floating, on its back, the small furry hands busy with something—kelp ribbon, its favorite sea urchin food, or a baby otter. Almost two and a half centuries of recorded observations agree in ascribing to this five-foot owner of the world's most valued pelt certain winning qualities we smugly call human: playfulness and lovingness.

Even the half-savage Siberian fur hunters, who raced greedily into Aleutian waters after Bering's survivors brought back the first load of furs, were known occasionally to remark, as they clubbed the defenseless otters to death, that they were "almost human." This did not, however, stop the *promish-leniki*—these human predators—from initiating the near-extermination of the species with a heedless brutality not often equaled in the sad accounting of man's inhumanity to other animals.

For centuries Aleut, Tlingit, and other tribesmen of the coast and its islands had hunted the sea otter for the beauty and utility of its pelt, and sometimes for meat. Nevertheless, the species flourished off the Aleutian and Northwest coasts and in the cool offshore waters all the way to central Baja California. Cousin of mink, weasel, and other mustelids, the sea otter is a former land mammal "returned" to the sea. It has mastered a habitat offering little competition and adapted so completely to its watery environment that it mates afloat and gives birth to its single pup as handily on a kelp dock as on the rocks ashore. And neither killer whale nor primitive hunting man had upset its balance. It was an utterly ruthless commercialism that brought it near the end in our time.

From Alaska south on this coast a human generation passed, with the sea otter unknown to it as a living animal. Then on a spring day in 1938, an observant person saw some animals on a kelp dock which were strange to him, although he was no stranger in that area at the mouth of Bixby Creek, Monterey County, some fifteen miles south of Carmel. The regional California fish and game warden verified the report—sea otter! Nearly a hundred of them! No one was more excited than Professor Edna M. Fisher of San Francisco State College, who spent four months zealously observing the herd. Her report the following year in the *Journal of Mammalogy* was a landmark study of the habits of sea otters on the California coast.

Since then, these delightful animals have often entertained beach-front residents at their picture windows in Carmel and Pebble Beach, and visitors to Point Lobos Reserve.

The picture grows from bits and pieces of chance discovery. One day, surely, someone scanning a kelp dock offshore in Oregon, or Washington, will see a dark shape moving as no kelp head moves, will focus intently, and if luck is with him he may see the little hands adjusting a stone on the wide chest, raising a shell—sea urchin, probably—and cracking it down. A baby might be close by, wound around with kelp ribbon to keep it from drifting away. . . .

The sea otter will have won back some more of its ancient ground.

ANOTHER great Pacific Coast comeback is in the making where pounding surf meets rock ledge and shelving beach, although its grotesque and outsized hero lacks the sea otter's endearing charms. He is the elephant seal.

Seal oil was valuable in the nineteenth century, and a three-ton bull elephant seal was a profitable haul. The huge but inoffensive animal had made its last stand on the California coast between Point Reyes and Baja's Cabo San Lazaro. By 1869 the observant Pacific whaler, Captain Charles M. Scammon, had to report the elephant seal "nearly, if not quite, extinct." In 1892 seal hunters killed seven out of eight found, after a long search, on Guadalupe Island. It looked like curtains for yet another animal species, with human hands on the pull. Fortunately, after the execution, Guadalupe Island was left in peace.

By good luck, the ornithologist Charles H. Townsend had landed with the 1892 party. Returning in 1911, he counted 125 elephant seals. In 1922 a scientific group found 264, and its reports won the cooperation of the Mexican government, which made Guadalupe a federal reserve with full protection for the giant seals. Dr. George Lindsay, director of the California Academy of Sciences, wrote in 1951 that this herd had grown to 1,600; a small herd was established on San Miguel, and another on Los Coronados,

forty miles from San Diego. And in 1961 Dr. Robert T. Orr of the Academy counted at least eighty hauled out on one beach of Año Nuevo Island, forty-five miles south of San Francisco. The story of the elephant seal, which now roams widely over the northeastern Pacific, appears at last to be one of a happy continuation, not a tragic ending. The big fellow may be, like the sea otter, reclaiming his former continental strands.

If one animal were chosen symbol of the freedom and mastery of the wild waves and rock ramparts of far-flung coasts, what would be more fitting than the sea lion? Picture the young male: plunging powerfully and skillfully through combers, up with a herring in his teeth, hauling himself out polished ebony–wet onto a spindrifted ledge, a sleek statue with foreparts balanced upright on angled flippers, head and pointed muzzle raised skyward—the fish engorged—to send his wild piercing, deeply resonant *ar-ar-ar-ar!* into the wind. Such is the California sea lion to those who know him where he is free. (Resemblances in this description to the "trained seal" of stage and circus are inescapable—he, or more likely she, *is* the amazing show-world "seal," combining agility, intelligence, and great teachability.)

Between them, the two sea lion species contribute a lot of color and action to the pulsing edge of our westward sea. With its largest numbers off Southern and Baja California, the California sea lion ranges from central Mexico to Washington state. The much larger Steller species characteristically seeks more remote shores, from the Channel Islands to the Bering Sea, with fifty of its estimated sixty thousand population in British Columbia and Alaska. Yet it appears before a large public in a few accessible places such as Oregon's Sea Lion Caves and Seal Rocks off Ocean Beach, San Francisco, where some may be seen from city windows.

ALONG single file of large birds glides, with infrequent wing strokes, inches above a rising wave. California brown pelicans, they had the long-beaked, heavy-bodied, underslung look of old Yankee Clipper or Catalina flying boats. "The bird is impossible," William Leon Dawson wrote in *The Birds of California* (1923), but "he can glide with incredible accuracy just above the surface of the water." More-

The sea otter, over five feet long, is surprisingly large in comparison with its four-foot cousin, the river otter. Once the world's most valuable and brutally hunted fur-bearer, the sea otter had been virtually exterminated by 1911, when the catch had dwindled from thousands to twelve skins. That year, the last pelt sold commercially brought $1,990 in London. And that year, the United States, Great Britain (representing Canada), Japan, and Russia signed a pact to prohibit sea otter hunting completely. Since then, the Aleutian population has grown to more than five thousand animals, and California's to more than one thousand.

over, "he is prepared to take care of an enormous haul" of fish—and did, offshore from central California to South America. Sadly, this is written now in past tense. It appears very possible from recent and careful observations that DDT concentrations in fish will write *finis* at least to California populations of this magnificent bird.

Other fishermen, the best that fly, stand on juts of rock among the waves once so keenly examined by pelicans—the cormorants. Three of the world's thirty or more species range the Pacific Coast from southern Alaska to Central America. They make the familiar upright silhouettes on rock and piling, wings sometimes spread-eagled. An S-curved neck, a slender and sometimes crested head, a long, slim, hook-tipped beak, face-skin or gular pouches colored red, yellow, buff, or blue, and eyes usually green— these features combine to give cormorants an archaic, reptilian character. Somewhat heavy fliers, they are at their best under water.

A better flier and perhaps equal swimmer and diver is the common or California murre, whose family is the Northern Hemisphere counterpart of the penguin's. In fact, the murre, with its full white front and similar shape and stance, will be recognized best as the bird of our North Pacific shore that looks most like a penguin—until it flies. The older generation of San Franciscans may recall it as the bird that supplied the city's eggs for nearly forty years after the gold rush. Russians and Aleuts who manned the Farallon sealing station during Fort Ross colony days, 1812 to 1841, doubtless recognized the murre because they had seen its enormous rookeries on the Aleutians and islands of the Bering Sea. Its eggs must have been among those few taken from the Spanish *Los Farallones* to Russia's never flourishing fort, but there were not enough consumers to have made the least dent in the also huge Farallon population of murres.

In about ten years on the lonely rocks (after which they chiefly procured eggs and sea lion meat), the Russians eliminated the fur seal from the area and from our story. Starting business in 1850, the Farallon Egg Company went through the murre rookeries with comparable zeal—that is, with total disregard for anything but large and immediate profits. More than half a million eggs were sold in less than two months of 1854. Of course, to those biologically ignorant people the supply may have seemed inexhaustible, but the rookeries never recovered.

We often take sides in nature's age-old wars, from a bias of sentiment or other commitment. Some people enjoy a sea lion as a noble example of wild free animal life. Others enjoy salmon for sport or profit, some of them calling for war on sea lions because they, too, enjoy salmon. Perhaps such people are simply unaware of research which has shown that sea lions feed largely on things less desirable to us: octopus, squid, hake, and lamprey, the latter a fish that kills much salmon. A human war on sea lions does not appear to be justified. Nor a war on sea otters to save abalones for us—the otters eat mostly sea urchins which destroy the kelp we prize. Nor even a war on gulls to protect the murres, the few that the eggers left. The essential thing is for man not to interfere with nature's checks and balances if he wants to continue to enjoy all life, including his own.

THE UBIQUITOUS GULL is everyone's symbol of the seacoast, from wildest beaches and rocky shores to bay mudflats and pilings in busy harbors. A gull's cry is a wild cry, and no one will forget it who has heard it on the wings of a storm. People who live near the Pacific shore, seeing and hearing gulls fly landward low overhead, glance to the darkening west: they know a storm is soon to follow. But those who get on close terms with offshore waters from the decks of small craft—yachts, motor launches, tugs, trawlers, sportfishing boats—also become acquainted with other birds, seldom seen at the shore except at their nesting sites. And those retreats may be in remote areas or on cliffs, headlands, and islands hard to get to and therefore seldom visited by man.

Soaring, gliding, banking against wind or wave, wheeling away for another pass, diving down, glancing off, touch and go, or following for hours—sea birds wing the traceless aerial wake of every ship, large or small.

Gulls seen well offshore may be kittiwakes—wings solidly black-tipped straight across—wintering southward from Bering Sea and Aleutian breeding

grounds, or, by good luck, Sabine's, our only fork-tailed gull. Offshore sailing leads to the realm of true open-sea birds, far-ranging, magnificent fliers. The wandering albatross, its wingspread of ten to twelve feet the greatest of any living bird, must remain for us in poetry and imagination until we go south of the Equator. But two smaller relatives sometimes appear within sight of our shore: the black-footed albatross and the short-tailed albatross. Other visitors of the order are fulmars, sailing close to the water to seek jellyfish, and shearwaters. Dawson has best described the latters' hunting organization: "a great revolving ring that drifts north or south with a movement as certain and imperceptible as the 'secular drift' of the stars. The circle may be a comparatively small one, so that you can see the returning line, the other side of the circle, a mile or so farther out to sea; or it may be very large, as much as twenty-five miles in diameter . . . a quarter of a million birds."

And there are the little dark storm-petrels themselves, whose principal generic name, *Oceanodroma*, means so poetically "runners on the ocean." They do in fact appear to run or dance on the surface, flying at touch-height with webfeet dangling. It is an experience to follow them to their island nesting burrows, and we shall in another chapter.

Two ocean birds are rare enough on our northern coast to make it a red-letter day when one sights either: the red-billed tropicbird—slender, white, its heavy red bill balanced aft by the two middle tail feathers, each one to two feet long; and (using its modern name) the magnificent frigatebird. Dawson (using its old name) said: "Without doubt, the Man-o'-war-bird is the Master Wild Thing a-wing." Fewer than twenty California sightings were on record when he wrote, a half-century ago. Of these, two were his, in August 1912 near Santa Barbara, California: "On each occasion one got only a quick sense of regal power and ease before the vision vanished, lost in the eye of the gale."

These qualities of wildness and threats of annihilation are easily read into the kaleidoscopic, ongoing drama of our offshore birds and mammals, a drama which has played continuously through recent epochs, unfolding in settings of unsurpassed grandeur, earth's most spectacular meeting place of land and water.

CHAPTER 6

EDGE OF THE TIDE

*The teeming world of algae and invertebrates
between salt-sprayed cliffs and lingering pools of low tide.*

To follow the receding tide by a random progress from one slippery rock to another— sloshing through seaweed, poising for a jump across a swift ebb-stream, making it to a more engaging vantage—is to build excitement and wonder at the vitality and variety of living things. Wonderment is roused most by the growing sense that here, between the splash zone and low water, there are greater numbers and more kinds of things alive than one has ever seen before in a small area.

The next thing to strike one is the apparent organization among both animals and plants, especially in their vertical distribution through high, middle, and low tide levels. Certain forms group together in communities, and each of these occupies a certain type of habitat; moreover, each inhabitant of a community has its own niche, or occupational role, which involves definite relationships with each of the others and with the immediate environment. The firmness of these ecological arrangements of tide-zone life strikes one as he scrutinizes them.

Anyone who has visited a few widely separated localities of the coast's intertidal realm and observed their habitat structure even casually has noted that the "zoning laws" of the tidal area hold throughout a wide range of latitude. All up and down the coast, the main divisions are recognizable. Within them, similar shoreline formations provide similar habitats, but these may be occupied by different species, even different genera, living the same life in regions remote from each other. The more than casual observer soon finds his way around each of the "neighborhoods" or zones of the intertidal area he visits most often, and recognizes similar if not identical forms in the same zones hundreds of miles away. As with television westerns, it's the same old plot, only the actors have different names.

Between the geographical extremes of the Gulf of Alaska and the Gulf of California, great biotic changes occur, but largely in a zone of overlap and transition from temperate forms to tropical. This extends from Point Conception to about midway on

SEA WATER, from great depths under pressure to the spray zone of occasional airy moisture, provides a nearly ideal medium for the life that is bound to it. All marine animals except those most recently evolved (the sharks and rays, the bony fishes, and mammals) have body fluids *isotonic*—equal in osmotic pressure—with sea water. They are free from the fresh-water animals' problem of dilution, and the land animals' one of excessive concentration, of salts in their systems. But they still have to cope with such ecological variables as absolute pressure, temperature, sea-water chemistry, currents, wave action, tidal movement, and the architecture of sea bottom and shoreline, as well as with the interrelationships of plants and animals themselves.

Baja's Pacific side. Even biologists have some problems sorting things out in this long changeover stretch. Fortunately, most of us are satisfied when we learn what pigeonhole to put some form of life in, and a few facts about the way it lives.

Before visiting the intertidal world, let us recall some background facts of the sea and its life.

*Where heavy surf beats against steep and jagged rocks, the sea palms are one of
the few forms of life—vegetable or animal—built to sustain such battering.
These algae have short "rubber tubing" stems, and long rubbery fronds.*

THE LONG CURVING SHORE

LIFE BEGAN in sea water, it is assumed, and its highest divisions evolved there before the first land-dwelling forms appeared in the mid-Paleozoic era. Sea life has had a much longer time to diversify into major structural types. However, owing to the far greater uniformity of its environment and the fewer natural barriers to its distribution around the earth, it has lagged well behind the late-coming land life in producing numbers of different species. Of nearly a million living animals known, only about one-fifth are aquatic, of both fresh and salt water.

The colder waters of the higher latitudes, such as embrace the larger part of this coast, make for fewer

THE SEA, with time and an all-embracing medium to work in, gave rise to every principal animal division, or phylum, from Protozoa to Chordata, and had experimented with several of them at length before sending trial balloons into the realm of air (Echinodermata, where sea urchins and starfish belong, is the only major phylum that has remained strictly marine). A wide range of radically differing structural plans and working models assured the eventual occupation of every sea habitat. Some were adaptable to withstanding colossal weights of water in the farthest deeps; others, to mastery of suspension and movement in mid-depths; still others, to riding the surface; and finally, a whole battery of forms, to taking up the most variable portions of the sea, its edges. (Land life, in its turn, met the challenge of infinitely greater environmental extremes—pressure excepted—by rapidly evolving new species on relatively fewer basic plans. It thus adapted to new conditions and habitat situations—aerial, earthbound, and subterranean. Some of its forms, paradoxically, have returned in whole or in part to their ancient mother, the sea.)

kinds of life but larger populations. (By the same token, on land, the northern temperate forests have no such wealth of tree species as tropical rain forests, but they blanket vast areas more uniformly.) Plankton, base of the ocean food web, is most abundant in those cooler regions where, consequently, the most productive fisheries are found. Where things are tough, the few well-adapted species tend to populate available habitats to the elastic limit. Thus, at some points along the northern rocky outer coast may be found large, densely populated beds of virtually nothing but mussels.

Extremes are always intriguing, and the Pacific shore has them, end to end. A tropical coral reef is one—Pulmo Reef at Baja California's tip, swarming with life in exuberant variety. A subarctic glacial sea-cliff is another—the calving of bergs around the Gulf of Alaska must exemplify the sheerest biological barrenness. But extremes mark boundaries; focus rests mostly on the broad in-between. Going from Cabo San Lucas to Point Sur, Cape Mendocino, or the western headlands of Baranof Island near Sitka, one finds few important differences in outer coast rock formations or in habitat zonation from high to low tide. Such long jumps in latitude, however, bring changes in species within intertidal communities.

Animals of the intertidal habitat have two things in common. They are invertebrates, except for a very few fishes; and they spend at least their adult lives within this narrow band of the seashore which extends from the occasional exposures of lowest low tides to the sporadic dampenings from the spindrift of highest highs. (A barnacle ending its free-swimming nauplius or larval stage to fix itself on a keel instead of a rock may of course continue its opportunities for travel!) Most replete with different forms is the zone of minus tides (a *minus tide* is one that falls below the average low-tide line); least is the nearly high-and-dry band wetted now and then by an extra high wave, or by spray from high-water surf.

As among men, the evolutionary drive seems to be toward improving one's lot. Some animals, by adapting to the sunlight and periodic near-exposure of tidepools, have moved up from the denser milieu of the lowest zone; even the subtidal bottom cannot imprison all its long-time inmates forever. And nonchalantly letting salt water dry on its back, the sand flea assumes airs of split-level living by sojourning freely many yards above the highest droplets of spray.

THE INVERTEBRATES of the Pacific Coast intertidal zone are distributed locally in accordance with three main factors (which also reflect the differences between East and West coastal tidal life):

Degree of wave shock. Prevailing westerly winds, tremendously long fetch of ocean waves, and wide expanse of unprotected coast all add up to wave shock upon this shore; it has been described as probably more powerful here than anywhere else in the Northern Hemisphere.

Type of bottom. This is critical in terms of what

animals and plants are able to anchor, cling, burrow, or otherwise secure themselves more or less permanently in or upon one or more of the available materials; in most areas rock, sand, and mud, separately or in combination, make up the bottom, each holding certain kinds of life.

Tidal exposure. Relative lengths of exposure time, in air and in water, determine the level at which each form occurs; under this heading also comes temperature of water as it fluctuates between summer and winter, especially in lower, warmer latitudes.

As we explore the band between high and low water, we find local conditions which, governed by these factors, determine the presence or absence of certain groups in the area. And we find also that the tide-zone habitats of one locality may be classed as belonging to *estuarine or bay shores;* to the *outer coast,* which may be *protected* from or *exposed* to wind and wave; and to the *open coast,* which most regularly takes the full force of strong winds and wave shock.

The relation of the changing levels of the tide to all these conditions and situations is next to be considered, very broadly. In simplest terms, four major tide levels are recognized, all up and down the coast:

Splash zone—rocks wet by the spray of high water breaking upon them; upper beach wet by storm waves only.

High-tide zone—area covered by most high tides and always exposed at low tide.

Mid-tide zone—always covered at high tide and usually exposed at low tide.

Low-tide zone—almost always covered; exposed by the lowest tides only. (The next lower—it may be called the below-tide zone—is always covered; this is the scuba diver's happy hunting ground.)

Leaving bay shores for visiting in a later chapter, let us go to the tide zone of some part of the shore that may be taken as typical of a large portion of the whole Pacific Coast—any one of the many places where beach walking and tidepool watching may be comfortably and pleasantly combined. For most of us, it is enough to get acquainted with the more conspicuous and easily identified forms of shore life. And watching the continuous assault of the waves on their chosen habitats, we wonder at their tenacity as well as their variety. (In these few pages, and the accompanying list of major forms of animals and plants

found in each of the tide-zone levels, it is possible only to hint at the number of them and how they live. Books for the reader's deeper interest are listed under Sources and Suggested Reading.)

SAND FLEAS or beach hoppers, exploding around one's feet in sandy areas above the splash zone, are "dry-edge indicators"—animals that seem to have broken the bonds of the sea but are still most at home near it. Where the rocks above high tide are wet now and then by fallout from the explosion of breakers against them, they may be dotted with small periwinkle snails. Strangely, while these apparently land-oriented mollusks must have gills wetted occasionally, they will drown if immersed too long. They are a sure sign of the splash zone. The fixed acorn barnacle, at a slightly lower level, is still of the sea: in this adult stage it can feed only by thrusting tentacles out to wave blindly in the froth for any edible passing by. Barnacle colonies give space to limpets, whose broad feet have tremendous power to grasp rock yet allow them to wander while scraping food from it. Barnacles and limpets both are adapted to wave shock; yet where they are numerous there is usually something to break the full force of ocean waves.

Whatever favors the splash zone and upper high tide forms also fosters the rich variety and abundance of life between high and low tides, which makes tidepools fascinating. Plants and animals both take advantage of protection, the rhythmically moving water alive with food, the long daylight, and intricate variations of foothold and living space.

In the high-tide zone the algae, minor on the damp rocks above, contribute the major colors and textures. The Pacific Coast is one of the world's richest in these plants, with some five hundred species; the different species are good markers of their tide zones. Trapping and holding much water as tides run out, seaweeds provide continuous wetness, shelter, and food for many animals. In this much-exposed zone one finds among the rockweeds (these algae thin out at the upper edge), besides turban snails, more barnacles, limpets, chitons, and many other animals, the scrappy little rock crabs. Great ones for wedging into crevices, these sharp-clawed arthropods can change from red to dark green and blend with seaweeds—triple security. They forage mostly at night.

THE LONG CURVING SHORE

The mid-tide zone is the truly teeming one. On this rocky coast, it is the zone supporting the largest populations of many different forms of life. Animals or plants, or both, cover every surface except the sandy bottom between areas of rock. Algae drape rock-tops and sides in rich variety and many colors. Squishing underfoot are dense colonies of a small anemone, a plant-like animal. A large starfish appears in red, yellow, and purple phases. Officially the purple seastar, this robust creature clings to rock and withstands wave-battering as few others can. Although the rock crab ranges into this zone, mid-tide rockweeds are the haunt of the purple shore crab. Another animal of both zones, the little hermit crab, grows bigger here; but a still larger hermit, of this zone especially, is the dominant one of its kind, residing almost exclusively in large turban snail shells.

Color characterizes the mid-tide zone. Bright red, purple, and coral encrusting sponges splash the sides and undersides of rocks and ledges. A vivid red nudibranch or sea slug—a snail with no shell—feeds on the red sponges. Other nudibranchs live in tidepools—beautiful little animals they are, one white with flaming orange-red appendages. For some reason these tempting-looking creatures are shunned by other carnivores. Among other animals of the zone are chitons; solitary corals in vivid yellow, orange, and red; brittle stars, which live beneath rocks and in the spaces between them, distinct mid-tide habitats that also protect long-fingered shrimps and several kinds of worms; and a blenny. This fish, long and much like an eel, is the first intertidal vertebrate one encounters. Another fish, not likely to be seen, is a small, blind goby, which shares a ghost shrimp burrow with a pea crab.

The low-tide zone, as a rule, is exposed to the air only by minus tides. Its denizens require the least in special adaptation for holding on to surfaces or avoiding desiccation. Subject to little wave shock, the zone affords a variety of niches for all classes of marine invertebrates. If one were to choose a single object worth the wait for an uncommon minus tide, the preparation, and the extra effort of going all the way out to where deep-cleft rocks are briefly exposed, it might be the great green anemone. En route, many things will be diverting: some splendid algae, giant red urchins six or seven inches in diameter, the many-rayed sunflower star spreading two feet and the largest of all starfish, huge gumboot chitons, a host of different crabs, and other fascinating things. Then, a ten-inch giant of an anemone fills one's eyes. In the sun or even in dull light, the delicately intense hue of the countless rays suggests something alive in its own right—and this is no fancy. For that luminous emerald is the response to sunlight of chlorophyll-bearing algae living symbiotically within the anemone's tissue, its intensity in proportion to exposure. Surely the great green anemone (it is sometimes almost blue) is the most beautiful animal of this coast's tide zones.

WHERE CLIFF and rock breast the long, strong winds from the open sea, surf batters mightily, unopposed, and nothing lives that cannot clamp powerfully to fronting faces of rocks—here a few plants and animals hold their almost exclusive ground. Among a handful of algae the brown sea palm braces against the most extreme wave shock at low tide. It is not tide level but maximum exposure to wind and wave action that ordains the open coast–rocky shore association of a hardy zone-marking trio: the common seastar, the California mussel, and the Pacific goose barnacle. It is an interesting community, with the starfish preying on the other two, especially the mussel—three widely divergent animals linked in successful adaptation to rigorous conditions.

As different as possible from this world of wave shock or the drier one of the splash zone is that realm which lies forever beyond the lowest of low tides: the realm of abalones, a red one growing to eleven inches; purple sea urchins, the major threat to young kelp on which they graze; the Dungeness crab, sometimes plentiful in the market place, sometimes scarce, according to a precarious ecological balance; cabezon, eel, and other fishes, many going into the scuba diver's bag.

Abundant as many of the animals and plants of the intertidal zones are, prolific as the edge of the sea appears, no realm of life is in greater need of our concern for its continuing good health—indeed, for the very survival of its living things. For its own sake and ours, we must guard the edge of the tide.

In the tidepools, it is often difficult to see just what is under water and what is momentarily exposed to the air. For the plants and animals of the intertidal habitat, life depends on the balance of adaptations to both milieus.

The scuba diver's blue-green world knows air only indirectly, and sunlight as an infiltration diminishing rapidly with depth, to a general limit of six hundred feet.

MID-TIDE ZONE
(usually exposed at low tide)

Brown turban snail (*Tegula*), zone marker.

Volcano limpet (*Fissurella*), opening at apex; also in low-tide zone.

Purple sea star (*Patiria*), or sea bat.

Plate limpet (*Acmaea*), flattest of the group.

File limpet (*Acmaea*), with coarse, overlapping ribs.

Sea star (*Leptasterias*), very small, six-rayed.

Purple shore crab (*Hemigrapsus*), among rockweeds; also in low-tide zone.

Horned slipper or boat shell (*Crepidula*); in southern area: onyx slipper and turban slipper (same genus).

Verrucose anemone (*Anthopleura*), aggregated on exposed rock surfaces.

Hermit crab (*Pagurus*, two species), abundant in zone, also in low-tide zone.

Chiton or sea cradle (*Tonicella*), on or under rocks.

Nudibranchs or sea slugs (*Rostanga*, vivid red; *Triopha*; *Diaulula*), inedible to other animals.

LOW-TIDE ZONE (exposed at lowest tides only)

Great green anemone (*Anthopleura*), zone marker, also known as solitary, and giant green, anemone.

Red anemone (*Tealia*), seen at most extreme low tides.

Anemones (*Epiactis*, *Corynactis*) and solitary coral (*Balanophyllia*).

Sea spider (*Pycnogonum*), found with great green anemone in some areas.

Giant red urchin (*Strongylocentrotus*) and purple urchin (same genus), closely related to sea stars.

Common sea star (*Pisaster*) and purple sea star (*Patiria*).

Sunflower star (*Pycnopodia*), largest of sea stars, with up to 24 rays; feeds on sea urchins.

Sun star (*Solaster*), less common than sunflower star.

Sea star (*Leptasterias*), a common, small six-rayed relative of one in the mid-tide zone. Less common: red sea star (*Henricia*), leather star (*Dermasterias*).

Red abalone (*Haliotis*), and others of the same genus; intensive fishing has greatly reduced their numbers.

Crab (*Cancer*), close relative of the Dungeness crab found in Pacific Coast markets and restaurants.

Kelp crab (*Pugettia*), one of the spider crabs.

Gumboot chiton (*Cryptochiton*), largest of sea cradles, sometimes 13 inches long.

Sea cucumber (*Stichopus*), some subtidal species are seen from glass-bottomed boats; others are intertidal.

MEAN LOW WATER

Hydroids (Eudendrium, etc.), including plume hydroid (*Plumularia*), one of the most delicate of intertidal animals, actually invisible under water; ostrich-plume hydroid (*Aglaophenia*, several species), for which the coast is famous: many others.

Other low-tide invertebrates: sponges; tunicates; worms; moss animals (bryozoans); rock oyster; fixed clam; snails; cone shell; spiny lobster; broken-backed shrimp; octopus.

Fishes: garibaldi; tidepool sculpin.

Brown algae: giant kelp (*Macrocystis*); ribbon kelp (*Nereocystis*); sea palm (*Postelsia*); feather boa kelp (*Egregia*); oar weed (*Laminaria*); "bladder chain" (*Cystoseira*); and others. Red algae: *Gigartina* (translated as "grapestone," in absence of common name); sea sack (*Halosaccion*); and some others, including coralline red algae. Flowering plants: eel grass (*Zostera*), low-tide level and below, in bays and estuaries; surf grass (*Phyllospadix*), on outer coast, sometimes down to 50 feet below sea level.

Encrusting red sponges (*Ophlitaspongia*, *Plocamia*) and purple sponge (*Haliclona*), in crevices and under ledges.

Proliferating anemone (*Epiactis*), grows its young in cluster around parent.

Solitary coral (*Balanophyllia*), bright orange-red; related to anemones.

Beach fleas (*Atylopsis*, *Ampithoë*), amphipods, numerous in rockweeds.

Brittle stars (*Ophioclus*, *Amphipholis*, *Amphiodia*, etc.), often aggregated under and between rocks.

Fixed snail (*Aletes*), attached to rocks, grows calcareous tube from mouth of shell; southern.

Other mid-tide invertebrates: pill bug; long-fingered shrimp; ghost shrimp; ribbon worms, scale worms sipunculid worms; terebellid worms pea crab.

Fishes: black blenny; blind goby.

Red alga (*Gigartina*), broad leaf with rough-textured surface, and red alga (*Porphyra*, nori to the Japanese), used in great quantities as a food.

LIFE OF THE TIDE ZONES

SPLASH ZONE
(wet by spray, storm waves)

Periwinkle snail (*Littorina*),
   on rocks.
Fixed acorn barnacle (*Balanus*),
   on rocks.
A small brown barnacle (*Chthamalus*).
Limpet (*Acmaea*, several species).
Owl limpet (*Lottia*), also on surf-
   swept rocks.
Green algae (*Enteromorpha*;
   Cladophora), sometimes
   present on wetter rocks.

UPPER BEACH (above spray)

Sand flea or beach hopper (*Orchestia*;
   Orchestoidea, several species).
Rock louse (*Ligia*), a large pill bug,
   ranges up from splash zone.

HIGH-TIDE ZONE
(covered by most high tides)

Black turban snail (*Tegula*), zone marker.
Large flatworm (*Alloioplana*), at upper limit
   of zone, under rocks on damp gravel.
Periwinkle snail (*Littorina*), another species
   replacing the one of the higher zone.
Limpet (*Acmaea*, etc.), many in this zone.
Hermit crab (*Pagurus*), often in turban shells.
Rock crab (*Pachygrapsus*), nocturnal in habits.
Porcelain crab (*Petrolisthes*), ranges also into the
   mid-tide zone.
Pill bug (*Cirolana*), an isopod, under rocks.
Beach hopper (*Melita*), an amphipod, under rocks.
Brittle star (*Amphipholis*), black and white,
   smallest of Pacific Coast brittle stars.
Worms (hairy-gilled, polyclad, serpulid, etc.),
   various kinds in various habitats in each zone.
Red alga (*Endocladia*), rockweeds (*Fucus, Pelvetia,
   Pelvetiopsis*), sea lettuce (*Ulva*), and a brown
   alga (*Ralfsia*) that forms dark crusts on
   rocks; also other seaweeds.

MEAN HIGH WATER

MEAN SEA LEVEL

*The retreating tide reveals not only tidepools, but often—
as here on the California coast just north of Bolinas Bay—
the geological structure of the shoreline as well. For a considerable distance,
the deposits of a former inreach of the sea were tilted in some later crustal uplift,
with a remarkable absence of warping in the other direction. When wave-cut to the present
terrace level, the harder strata edges are as straight as concrete walls.*

Sea palm, a brown alga.

Oar weed, a brown alga.

Red sea fan, a red alga of the lowest tidal levels.

Rockweed, a brown alga of the upper mid-tide zone.

*Oar weed and surf grass; the leaf is
in a late-winter to early-spring stage.*

*Bed of oar weed exposed at very low tide,
with surf grass overhanging.*

64

Two members of a characteristic open coast community: the Pacific goose barnacle,
gray-white, and the California mussel. The third member of this trio, the common sea star,
does not appear in the picture but is undoubtedly close by—the other two animals are its chief sustenance.

Orchid nudibranch, low-tide zone.

Red sea star or blood star, low-tide zone.

Giant red urchin, largest on this coast; low-tide zone.

Nudibranch, mid-tide zone.

Webbed sea star, sea bat, or batstar; mid-tide zone.

Giant green anemone, low-tide zone.

Black oystercatchers—possibly a pair, since the sexes dress alike. This rather large shorebird ranges on the Pacific Coast from the Aleutians to Morro Bay, California, and on the offshore islands southward to Baja.

Elegant terns breed on Baja's offshore islands but in the fall wander as far north as San Francisco Bay.

CHAPTER 7

BIRDS WITH WET FEET

*Winged creatures that follow the edge
of the sea and fish the ever-moving surf.*

IT IS THE SIZE of a crow, but its all-over hue is more sooty than purplish, becoming slightly brownish on the back. Its slender legs and three-toed feet are pink, and its long, straight, heavy beak a bright vermilion. Alone, picking its way among the mussels, barnacles, and dark algae on the spray-wet rocks, sounding a repeated sharp whistle, it seems to proclaim its exclusive right to that part of any rocky shore. A bird-wise watcher—at California's Point Lobos, it might be—calls out with delight, "Black oyster catcher!"

Resident of island and mainland shores all the way from Baja California to Attu in the western Aleutians, with five other species of its kind on coasts around the world, our black oyster catcher is interesting for more reasons than its relative scarcity. For one thing, it is perhaps the most easily recognized of our Pacific shorebirds; no other species closely resembles it. Yet it represents a very large bird order, Charadriiformes. Widely dispersed but nowhere in large numbers, it occupies a well-defined niche of the shore world. Unlike so many sea and shore birds, it is something of a loner. So even to an experienced birder, an oyster-catcher day is a good day at the seashore. The bird is, moreover, misnamed. It is not one to frequent mudflats or oyster beds; and as Dawson said, "oysters are not much given to sprinting away." Mussel rocks are its milieu. The name should be "mussel muncher."

Its chisel-bill is higher than it is wide, for knifing between the mollusk's valves and snipping the powerful adductor muscle in one stroke. Not only mussels but other bivalves, worms, and crabs know the strength and efficacy of that instrument. In its feeding the oyster catcher is a bird of the upper tide zone. Nesting is not far from high water, preferably on coarse gravels where the spotted eggs gain some benefit of camouflage. Plover-like, the mother bird uses various tricks to draw intruders away from the stony nest.

A globe-encircling order, Charadriiformes (the curious name refers to the cleft in each one of the pair of nasal bones) includes plovers, turnstones, and surfbirds of the type family Charadriidae, besides such widespread forms as phalaropes, avocets, stilts, snipes, sandpipers, curlews, gulls, terns, auks, murres, and puffins. It embraces such extremes, travel-wise, as the stay-at-home oyster catcher and that long-distance champion of all birds, the amazing arctic tern—that lithe flier wings ten thousand miles south each year to find a second summer in antarctic regions, one of its routes being off the Pacific Coast. Many of the birds one commonly—and some not so commonly—meets on a tidepool excursion, a beach walk, or near the margins of tidal mudflats and salt marshes belong to families of this giant order. Other major groups are represented, but the charadriiform birds dominate these habitats. They are truly the masters of the very edge of land and water.

When in oyster catcher territory—on the rocks—one should be on the watch for surfbirds. Not that the chances of a meeting are very good, even in winter when they are spread along the Pacific coasts of both Americas all the way to the Straits of Magellan.

*Strong fliers, the gulls are worldwide birds of salt waters, including such inland "seas"
as the Great Salt Lake in Utah. A score or so different species live upon the Pacific Coast.
Omnivorous, they are scavengers of the beaches, and parks and picnic grounds of coastal cities.*

THE LONG CURVING SHORE

The common, or American, egret, along with the smaller snowy egret and the great blue heron, has established one of its West Coast rookeries in the treetops of a small area of Bolinas Lagoon just north of the Golden Gate. Through the efforts of many conservation-minded people, a large property surrounding the site was purchased and dedicated as the Audubon Canyon Ranch. This area has become a center for nature study and ecological research.

Although this bird, which looks like a large sandpiper, appears rather regularly at favorite rocky shore points in California in late spring and early fall, it is not numerous nor easily befriended.

First known to science in 1789, when the records left by the naturalist Gmelin of Bering's Siberia staff (1733–43) were published, the surfbird kept its breeding grounds secret from the world until 1921. That year a young zoologist, Olaus Murie (a renowned conservationist who died in 1963), was working above timberline in Mount McKinley National Park. It had long been rumored that, when they mysteriously disappeared for the summer from the Alaskan coast each June, the surfbirds went up to the mountains to breed. Nevertheless, it was a sudden surprise when Murie flushed an adult pair and a "downy young one" high on a mountain slope so far from the sea. Confirmation came in late May of 1926; Joseph Dixon, another eminent western zoologist, and George M. Wright found the first surfbird nest ever known. So was discovered the strange secret of the bird that lives most of its life to the rhythm of surf on rocky shores of two continents, yet every summer seeks equally rocky heights of four thousand feet or more, as much as five hundred miles from the sea, to rear its young.

Sharing the surfbird's ocean shore domain—and breeding on the coast like proper shorebirds—are the two turnstones. The black turnstone keeps to the West Coast, while the ruddy one ranges around the Northern Hemisphere, wintering on the Pacific shore from San Francisco Bay to Baja California. This is the shorebird that leaves no stone, small driftwood bit, seaweed clump, or other beach debris unturned in its energetic search for sand fleas and more small delicacies. In spring the ruddy turnstone wears breeding plumage with a Harlequin look, strongly marked black-and-white and cinnamon red; the sober cousin is all-over blackish or dark gray except for its white lower breast and belly. It may be seen around tidepools along with the surfbird, the wandering tattler, and sometimes the spotted sandpiper, which is the most widely distributed shorebird of our continent, especially on inland waters. All these birds are loners, more or less.

On that precise edge where the Pacific Ocean thins out to a lingering wetness upon beach sands and gravels, a largely different crew—a motley mob—takes over. It may be any one of dozens of smooth or pebbled beaches curving away from a sheltering rocky point on the Oregon or California coast, the cast of birds varying with latitude and season. As each new

Whether feeding at the edge of the tide or flying in large groups, sandpipers form lively flocks. The small shorebirds are attractive in all their many species.

*Avocets exemplify the specialization in feeding habits and adaptations
that enable enormous numbers of shorebirds to occupy the same stretches
of mudflat, salt marsh, freshwater wetlands, and similar habitats without
the conflict of undue competition. The upcurved avocet bill is designed for
probing and stirring up food as the long-legged bird stalks the water's edge.*

The great blue heron, largest of its kind, is a versatile fisherman. Extremely long-legged, it may stand motionless for an hour in a pond, stream, or tidal flat, then suddenly spear a frog or fish with its beak. When such waters dry up, the heron will take to pasture lands and the hunting of rodents; or it may go the opposite way—to the kelp beds just offshore, for a different kind of fishing.

wave flings upon the hardpacked ground some bits and fragments of sea harvest enmeshed in rags of foam, the birds flock and peck like chickens after grain in a barnyard. In a body they race seaward with the whispered retreat of the undertow, wheel, and scramble for the tidbits left there, just ahead of the next wave's sally. They don't want to miss a morsel, and they don't want to get their skirts wet.

Whatever gathering of species—knot, black-bellied or semipalmated plover, marbled godwit, ruddy turnstone—is enjoying the fringe benefits of the tide at any time, only one is almost certain to be there, on virtually every beachhead in the world. This is the sanderling, a sandpiper of cosmopolitan range. "The model Shore-bird," Dawson calls him, ". . . because in structure and habit he is most exactly adapted to those special circumstances which constitute a shore . . . . For within this special belt there is a very special line which not in all Earth's history was ever twice the same, a line which has broken into a billion new curves while these words are being read. It is the edge of the wave which the Sanderling follows, and he is *the* Shore-bird *par excellence*, . . . a part of the tidal mechanism." Doubtless it is misleading to speak of this bird in the singular. Wintering flocks on the beaches will run from one to three or four dozen; migrating, they travel in hundreds.

"To the ends of the earth and back again extend the migrations of the sanderling, the cosmopolitan globe-trotter; few species, if any, equal it in worldwide wanderings," Bent says. Everywhere, "one of the characteristic features of the ocean beach [is] a little flock of feeding sanderlings. . . . At all times the surf line attracts them, where they nimbly follow the receding waves to snatch their morsels of food or skillfully dodge the advancing line of foam as it rolls up the beach, . . . their little black legs fairly twinkling with motion."

And so the patterns repeat: waves roll shoreward to break their last on beaches; birds flock and run back and forth along the broken edges to feed on what the sea brings. Waves follow certain laws of physics in the same way the world around; beaches are built by one set of forces—physical, hydrological, geological—on every continent and most islands. Birds repeat the imperatives of their evolution and the drives of their distribution, so that similar, and often identical, forms meet similar situations in like ways a hemisphere apart. At the very moment when someone is watching, with amused delight, a flock of sanderlings skittering back and forth—like clockwork toys, an observer has said—at waves' edge on an Oregon beach, another may be enjoying the same act on a strand in Chile or Hawaii.

Thus our Pacific shore combines, as every shore does, particulars and universals. Nature's world is one world; yet every part of it, and every moment of its time, is something quite unique.

CHAPTER 8

THE MARCHING SANDS

*Living dunes and beaches — the elements
and evolution of the land between two worlds.*

BETWEEN TWO LIVING WORLDS — the intertidal one of algae gardens, tidepools, and surf electric with plankton and fishes, and the upper world of land-dwelling plants and animals — there is another, a relatively lifeless one. This is the narrow world of beaches: the wandering, much broken, often unstable boundary between the life-bearing realms of sea and land.

The hard, enduring, yet fluidly mobile stuff of this borderline world is sand. Edging the seas, it is perpetually wet down and packed solid by the tide. Bounding the land, it is perennially dried by sun and loosened by wind, and these give it what life it has. In the dry-sand world, lifelessness and life sharply alternate, as plants take hold and make little oases to attract other plants and such things as ants and beetles, lizards and birds. But sand itself has a particular essence and fascination.

It is formed by weathering of cliffs, erosion of mountains, wave-battering of rocks and reefs. It is carried to the sea where it enters the flow of longshore currents and the endless wheeling of surf. Sorting silt from sand, the sea layers its deeper bottom with the fine, builds its strands with the coarse — builds, tears down, and builds afresh. Winter seas pluck tons of sand from the berms of beaches, roil it above the shallow intertidal stratum, and put pounds back. The rest is banked for the season in offshore bars. Lazier spring and summer waves gently reverse the process, restoring tonnages of sand to drying outer edges of berms, where onshore winds pick it up and carry it landward to widen beaches and build dunes. On crisp days of strong wind, one can feel it sting ankles, hear its dry, sleety rustle through bending grass stems as it hastens to dune crests and gently drops down lee slopes on the landward side.

Sand beaches, one observes, mirror in color and texture the coastlands they edge. Thus the famed black sands of Hawaii's Puna shore reflect the island's coal-colored lava flanks, where Mauna Loa and Kilauea have spilled into the sea in recent time. Fronting the Washington and northern Oregon coasts, more ancient basaltic headlands have yielded to the pounding surf grain by grain; currents have spread the fine, dark greenish-gray sand along hundreds of shore miles to build broad strands, flat and firmly packed. Southward, between the Siuslaw River and Coos Bay, Eocene sea deposits, the erosion products of still older formations, now lie loose and mobile in the pale buff fifty miles of the Oregon Dunes and their wide outlying beach. From Cape Mendocino to Point Arena, California's coastal bluffs are chiefly shale, conglomerate, and a dark gray sandstone called graywacke; rock-studded beaches run gray to brownish, fine or coarsely shingled.

Many widely differing coastland rocks have made beach and dune sands for the most part warmly light-toned from central to southern California. They contain much quartz and feldspar from the breakdown of granite that along the coast is not coldly white but yellowish. These sands are coarse, angular, and tend to steep-faced beaches. At the same time, during long coastal summers, they may in many

*Coastal dunes north of Fort Bragg, California. The ripple marks and shadows reveal that:
the view is to the south; the prevailing westerly wind of this coast is from the right of the
viewer, as shown by the long slopes of both ripples and dunes; the short slope is on the lee side.*

75

places form exceedingly broad berms of loose, dry sand, making pleasant playgrounds above reach of all but unusually high tides. Especially in Southern California, from Santa Barbara to Coronado, where there is much less rockiness than farther north, these great beaches early reinforced the familiar American idea, spawned on both Atlantic and Gulf coasts, that a proper beach is a long expanse of "white" sand.

I
N ANY GROUP of beachcombers—driftwood brows-
ers, glass float hunters, shell fanciers—one is sure to find a pebble picker. The devotee of bright bits of stone is knees down at once on spotting a windrow of the smoothed and rounded objects, their hue and polish heightened by a moment's wetting.

Cobbles, pebbles, fine gravel, coarse sand, silt— the stuff of shingle, beach, and tidal flat is for the most part the breakdown product of rock. Larger pieces—boulders, cobblestones—and most smaller particles are random rubble of land's edge in stubborn retreat before the sea. Some stones are tumbled and washed into the ocean by rivers and swift, steep coastal streams. The finest sands and silts, collected as habitable stratum beneath intertidal rocks if not washed down to the deeper offshore bottom, hold particles that passed long interim ages in soils, perhaps far inland. Bits and pieces of molluscan shell and tiny fragments of hard urchin and crab exoskeleton are mixed in varying proportions with the inorganic mineral grains of the beach. Usually the flat or slightly curved opalescent "pebbles" on our coast are pieces of abalone shell. Mussel shell flakes are darker violet- or greenish-blue.

Life's shadow persists in sand. Every particle holds a secret story of its origin—it may be recent, or incredibly ancient. Gather a handful of the variously colored and textured pebbles: a cupped palm may contain both the shard of a life contemporary with one's own and a fragment of earth crust antedating all life by a billion years.

There is a wondrous if illusive finality about the bits of stone one finds along the beach. Exceedingly hard, shaped to characteristic flattish ovals by countless years of jostling together in moving water, many of them become "frozen" for an interlude. Taken out of circulation for perhaps a few, perhaps many million, years in the dry vault of a conglomerate forma-

tion, to be washed free again by the same or a different sea or river in another age, they seem now irreducible, past change. Size and shape as well as hardness may enable them to withstand further fragmentation. Only eons of continuing abrasion can buff them smaller until, eventually, under the intense heat and pressure of some metamorphic process, their molecules flow, and they become veins or marblings in an altered rock. Nothing is truly permanent.

B
RUSH AWAY a surface layer of pebbles on a sandy
beach. Smaller ones, and still smaller ones appear beneath, sorted and sifted down into the sand. At first the matrix of sand seems nothing but miniature pebbles, minutely reflecting forms and colors. But not so: sand's distinctive character becomes evident. Sand is sand, not an infinitude of minuscule pebbles. Beach pebbles may indeed be chance wanderers from many parts of space and time within the region, but the vast bulk of sand represents either a substantially homogeneous native source or a mass migration largely from a single, more distant one. American beach sands are to a great extent granitic, with quartz and feldspar giving them paleness. Much of this granite sand—lightweight, angular, easy for water or wind to pick up and move—harks back to rock formations gone from the scene ages and ages ago. And just as pebbles "did time" in conglomerate lockups, some of this sand has rested through geologic periods bonded in sandstone. Earth's building materials are constantly reused.

As hole diggers and castle builders know, sand behaves as a solid when cemented with just the right amount of water. But dry sand is fluid, like water or air. It flows through the neck of an hourglass, and when heaped above its angle of repose—32–35 degrees—it cascades downslope like a liquid. This is one mechanism of the movement of dunes. Another is the flow of individual sand grains in a windstream as they move like separate molecules on the disturbed surface of a liquid mass.

A dune is a wind-piled hill or ridge of sand, and may consist of any sort of material responding in certain ways to wind—anything, that is, with the granular size and other characteristics meeting the idea of sand. There are dunes of Italy's volcanic olivine, Florida's shell particles, coral of tropic atolls, pure gypsum in New Mexico's White Sands, and the fine dry ice crystals of Antarctica and the Arctic, where water becomes a geological material (as it does also in glaciers).

Once it gains speed of at least eleven miles an hour, wind begins to pick up surface grains and arc them forward. Landing with an elastic bounce, a grain strikes another grain and so helps the wind, made turbulent by the granular surface, pick that one up in turn—and so on. This process of sand movement is called "saltation" (leaping) and is the means by which a dune builds up and moves, layer by peeling layer, to the crest and on down the cascading slip face which leads its forward motion.

Dunes form when three things meet: a supply of sand, wind with the force to move it, and fixed objects such as plants to arrest it long enough to start its hummock and ridge building. Plane surfaces tend to be swept clean; without projections to trap and collect it, sand flows evenly across while the wind holds. If winds are usually gentle over such a surface but sometimes just brisk enough to move sand, a deposit of it may grow there and form ripples in response to superficial irregularities. Ripples form on dune surfaces during periods of light wind (under eleven miles an hour), echoing dune ridges in profile.

THE SANDY BEACH and coastal dune habitat is one of harsh and almost constant wind and salt spray, not of organically enriched soil but of uniformly sterile and mechanical stuff. Sand's main, if not only, advantages are that plant roots can penetrate easily and that it can absorb and hold the water of rain, fog, or dew. It all adds up to comparatively thin living at best. And while psammophiles—sand lovers—thrive in their impoverished habitat, they are not a numerous lot, in either species or populations. They include some common forms adapted to either soil, desert sand, or salty coastal conditions; others found only in sand, of both desert and shore; and a few that live only in the sand of seashores and coastal dunes. In type, and not seldom in species, they find their sandy niches the world around.

Only in a few places on this steep and rocky coast are classic conditions met to build dunes more than a few rods landward. Many great and small Pacific beaches and spits are dune-capped, so that true if

lesser dune formations may easily be seen. These are favorite recreation places. All too many of them, however, have been destroyed or are being lost in some kind of human exploitation, such as beach-front subdivision. The beginning of the end of a wild dune area is the planting of grasses, shrubs, or young trees to "stabilize" it—in other words, to change it altogether. When plant cover takes over, dunes are done. A dune is no longer a dune when it stops both building and moving, when it has yielded to some plant matting its pristine freedom to fly before the wind.

If we hold that among the prime values of this great Pacific shoreline are those linked closely to its remaining wildness, to the freedom of nature to go on expressing itself in abundance and variety, to our opportunity to experience here certain unique and revitalizing personal dialogues with earth and sea, wind and sky—then at once we find a basis for judging what must be kept and how the rest must be used. We know that bold cliffs and lofty headlands are splendid for viewing; tidepools are rich as jungles for studying life; wide sand beaches are the most inviting and relaxing of playgrounds; dunes wild with wind and sun, primroses and restless sand, are inspiring oases for the trammeled soul.

A National Park Service survey of 1959 detailed 74 areas "possessing important remaining opportunities for recreation and other public purposes," including scientific study. Nine were in Washington, 17 in Oregon, 48 in California, and they totaled 527 miles of shoreline. The next ten years of preservation effort brought in the expected mixed bag of success and frustration, with the balance at least on the plus side. A few of these areas are scenic rocky shore, but most are mainly beach or beach and dune. Although mass recreation needs become more critical each passing year, something must be spared also for the few whose delight is a serendipitous stroll along the high-tide line, following a short-eared owl's daylight hummock-hopping from one lookout to the next, or soaking in the sun-warmed peace of a dune hollow beyond the last jeep track.

KNOWING WHAT materials and conditions must combine for the building of dunes, one can spot on a good relief map of the three-state coastland the areas where major dunes should be. Given the first

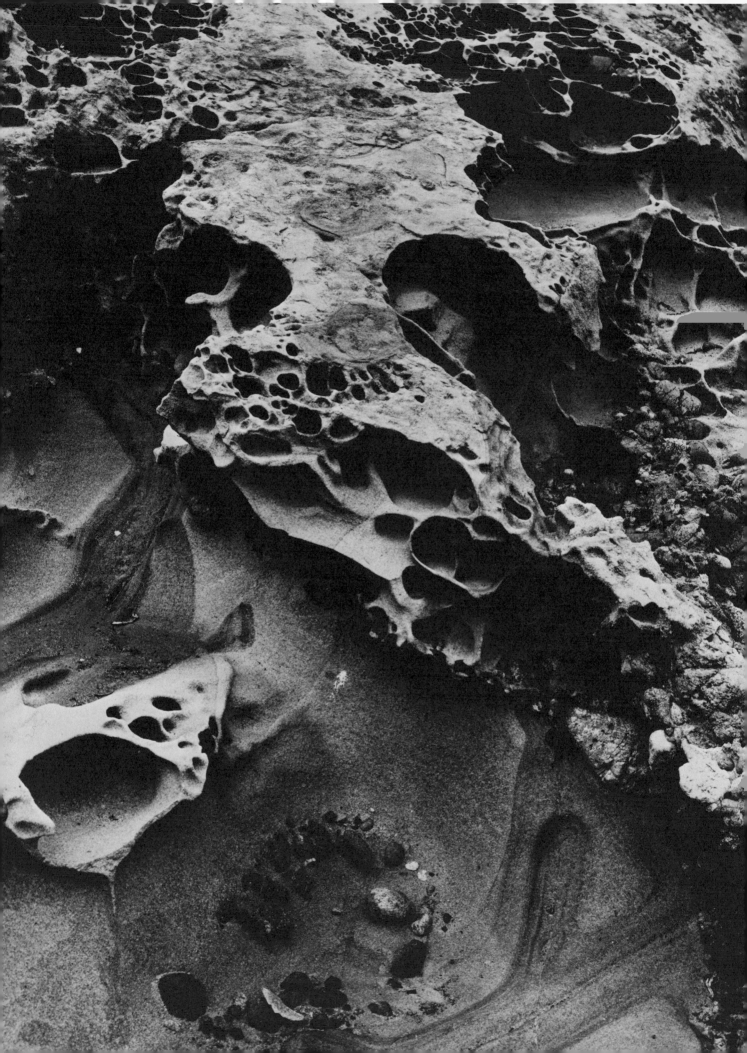

essential, an all but limitless supply of sea-borne sand, the receiving end of the combination calls for the open breezeway of a broad, low river valley headed into the prevailing westerlies. A look at the map for a place fitting topographic requirements might quickly focus on California's Santa Maria River.

Just north of Point Sal, up the coast from the great bend of Arguello and Conception, the Santa Maria River plain slopes to the sea and fans out along a fifteen-mile beach front. Here the coastline cuts one of its many north-by-east steps, from Point Sal up to the shore communities of Oceano, Grover City, Pismo Beach, and Shell Beach, where it turns westward again to Point San Luis. The valley plain is rather heavily farmed and grazed. Midway, three miles from the shore, a huge refinery stands. From its cracking towers the oil men can look gravely seaward, in a calculating arc from northwest to south, at ridges rising a hundred feet and more above their ground level—ridges of migrant sand.

The refinery workers can in fact see, a mile away on either side, horns of the larger dune mass pointing landward in line with the plant. However, this is in no foreseeable danger of being engulfed. It is built on a dune-free tongue of open flat land reaching two and a half miles seaward to Oso Flaco Lake, which forms an effective barrier to dune drift at a point only a half mile from the tide line. In time, sand may fill the lake from windward, but cannot blow across it. Instead, the great drift splits to send its long horns inland, high sand ridges moving downwind. These and others to the south finger their way through partial scrub cover. Some are grounded altogether, others blow out of weak places in the cover to resume their march. The ongoing ridges have reformed as dunes, drifting as far as three and a half miles from the sea near the oil town of Guadalupe. To the north of Oso Flaco Lake, a group of a dozen smaller lakes and ponds with bordering marshes presents another barrier to the Nipomo Dunes.

Through the efforts of a few devoted people over many years, Nipomo Dunes are still there to enjoy. Certain back roads lead in, such as one to Oso Flaco Lake; there is also a route from Guadalupe, but the oil field should be avoided if one is looking for wildness. On the Santa Barbara County side of the Santa Maria's dry, sandy wash, jeep trails go down Cor-ralitos Canyon to Mussel Point and the south end of the dunes, less than two miles from Point Sal. Easiest of all is the short beach hike from Oceano. One can walk down along Pismo Beach State Park and soon be far from beach-side shacks and parking strips. Even solitude can sometimes be found.

THE PLANTS of the dunes have by both internal and external means made this area their own. The one most likely to be found nearest the reach of the tide came here from the Old World: the sea-rocket, an annual of the mustard family. From summer to late fall, one species livens the strand from here to the Mendocino coast with its half-inch pink to purplish crosses.

Representing the rose family in this outermost sand habitat is a Pacific Coast native of particular importance, the beach strawberry. From the Pismo Beach area north to Alaska, visitors are attracted by the familiar-looking low plants. The good-sized berries have a delicious flavor, but they scarcely compare in tender succulence with the product of hundreds of cultivated California acres.

A common enough shore plant, the sea-fig, can now be seen in large masses on freeway interchanges and cutbanks, where it is planted to prevent erosion. It grows naturally on beaches, dunes, and bluffs, from Oregon to Baja. An annual of the same genus ranges along the coast from Monterey south to Baja. Its crystalline vesicles, which look like dew on its spatular leaves, give it the name "ice plant."

There is a morning glory on the upper beach that is not a trailing, thin-leaved vine but a prostrate mat of glossy and fleshy foliage. In form this and other plants of the coastal strand have adapted themselves to a peculiar condition of dryness. Among them are two primroses. One is the typical evening primrose of moist places like stream banks and seacliff seeps; the other is prostrate and spreading on the sand.

Dune sands march in from the sea and living things strive for foothold on their loose and shifting mineral substance. On the beach side, life finds the sand environment unstable, often precarious. Going inland, stability increases, except on the most windwardly exposed dune faces and the high, ever-shifting crests. Sedges appear, with far-creeping rootstocks or stolons reaching out to seize the mobile surface.

Part of the endless recycling pattern of earth materials: sandstone at the upper tide level is being broken down by wave action into its separate component grains of sand. In some future time the grains will again be compressed as sandstone.

THE LONG CURVING SHORE

Rushes occupy moist dune swales, not infrequently staking out clean new sand slopes, with little upright stems at stolon-ends. A number of grasses, good sand holders, have their place here, among them bluegrass and rye grass, their slender rhizomes probing just beneath the surface to extend mattings of turf. Most widely conspicuous is beachgrass, first brought from Europe as a sand-binder to prepare for the planting of San Francisco's Golden Gate Park and, since then, introduced extensively up and down the coast. It is the tall, dense, light green to yellowish grass whose spike-shaped but soft, thick panicles plume the tops of so many dune hummocks along the back of the beach. Most of us accept it as a natural element of Pacific Coast beach and dune scenery, as we do another immigrant, Argentina's pampas grass, whose giant domed tussocks appear quite at home in flattened, somewhat stabilized dune swales.

On a dune walk one is sure to be attracted by little lacy balls of minute pale-pink flowers on woody but slenderly branching, small-leaved bushes—wild buckwheat. The family is large in the dry West. Among the composites, or sunflower family, are a mock-heather—a slight bush with many small leaves and yellow ray-flowers—and groundsel, or senecio, its clusters of six-rayed yellow flowers obscuring almost threadlike leaves.

These are but a sampling. It is impossible to list here all the great many beach and dune plants of this coast. Some excellent guides to them are listed in the back of this book.

EARLY IN THE DAY before the sea breeze erases the night's graffiti on the sand, when small crinkles cast long shadows, or at any time in pockets and swales where the wind touches but lightly, the stipplings of myriad tracks reveal a surprising variety of animals for so lean a habitat. Traffic patterns may seem at first glance quite aimless; closer study reveals purposes and cross-purposes, small but resolute, frequently grim. A western toad may have shifted gears from awkward walk to clumsy hop and captured an equally graceless darkling beetle—the dull black *pinacate* also seen on dusty roads. Pocket gophers and harvest, meadow, and white-footed mice represent the rodent kind. The kangaroo rat is perhaps better known to human "desert rats" than to any

beachcomber; the grass- and shrub-mantled dunes, from Nipomo north to their recurrence on the south side of Morro Bay, have their own exclusive species of this captivating and quite un-ratlike little rodent, the Morro Bay kangaroo rat. Those who have watched any of the group jump and dance by the light of the moon are lucky. On the dunes in the dewy morning, one might pick up and try to follow a wide-spaced series of three-point landings—tail and two hind feet—which zigzags across the sand.

Larger tracks tell of similar if weightier survival errands. Raccoons, weasels, bobcats, striped skunks, black-tailed jack- and brush rabbits all have business on dunes and beaches. One will surely see the chisel marks of deer hoofs. The largest tread may be that of a black bear, especially where northern forests edge the strand.

While hunkered down to trace a garter or gopher snake's sinuous furrow, or to sort alligator and fence lizard tracks from killdeer and quail, one falls to musing about the community of life that makes a go of it here, somehow. The sea's surface, too, is wind-shaped and ever shifting, but it is richer by far, with its myriad zoo- and phytoplankton, its pelagic fishes, birds, and mammals. The ocean is rich in depth, too; here, on this sand, nothing lies beneath but more sand, salt, and a water table above bedrock to be reached for, if not too deep, by a few stretched and thirsty taproots. Here is no mold-meaty soil, and no earthworms to ply it. But there are mineral nutrients, given by the sea, and there is sunlight. It all adds up to a viable culture, with everything playing its ecological part.

Consider the kangaroo rat, for one. The fur-lined cheek pouches hold a good many seeds, and the little jumper is highly mobile. Rodents have much to do with the density and distribution of their favorite seed-bearers, reducing the number of seedlings in one place and unwittingly planting a new crop in another. The kangaroo rat stores seeds in its burrows, after curing them for a time in thimble-size holes in the hot ground. Between crops it eats grass and leaves, a further check on vegetation. And it consumes no water as such, converting what it needs from its food. The total ecology of the sand world is made up of countless interrelationships, some universal in nature, some peculiar to this environment.

Sturdy old beach pines are being engulfed by sand on the crests of the Oregon Dunes. When they are dead and their bark is stripped away, the dry wood is sandblasted to a silvery white. The wind is from the left in this picture.

Sand dunes along the California shore, ten miles north of Fort Bragg.

CHAPTER 8: THE MARCHING SANDS

From the lee shore of the sand sea, the slip-faces below the sharp crests of those dunes farthest advanced upon the land, a different world appears. On the coast's far north, one might look into a dense forest of spruce, hemlock, and fir. In California, the scene may still be open beyond the dunes, with scattered beach, bishop, or Monterey pines dark on the pale sand hills where their dune-march has ended. In the merging valleys of the Arroyo Grande and the Santa Maria, the Nipomo Dunes' edge is dense scrub-matted ridges, aromatic under the sun, and a string of small lakes with willowed banks. The blending of two environments at a common border is exemplified by the willows, which seem to climb dry-footed up the steep sand slopes. Although they must start seedlings in the wet, these ever-flexible little trees can elongate their shoots to push through and over the sand as it moves into their domain.

Here the surf is a distant hum, if heard at all, and the ocean wind slacks to soft land breezes. Though the land world is more intense and complex with all sorts of life, there is a sense of loss as one leaves the dunes. Lost is contact with the great sea, and gone the feel of wind as a moving and shaping power, the sense of life struggling against particular odds, the clean simplicity, and wildness. What lies ahead looks deceptively static, overabundant, too ready to let man take over and alter it to his needs.

But nature has even greater forces for change in reserve—forces more awesome than man, or wind, or waves. Look from the high dune crest, eastward for a mile, then upward another hundred feet. There, facing down, and over these "new" dunes to the ocean, is the rim of Nipomo Mesa. Now a cultivated plateau lying between arroyo and river drainages, this is a structure of old sedimentary deposits capped by sand hills—ancient coastal dunes. Gradually it was raised in one of the periodic crustal uplifts along this shore, so that when a new terrace emerged, on which dunes are now building, that old one had become too high and too far from the replenishing sea. Tectonic force was the stronger, a force that may even now be lifting the present Nipomo Dunes in turn. But if we, and future generations, let them live, the beauty and magic of the dunes will keep for as long as man is here to enjoy them.

The sea-fig, an introduction from the Southern Hemisphere, has become naturalized on this coast from Baja to Oregon. Widely used to hold the ground along road cuts and freeway interchanges, this magenta-flowering succulent and the closely related hottentot-fig, with its large yellow blossoms, spread rapidly by running stems along the ground in all directions. Photographed at Asilomar, California.

The Oregon Dunes, near Florence, with sandblasted beach pines.

Dunes at Dillon Beach, California, looking south toward Tomales Bay.

*Pebbles on Fort Cronkhite Beach, Marin headlands, on the north side
of the Golden Gate — a favorite place for pebble hunters.*

Dunes, almost snow white, edge the shores of Bahía de Sebastián Vizcaíno.

CHAPTER 9

SEACLIFF WORLD

*The bold palisades—their formation and changing facades
from Baja California to the Northwest Coast.*

THE FIRST OBVIOUS and distinctive life of both island and mainland seacliffs to strike explorers of this coast—sailors and naturalists alike—was probably the oceanic and shore birds in their teeming rookeries. From beach, shingle, or surf line to topmost pinnacle, every ledge or cranny of cliff, stack, and offshore islet was likely to be so crowded that birds jostled each other, and probably not a few eggs and unfledged nestlings went over the side, casualties of an avian population explosion. The seafarers' hunger for fresh protein began early to take toll. Eggs were a welcome change from salt pork or no meat at all. Men risked necks to get them.

Fortunately for the abundance, variety, and balance of coastal and offshore life, there are some places where ancient ecological patterns hold. Chief among them are offshore islands and their satellite islets and rocks. One such is rocky Prince Island (a half-mile from San Miguel Island off Santa Barbara) 650 yards long, 288 feet high, with steep seaward face. For sea birds the islet is a fine residential complex, with a distinct "social stratification." Each proprietor in the condominium has its suited level.

Prince Island cliff manor is a full house. The dominant, aggressive western gulls hold the penthouse crest, a vantage giving these roost robbers easy access to the eggs of the next lower tenants, Brandt's and double-crested cormorants that occupy shoulders and sloping sides. Better protected but most precariously situated, the smaller, shier pelagic cormorants cling to every little ledge and toehold of sheer cliff face where, it has been aptly said, they

perch upright "looking collectively like black bottles on a druggist's shelves." Also relatively safe from the lords of the manor are the tufted puffins, which stash their eggs deep in cliffside burrows and caves. Vulnerable but holding their own by sheer numbers are California murres on the open ledges. Leach's petrels and Cassin auklets dig in where grassy slopes afford some loose soil. The ground floor, virtually at surfside, is home to occasional pairs of pigeon guillemots. These dove-like sea birds are awkward afoot and in short flights about their rock and cavern habitat, but masterful swimmers and divers in the surging water.

This islet's avian tenancy exemplifies the life of countless similar situations on islands, rocks, and headlands far up and down the Pacific shore. Some species range over most of it, some nest in the south, some in the north. But whatever the latitude, these windy, surf-splashed rock battlements of the outer coast are primarily a sea bird's world. Those wild winged creatures alone have mastered that uneasy and challenging environment.

WHERE LAND PLANTS have won footing on seacliffs, bluffs, and even wave-washed rocks and stacks above the level of marine vegetation, they live and often thrive amid habitat hardships of their own. Strong wind is one of the most obvious. Where shrubs and trees directly face the wind's unobstructed drive across the sea, it warps and gnarls them just as it does on alpine slopes. *Krummholz* (twisted wood) along with cliff, rock, and surf, is part of much prime coastal scenery. No less striking are dense stands of certain

Pelagic cormorants on their cliffside nest on the Farallon Islands, off the Golden Gate.
One of four cormorant species on the coast, the pelagic ranges from Japan,
around the Bering Sea, to Los Coronados, Baja's rock islets near San Diego.

trees, such as coast live oak and California laurel, which are wind-cropped to crew-cut evenness at the top and appear plastered against hillsides and canyon walls to windward. Individual trees are, moreover, stunted almost to shrub size by wind-drying, their slim trunks all leaning downwind, usually up-slope, in impenetrable thickets.

One of the most notable of such wind-shaped coastal "pygmy forests" is a dense, well-watered growth of California laurel in Steep Ravine on the Marin County coast north of the Golden Gate. Typically, this is a large tree growing spaciously in sheltered Coast Range stream bottoms and moist canyonsides. Here, as it chokes the narrow ravine plunging down the sea slope, the laurel "forest" is pruned like boxhedge by the drying westerlies. Crowding and wind combine to prevent normal growth.

The lopsidedness of both alpine and coastal woody plants is, in fact, due more to the drying effect of constant wind than to its force. A tree may stop growing altogether on its windward side. At Cypress Point near Carmel Bay, a Monterey cypress was found, when it was felled, to have a trunk six feet and 304 growth rings thick on its lee side, and *three inches* and 50 rings to windward of its heart! The opposite diameter was nine inches. This seacliff bole was shaped like a reverse airfoil.

It is something of a paradox (timberline comparisons aside) that the same winds which dry coastal plants so markedly also bring much water to their exposed situations. Shrubs and trees desiccated to desert-like growth by sea winds are sometimes festooned with mosses and lichens nourished by the fog swept in from the ocean. On steep bluffs especially, this fine, enveloping moisture of the sea air is more important to plants than a low seasonal rainfall which runs off quickly with little penetration of the almost vertical ground.

Like those of beaches and dunes, plants of lower seacliff and coastal bluff levels are greatly affected by salt spray, so that among them, too, are many succulents. Some forms show adaptation to this salty, ecologically near-desert environment on the part of groups that are not normally succulent. Others belong to certain genera of fleshy plants widespread in places of much rock — plants with such names as live-forever, hen-and-chickens, bluff lettuce, chalk

lettuce. Another is the stonecrops, adept cliffhangers, which may be found loosely and shallowly rooted in tiny pockets of soil, or seemingly in none at all, within sheer-cliff crevices or even beneath overhangs, and along the breaks just below a terrace or plateau edge of rock.

Another common adaptation to windy, drying exposure is seen in the suffrutescent perennials, plants whose upper branches die back after flowering or during "hard times" of severe drought or wind-drying, leaving woody lower stems and base to maintain their leasehold. On the Channel Islands, most herblike perennials of the western headlands manage to survive this way.

Soil is another essential in short supply for cliff-dwelling plants. Even on less sharply vertical slopes, gravity is plainly against the buildup of soil to any depth. Erosion is usually rapid, with or without rain, varying with soil material and the geological structure of a cliff. Wave undercutting can be suddenly catastrophic. Wherever a little soil forms, in pockets, on ledges, on sloping bluffs, the finer material is constantly winnowed out by the wind to leave the coarser. Scant, the soil may also be spray-salted to some height above the tide and though temperature extremes may be close, the evaporation rate is high. Plants gaining foothold despite such conditions are usually low, compact perennials, commonly succulent and hairy or fuzzy, or suffrutescent. Their spread by seeding is very limited, especially since seeds seldom travel laterally across such steep slopes.

Here and there, especially to northward as rainfall increases, ground-water percolates through rock formations to emerge in seeps and springs on the cliff faces. At such points rich and varied concentrations of plants may grow in the sparse soil, following the wetness down in cascades of flower and green until it disappears or blends into the spray zone. Where seepage is constant and in volume, its path down may resemble a pond outflow complete with algae and horsetail. If cliff material contains clay or shale, the seep is likely to bring down and pile upon the strand an elongated fan or talus of mud. And the farther one goes to the north, the more seacliff waterfalls there are to enjoy, supporting a variety of ferns and moisture-loving flowers.

The green mantle some seacliffs wear is seldom

thick enough to hide their rocks or obscure their structure. Like the cliffs of the Grand Canyon, they are an open book of geological history. The shore's landforms and their building material tell the story of a coast rising along lines of structural deformity of the earth's crust, of its continuous attack by the ocean and of its constant renewal by uplift. There are old cliff faces well back from the sea, old terraces above the tide level reaching seaward to newer faces, and so on until today's face rises above the present shoreline. And so it is along very much of this coast.

The varying rocks themselves give particular character to the cliffs they form. Sandstones, shales, and other sedimentaries are a large part of the stuff which has been cut away from these faces by waves and redeposited offshore to build the rock of future terraces. Or they may come back from sea-bottom to dry land—uplifted, sometimes much warped or tilted—as a veritable mausoleum of some period, to excite geologists prying into a shaly cliff face with pick and hammer.

Angle, thickness, hardness, kind of rock—these characteristics of strata give form and texture to cliffs. Already noted are sea stacks and arches, caverns and blowholes. Alluvial outwash plains of Southern California, granitic uplifts in their remnants such as the Point Reyes Peninsula and the Farallon Islands, deep-layered volcanic basalts of northwestern Oregon—each formation gives its special stamp to some part of the composite profile of the long coast. And one must not forget the blue-white crystal ice cliffs of the Alaskan shore, where massive glaciers calve their towering bergs into the sea.

Of the Pacific Coast it has been said: "When you go to the beach you have to walk down steps or scramble down a path worn by thousands of eager feet." It is indeed one of the longest largely cliffbound coastlines on earth.

IN MANY WAYS the west coasts of North and South America mirror each other: cold offshore waters, cliffs, fog. South America's, however, is by far a more desert coast, at least from Peru to a long way south in Chile, despite a heavier and colder fogginess owing to the very cold Peru (Humboldt) Current. This arid austral coast lies in the rain shadow of the Andes, unreached by the Atlantic easterlies. On our more temperate North American coast with its humid onshore westerlies and its rainfall—slight in Baja California's desert latitudes to quite heavy from the Olympic Peninsula north—even the cliffs reflect the varying degrees of life-giving moisture. Plants respond in type and density to the amount of water they receive.

Start a cliff-exploring journey northward from somewhere on Baja's coast, El Rosario perhaps. Here cacti and gray lichen grow along the cliffs. Some people, after a passing glance, would call this a desolate landscape. Life is here, however, not in effusive abundance but in quiet and sure possession of this edge of land.

Around San Quintín the ecological picture improves for both nature and man. Clifftop attempts at dry farming produce some beans and other field crops where the ground is not covered with dense agave. Although this is a weird-looking place with dead agave stalks tilted in all directions, a kind of beauty crowns the parched land in spring when they stand tall and yellow flowered.

From the Baja California–San Diego County line to Santa Barbara and its western suburbs, the cliff world is seldom free from human disturbance. One seaside town or city after another perches on the bluffs or spills over to the high-tide mark. Around the northwest-trending curve of coast from Point Loma to the broad low flat of the Los Angeles Basin, moderate cliffs and bluffs form the seawall of a tableland frequently cut by deep arroyos. Midway between La Jolla and Del Mar, where the mesa drops as much as three hundred feet to the ocean, its V-clefts are filled with the wind-contorted shapes of the first native tree one meets on this northward journey along the bluffs—the rare relict Torrey pine. Some three thousand of these strange little trees seem to be struggling upward, by every small foothold, to escape salt spray, only to be taken into camp in the end by the wind blasting across the mesa top. Another few score of them cling to the eastern face of Santa Rosa Island; the two sites, with ocean between them, are all that remains of this pine's once wide coastal habitational range.

Torrey Pines State Park hopefully preserves for good the larger, mainland stand of the tree, much of which was early lost to development. Other bits of

The bluffs near Point Sur on the Monterey coast, California, are protected from rapid weathering by a dense blanket of coastal scrub or "soft chaparral," which is found on lower, moister slopes than the true chaparral on the coastlands.

wild Southern California coastline are protected at least for the present in military reservations. But sea-cliffs are largely defaced by roadways, buildings, oil-well rigs, and other industrial construction. The climax of almost total obliteration of everything natural comes at the edge of the Los Angeles Basin, from Newport Bay to Santa Monica. Much of the low bluff-line in the Long Beach area has been bulldozed to oblivion. Even that high bastion of the Southland's cliff world, Palos Verdes Hills' sea-face, is yielding more and more of its remaining naturalness to a well-heeled human desire for homesites facing sunsets and ocean breezes — and fighting back in Pyrrhic style by giving ground to slippage.

On the angular flanks of the Santa Monicas plunging into the sea, chaparral and coastal scrub come into their own as the hallmark of Southern California highlands. Most typical vegetative expression of the coastal climate called Mediterranean, chaparral deserves its own chapter. It is enough to say now that,

from this area where it is so clearly dominant, on north at least to Marin County, chaparral is seldom absent from one's view of ridgetops and upper slopes of the ranges from the coast highway.

SINCE 1937, when a five-year project was completed and California State Highway 1 was finally blasted out of these cliffs and carried almost the entire length of the state, across many canyons over lofty bridges, it has been an easy few hours' drive between Morro Bay and the Monterey Peninsula. Until then, from the day in September, 1769, when Portolá's party found itself blocked from its coastal march by the Santa Lucias' plunging flanks and had to strike inland up San Carpoforo Creek and over the range to the Salinas Valley, this hundred miles of coastline was not for human passage. For the long years that the road south ended at Big Sur and the road north led only to cattle ranches beyond San Simeon, it seemed that the wild and precipitous stretch between was destined to remain forever trackless. But the day came when the men, the machines, and the money were marshaled for assault on this ancient rampart of cliffs.

After one has "landed" at Monterey from this route hung between sky and sea, the coast journey north is resumed in a wide, mostly flat, semicircle around Monterey Bay to Santa Cruz. Just west of that pleasant seaside city are the well-known arches and stacks. One may go down to the beach and explore in safety at low tide, or walk out over the old raised terrace, which is still a long way from falling in to make new stacks out of old arches. At high tide, the surf thunder in the raceway beneath is exhilarating.

No match for the Monterey section, but still the favorite route to the Golden Gate for many who love an open road—now close to beaches, now skirting cliffs and bluffs—Highway 1 skims on to another landing beside San Francisco's Ocean Beach playground. At the southern gatepost of the Golden Gate, are reminders of the city's cliff-consciousness. From the beach, generations of San Franciscans and tourists have watched Steller sea lions lolling on the surf-washed ledges of Seal Rocks. From here around the bend to high Lands End, the cliffs are very steep with sea caves cut in their feet—a truly perilous attraction to incautious climbers. Those lofty bluffs—grass and scrub covered, rock-cliff footed—of Marin County, across the Golden Gate, stand in stark contrast to the solidly urban south side of the Gate. Farther north, near Drakes Bay, these Marin seacliffs are a light buff color, quite steep, their bold faces little relieved by vegetation. Here the land comes to a clean, sharp edge.

Beyond Bodega Head and the Russian River mouth, Highway 1 resumes its intimacy with cliff faces, rocky headlands, wave-cut terraces, and the canyons that rivers and streams have worn across these barriers in order to reach the sea. Here there are more such clefts than there were in the south, with fair-sized and flowing rivers—evidence of higher rainfall. More obvious evidence is a heavier, more varied plant cover. Bishop pines are dark upon bluffs and landward slopes. Redwood and Douglas-fir fill river bottoms, where lumbermen are waiting for second and sometimes third growth to mature. Coast towns are frequent, some on the bluffs, some beside river

mouths. In settlement, resort-going, farming, lumbering, fishing, the patterns of human ecology are widely evident, but with a kind of rugged simplicity at one with land and ocean shore. Yet there is still much wildness on this northern coast, of Sonoma and Mendocino, before the highway leaves it to cross the outer range and join U.S. 101 midway in the great Redwood Belt.

Beyond direct reach of State Highway 1, from Rockport to Shelter Cove and the ocean front of the four-thousand-foot King Range, the wilderness cliff world comes again into its own. On steep-sloping bluffs the northern coastal scrub is intermixed with various timber trees where soil, moisture, slope, and exposure are favorable.

From northern California on to Alaska, plants of the coastal strand and cliff world are progressively less marked by certain adaptations than they are toward the south. Cliffs and bluffs are still windswept in the north. Steep slopes have their soil and erosion problems, in any latitude. The thing that makes the great and so clearly visible change, south to north, is precipitation. The mean annual figure ranges from well below ten inches south of San Diego to one hundred along the coasts of the Olympic Peninsula and Vancouver Island. Obviously, the farther north on the coast they grow, the less plants need to make either external or internal adjustments to drought. The factor of salt spray is, literally, washed out of the picture. Plants of the northern strands and bluffs have little need for succulence.

In the south, the cliff world appears bold, open, cleanly divisive between land and sea. Along the northern coast, where great forests march to the edge of bluffs and the backs of beaches, and the sheerest cliffs may be hung with wild cucumber, vine maple, and other trailing things, and studded with ferns and delicate herbs, one is more conscious of simple termination than of change. Land's edge is darkly but softly verdant.

Taken all together, nothing more powerfully identifies the Pacific Coast than its great seawall of cliffs and steep bluffs. And between the extremes of Baja Californian desert-by-the-sea and Alaskan seafronting glaciers, the shifting latitudes are most visibly marked by the climate-controlled changes on the bold outer face of the cliff world.

CHAPTER 9: SEACLIFF WORLD

A sheer cliff face exposed by a landslide and finely sculptured by rain and runoff.

PART TWO:

ISLANDS
AND INLETS

*Where the sea has broken the barrier of the continent's
edge to carve inlets—as here in Puget Sound—labyrinths
of waterways and islands are formed.*

CHAPTER 10

ISLANDS BEYOND THE EDGE

*The continental shelf and the sea —
changing topography both above and below the ocean surface.*

SOMEWHERE in every heart or imagination there is an island, symbol of romance, escape, tranquillity. Robert Louis Stevenson may be in part responsible; he who launched youthful spirits to a "Treasure Island" chose, moreover, to live his own last days on Samoa. But for the naturalist, islands have a different fascination: many are ideal places to watch evolution at work.

These Pacific islands of the Americas are few. Great island arcs and archipelagoes fringe the Pacific's Asian and Australasian shores. From its center southward and westward this ocean is studded with islands and atolls as no other is. But our Eastern Pacific's islands are quickly named. Off South America lie Sala-y-Gómez, Juan Fernández Islands, San Félix and San Ambrosio, the Galápagos archipelago, and Malpelo; southwest of the Isthmus of Panama, Cocos Island; off Mexico, Clipperton, Revilla Gigedo Islands with outlying Clarion, and Guadalupe. All are volcanic, some recently active. They are, it might be said, the ones that made it to the ocean surface, broke water, and have not yet eroded away or sunk by their own weight back into the yielding basalt. These are the few, the high and dry, named on navigation charts. They are not as lonely as once supposed, however. Since World War II a great deal of ocean bottom sounding has been done, in a program climaxed by the work of the International Geophysical Year but still going on. The Eastern Pacific ocean floor, long thought to be relatively featureless, shows on echograms as bristling with whole ranges of mountains and veritable archipelagoes of islands, under the sea

off Baja California and again in the Gulf of Alaska.

Islands, subocean rises (scarps, ridges, seamounts, tablemounts), and the recently discovered fracture zones of the Eastern Pacific—all are related in various ways to the great volcanic and seismic belt circling the Pacific Basin. The mainland has seen much action along this belt. San Francisco, Katmai, Lassen, Santa Barbara, Parícutin, Anchorage, Irazu—these names recall spectacular events which were in fact mere incidents of an ongoing process. But on the seaward edge of the belt—platform for islands—most activity is deep under water, known to us only through instruments. On February 6, 1964, Honolulu seismographs picked up a strong earthquake, Richter magnitude 6.5, in the Gulf of Alaska a hundred miles south of Kodiak Island. Seven weeks later the March 27 quake not only devastated Anchorage but lastingly scarred and changed the rim of the gulf and offshore islands.

By chance some striking volcanic activity has been observed on islands far to the south. Beebe and others have vividly described and photographed Galápagos eruptions. In August, 1952, a tuna clipper radioed to California that San Benedicto, one of the four uninhabited deep-sea Revilla Gigedos, south of Baja, had shot off violently. Scientists flying in during the action found the little island blasting away through an old cone to form a new crater (they named it Boqueron —"Big Mouth").

The Eastern Pacific's floor and adjacent continental slope and shelf, with their deep submarine canyons and other structures right to the shoreline, are now a tremendous laboratory in which researchers are at

Steaming intermittently, four-thousand-foot Kiska Volcano, near the western end of the Aleutian chain, is one of eighty volcanoes in the arc formed by those islands and the Alaska Peninsula. Of these, forty-seven have been reported in action since 1760.

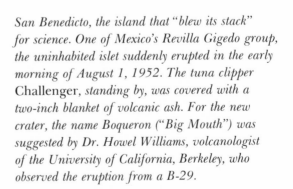

CHAPTER 10:
ISLANDS BEYOND THE EDGE

*San Benedicto, the island that "blew its stack"
for science. One of Mexico's Revilla Gigedo group,
the uninhabited islet suddenly erupted in the early
morning of August 1, 1952. The tuna clipper
Challenger, standing by, was covered with a
two-inch blanket of volcanic ash. For the new
crater, the name Boqueron ("Big Mouth") was
suggested by Dr. Howel Williams, volcanologist
of the University of California, Berkeley, who
observed the eruption from a B-29.*

work with everything from scuba gear to ship-borne drill rigs and echo-sounding devices. They are throwing new light on this vast and varied foreground to our Pacific shore and offshore islands.

A N OCEAN APPROACH to this shore by ship or jet gives no inkling of what lies below the surface. So imagine a Jules Verne exploration of the bottom. If we submarined down the 18,240-foot undersea slope of that monarch of ocean islands, Hawaii, and headed northeastward to the California coast, we would first cross the Hawaiian Deep, exceeding 3,000 fathoms in places. Then we would travel 1,700 or 1,800 sea miles at a gentle average upgrade to around 2,500 fathoms. With central California our target, the smoothest going would probably be up the valley, 500 miles wide, between the Murray Fracture Zone to the south and the Mendocino Seascarp, an escarpment 1,500 miles long, to the north. Imagining that submerged landforms loomed above the great plain of the deep bottom as visibly as in air, we would view that east-west ridge as a band on the distant horizon to our left. Nearer, on the right, a number of tablemounts would rise like mesas on a Southwest desert landscape to mark the Murray Fracture Zone.

As we climbed the continental slope between the two zones, the sharper peaks of a few widely spaced seamounts would come into view, standing guard offshore in front of the still higher mass of the coast ranges—unseen above the ocean surface—rimming the continent itself. One might be Davidson Seamount, rearing more than a mile above the 2,000-fathom line sixty miles off the Monterey coast. Another would be Pioneer Seamount, a like distance outside the Golden Gate. An approach to the south of Point Conception would bring into view a scattered group of these undersea mountains outflanking the Channel Islands not far off their elevated platform. But, leaving that Southern California island world for later exploration, we shall now turn northward to where undersea islands are many, not few. First, a glance back will emphasize the contrast.

Our route from the mid-Pacific has been over the Deep Plain. Smooth and sloping gently upward to the California coast, this broad oceanic valley lacks true islands and shoals. Besides the two named, only three

other elevations that deserve to be called seamounts have been found rising upon it. These mounts, ranging from a half to a full mile high above their bases, show echo-sounded profiles like peaks of the Cascades. They would have been offshore volcano-islands, had they made the last few hundred fathoms up and broken water. They form a line roughly paralleling the coast and seem related to it rather than the ocean floor.

Venturing north, we come to a broad belt, much more thickly studded with seamounts, lying upon a greatly widened platform off the continental slope. Geologists have given the name Ridge and Trough Province to this region, which stretches from the Mendocino and adjacent Gorda escarpments to the area southwest of the Queen Charlotte Islands. This is a region of rather complex bottom structure, relatively youthful in its southern part at least, and seismically active. Long narrow ridges trend north with the continental slope and coast, rising from the bottom, which is a plain except for these and the further interruptions of deep troughs or depressions.

Northwest of the Ridge and Trough Province and comprising most of the gulf is the Gulf of Alaska Seamount Province. In general this part of the northeastern Pacific's broad bottom is smoothly and deeply covered with sediments grading gently down and away, southwestward, from the continental shore. But this otherwise even slope is dotted by no fewer than thirty-six volcanoes, which would be called majestic if they rose to view on land. Quite old, none reach higher than 227 fathoms below the ocean surface. Eleven of them are flat-topped. These few, called *guyots*, are now half a mile beneath the sea, but their shape indicates planing by wave action. Once volcanic islands, they have sunk deep while the sea level has greatly risen. Indeed, it is thought that the entire northeastern Pacific Ocean floor has gradually subsided. There is no evidence of recent volcanic activity in the province, nothing to indicate new islands building. It is a silent landscape of ancient volcanoes beneath the ocean, many of them more than two miles high.

T HE ALEUTIANS and the Bering Sea, with its continental shores and islands, lie outside our limits, but certain things of their geology (and of their life,

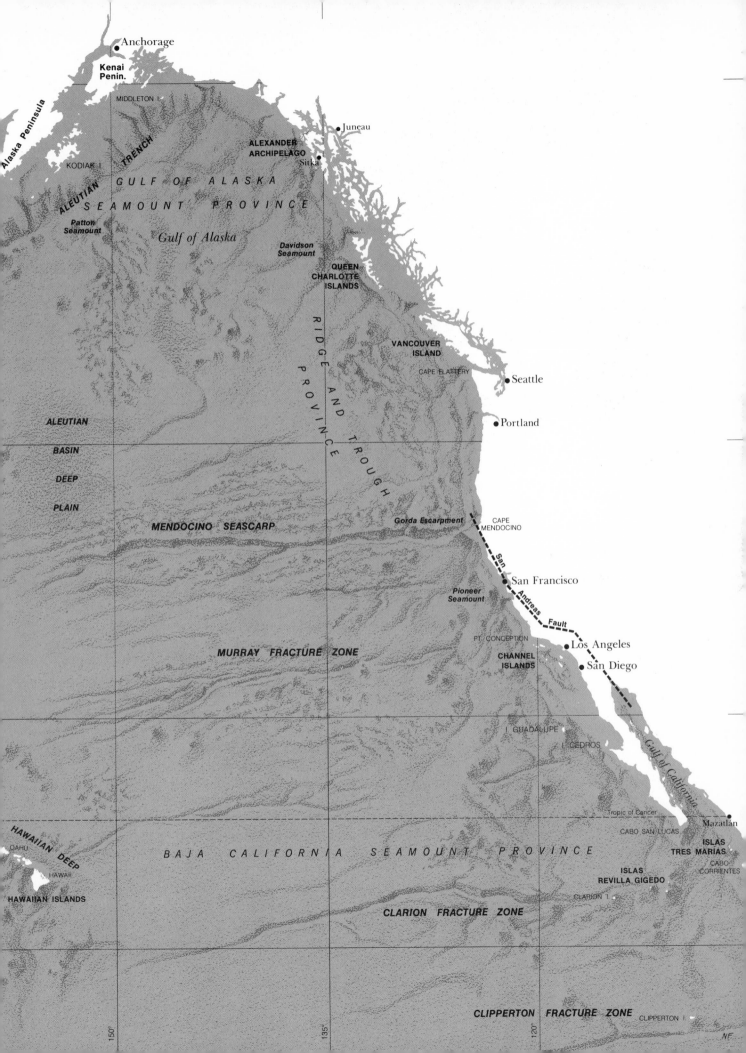

Anchorage

Kenai
Penin.

MIDDLETON I.

Alaska Peninsula

KODIAK I.

ALEUTIAN TRENCH

GULF OF ALASKA

SEAMOUNT PROVINCE

Patton
Seamount

Gulf of Alaska

Davidson
Seamount

Juneau

ALEXANDER
ARCHIPELAGO

Sitka

QUEEN
CHARLOTTE
ISLANDS

VANCOUVER
ISLAND

CAPE FLATTERY

Seattle

RIDGE AND TROUGH

PROVINCE

Portland

ALEUTIAN

BASIN

DEEP

PLAIN

MENDOCINO SEASCARP

Gorda Escarpment

CAPE
MENDOCINO

San

San Francisco

Pioneer
Seamount

Andreas

Fault

Los Angeles

PT. CONCEPTION

San Diego

MURRAY FRACTURE ZONE

CHANNEL
ISLANDS

I. GUADALUPE

I. CEDROS

Gulf of California

HAWAIIAN DEEP

OAHU

HAWAII

HAWAIIAN ISLANDS

Tropic of Cancer

Mazatlán

CABO SAN LUCAS

ISLAS
TRES MARIAS

CABO
CORRIENTES

BAJA CALIFORNIA SEAMOUNT PROVINCE

ISLAS
REVILLA GIGEDO

CLARION I.

CLARION FRACTURE ZONE

CLIPPERTON FRACTURE ZONE

CLIPPERTON I.

150°

135°

120°

NF

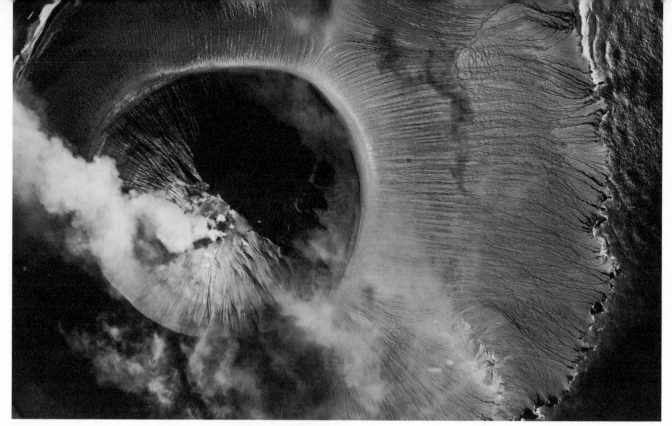

*Boqueron Crater was still steaming seven weeks after the eruptions of
San Benedicto began, and showed a congealed lava plug in its throat.
However, no lava had flowed during the island's period of activity.
The fine blanket of ash shows erosion streaks from the runoff of rain.*

as we shall see) do not. The Aleutian island chain is
in fact the major part of the Aleutian Range of volcanic mountains, whose 1,600-mile length begins with
Mount Spurr near Anchorage and ends with Attu
Island, which is closer to Asia's Kamchatka than to
our Alaska Peninsula. Older rocks, chiefly volcanic
and so much eroded that they play no part in present
landscapes, support this range of very active volcanoes. Since the Russian explorers and fur traders
first began to observe them in 1760, at least forty-
seven of the eighty distinct volcanoes in the chain
have been reported as steaming, erupting, or otherwise active. Fifty-eight have kept their pristine volcano form, while venting ash or lava, ever since the
last Pleistocene glacial retreat.

The many passes—some deep, some shoal—
through this tightly-linked chain of storming, steaming, smoking volcano-islands are hell-gates to the
more placid realm of Vitus Bering's sea. Waters of
the Aleutian Basin on the north of the long island
arc, near the International Date Line, sound a little
over two thousand fathoms; then the Bering Sea
floor rises rather abruptly to the 100-fathom line,
trending northwestward from Unimak Pass almost to

the Asian shore below Cape Navarin. This line marks
a shelf that stood high and dry in Pleistocene time as
the edge of a land bridge between the two continents.
Upon this present 100-fathom shoal are several
islands: large St. Lawrence and Nunivak, the very
small Diomedes between which our boundary with
the Soviet Union passes, and the Pribilof Islands.
Now standing at most between five hundred and a
thousand feet above Bering Sea tides, some much
less, the five little Pribilofs may once have appeared
as low hills on the southern horizon of the Bering
land bridge. They now mark the southward limit of
Bering Sea pack ice. But their importance to our story
lies in their role as breeding ground for some of the
conspicuous animals of our Pacific waters and shore.

From Hawaii, monarch of a great mid-Pacific
island chain that is enormously significant as a
crucible of evolving life, we have journeyed eastward
then north to the far edge of our Pacific island world.
In our view from the bottom of the ocean, briefly
glimpsed shapes that rise toward the sea surface have
hinted at the forces forever at work building islands—
forces of great energy within the earth's crust which
ceaselessly change its outward form.

*The Alaskan brown bear is fond of salmon; but the answer
to the frequent charge that he seriously depletes this game fish
is that most of his catch is of dying or even dead salmon after spawning.
Thus the bear is performing a beneficial "cleanup" function.*

105

Lake Crescent, the northernmost scenic attraction of Olympic National Park, lies between the mountains and the Strait of Juan de Fuca. Biologically speaking, a lake is an "island" — a body of water surrounded by land — and may hold some unique forms of life in isolation. Such a form is Lake Crescent's famous Beardslee trout, a great game fish.

107

CHAPTER 11

LIFEGUARD ISLANDS OF THE NORTH

*The Queen Charlottes—where life found refuge in the Ice Ages;
and the remote Pribilofs—where fur seals still breed.*

THROUGH THE PASSES of the Aleutians the Pribilof fur seal herd takes the open sea road toward a southern winter. The animals scatter in a wide fan, some to make the far Japanese islands, a few turning up along the Hawaiian chain, but the greatest number streaming down off the North American coast all the way to the Mexican border. Generally the old bulls keep more to the north, but cows and young seals may occasionally be seen in small groups anywhere from fifty to as close as ten miles from the California shore.

The Alaska fur seal belongs to the deep-sea surface and, come breeding time, to a few islands in the Bering Sea—over 90 percent to the Pribilofs. For two centuries these relict jots of volcanic land, hidden by almost perpetual mist in a lonely side-pocket of the Pacific, have had a material importance to man out of all proportion to their size and intrinsic worth. For a brief season, with unfailing regularity, they are the focus of a large animal population which for most of the year is dispersed widely and freely over a considerable part of the greatest sea. Such is the ineluctable rhythm of nature and time.

Tides washing the Pribilofs' rocky shores and rising and falling in Aleutian passes are home, feeding ground, and carrier for a legion of pelagic and off-shore animals. Also of the family of the eared seals but larger than fur seals are Steller sea lions, found mainly in Alaskan waters. Fortunately for their survival, they lack the precious soft underfur which gives the pelt of the fur seal a value second only to the sea otter's among marine fur-bearers.

Old male sperm whales also pass through the Aleutians to their Bering Sea summer grounds. Killer whales find good hunting among the lesser mammals of island waters—hair seals, sea lions, and others. The bowhead is coming back from the serious depletion of whaling days, along with the right whale, the California gray, and several more.

Of fishes about the Aleutians, the mackerel, cod, herring, halibut, and salmon are in good supply as food for men and other mammals. Shellfish crowd the inshore—shrimp, true crabs, and the giant king crab, a "living fossil" in a class all its own, with wondrously long, meaty legs.

"The climate of the Aleutians," one geographer tells us, "is a succession of unpleasant weather." Forming a boundary between the cold Bering Sea and the warmer North Pacific Ocean, the chain suffers the turbulence normal to a climatic border zone. Moist winds warmed by the Japan Current and tangling with colder arctic air bring quantities of fog, rain, and snow to the islands a full two-thirds of the year. The overcast umbrella covers the Pribilofs, too; the cool, damp, largely sunless summers are part of the islands' attraction to the fur seal herd. These animals must come ashore to breed and give birth, but they do not take to direct sunlight.

This Bering Sea climate is not for trees, nor for the lush growth of very much else. Here such things as willows and birches are ground-creeping shrubs. Grasses and sedges are chief among the Aleutians' plants, which number less than five hundred kinds. During the short growing season, various flowers

*In the highland hearts of some of the islands and peninsulas of the Gulf of Alaska
and Northwest Coast, many forms of life were somehow protected from the glaciers, and
lived to repopulate the land. Even such forms as this spotted coral-root orchid survived.*

bloom in sheltered valleys, but almost nothing clothes the heights except lichens and mosses. Unlike the teeming seas surrounding them, these island pinpoints of land are hostile to most forms of life.

THE KODIAK ISLAND group to the east contrasts with the stark Aleutians in many ways. Along the mainland end of the Aleutian–Alaska Peninsula volcano chain, Kodiak, Afognak, and their smaller satellites form a compact cluster of partially submerged fault-block mountains, the sea-plunging extension of the Chugach-Kenai range. In the Mesozoic era, strong lateral crust movements wrinkled the Alaskan Gulf rim into alternating arcs of highland and valley. Where the Chugach-Kenai-Kodiak chain now stands, a deep trough was formed and the sea filled it. Erosion of the bordering heights deposited many thousands of feet of sediments in this trough—beds later raised to form the present ranges. During that time the land was eroded down and further uplifted, in several stages; then in the Pleistocene it was heavily glaciated. Although the mainland part of the chain rises sharply to over 13,000 feet on some of its peaks, the Kodiak group reaches only 2,000 to 4,500 feet above the sea. Ice covered it almost entirely during the Pleistocene. Glaciers scoured its flanks and gouged deep clefts which, as the sea rose in the great postglacial melt, formed narrow channels cutting the mass into its separate islands and shaping the long fiords that nearly divide it many times again.

Thereafter, climate and landforms conjoined to make Kodiak and Afognak (with a small bit of the sheltered peninsular shore opposite) a southwest-pointing spur to the northwesternmost ice-age refuge of the Pacific Coastal Forest in the Kenai mountains. The one cone-bearing tree to seize this new outpost was the Sitka spruce.

Arctic winds beat fiercely against the icy Bering Sea side of the high Alaska Peninsula, but on the southeast the waters of Shelikof Strait and the islands are warmed a little by the northward offshoot of the Japan Current. Pollen studies show that sometime after the last glacial retreat, the moisture-loving and generally maritime Sitka spruce moved down from the Kenai Peninsula to find a congenial niche on its Kodiak-Afognak extension. A pure stand of it now grows tall and straight on the muskeg at Cape Gre-

ville, of lowland northeastern Kodiak. Higher up (to its 3,500-foot limit) it becomes more and more stunted and irregular as dampness lessens and winds increase. It may, in fact, have appeared at this far end of its range long after the ice sheet vanished, the climate having grown cooler and moister again with the passing of time, and thus more favorable to this tree. Some of its southward spread has been seen in historic times.

Among those who would not wish the spruce forest to take over all the lowlands of the Kodiak group are stockmen. A good native grass, locally called beach rye, provides the year-round grazing that makes the two largest islands—especially Kodiak—a major Alaskan beef and dairying center. This economic fact also gives rise to mixed feelings about Kodiak's most feared and yet highly respected native inhabitant, the Alaskan brown bear. The largest of all carnivores, this splendid animal is itself an economic as well as aesthetic asset to Alaska. Better known as the Kodiak bear, it has long been a prized quarry of the world's hardiest hunters. Guide fees and outfitting money going into Kodiak pockets more than offset the yearly loss of a few head of cattle and even a considerable quantity of salmon. With regard to the bear's unquestioned fondness for that valuable fish, biologists have replied to complaining fishermen that salmon are overfished by people, not bears. In any case, Kodiak, like all of Alaska, is still a land where nature runs large and competing man is relatively small. And while some Alaskans have demanded the extermination of Kodiak's magnificent bear, many others fortunately have championed him as symbol of the rugged wildness that is truly Alaska's most vital asset. It must be hoped that not even the all-out exploitation of arctic oil fields will reduce the state to an unexciting and unchallenging tameness. Nature needs wilderness, and so does man—body and soul.

ISLANDS long isolated from the mainland have played signal roles in the evolution of life. The outer islands of our Northwest—Pribilofs, Aleutians, Kodiak, Queen Charlottes, Vancouver—are, in their close-knit groups and chains, quite near the continent. Theirs has been a history of continual upheaval, volcanism, glaciation—disturbances of landform and environment not favoring patient evolutionary change. Nevertheless, these islands are, and have been, guardians of life and the living, and have had some part in fostering new forms of life, as well.

The vital factor for each island is being where it is. The fur seals must have their Pribilofs, haven for breeding; offshore and intertidal animals cling to the Aleutian anchor chain, which greatly extends their range; but for Kodiak's welcoming shores, the Sitka spruce might have retreated instead of advancing. These islands stand upon, and soften, the borderline between a rough sea and a harsh land, inviting oases to the life of both. Vancouver Island and the Queen Charlottes were among the last coastal refuges for terrestrial animals and plants in a desert of ice.

Ten or twelve thousand years ago, the retreating ice left this northern coast a wasteland, a cold, wet desert of naked rock and glacial till. How did life come back to these shores? From where did the animals return? How did a luxuriant forest spring to living climax in so short an ecological time? Whence came its seeds—hundreds of miles from a warmer, unglaciered south? To go the whole distance would have required, for vegetation, more millennia than the postglacial epoch has provided.

The answer appears to lie in a theory advanced by E. Hultén of Sweden in 1937, when knowledge of the regional geology and glaciation patterns was still quite sketchy. He proposed that certain biotic refuges were spared by the glaciers; and from these, after the ice had gone from the areas around them, life moved outward to reclaim its own, as it will when conditions favor its spreading. One of the ice-free areas, or *refugia*, was thought to be centered upon the Aleutians in the southern Bering Sea region. Another was in the south central Alaskan region of the Kenai Peninsula and the adjacent area of Prince William Sound. Lesser refugia may have occurred around Lituya Bay, in southeastern Alaska, and along the coast from British Columbia to Puget Sound, the southernmost reach of glaciation. More recent studies, which show beyond a doubt what areas the glaciers claimed, give this theory strong support.

On mapping certain plant assemblages, Hultén found them to be zoned in a concentric relationship, clearly indicating their migration from a common center. Here was biological evidence for the existence of ancient "islands" of life which had withstood the

ISLANDS OF THE NORTHEASTERN PACIFIC OCEAN

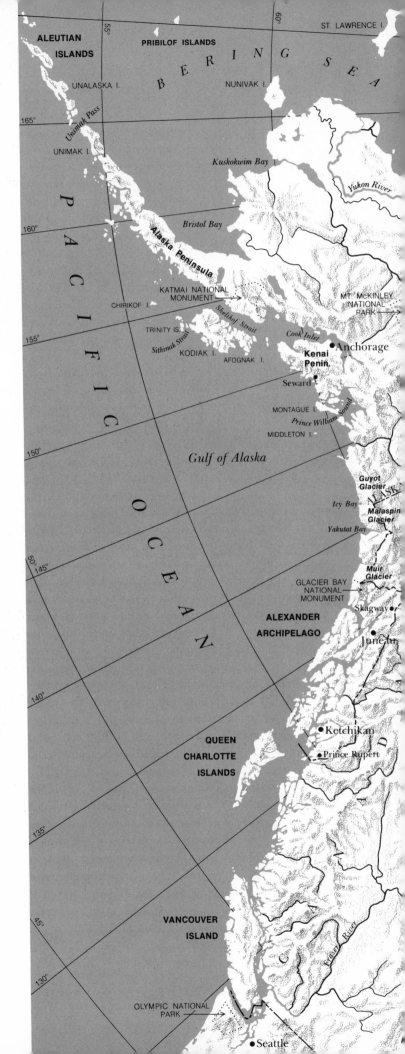

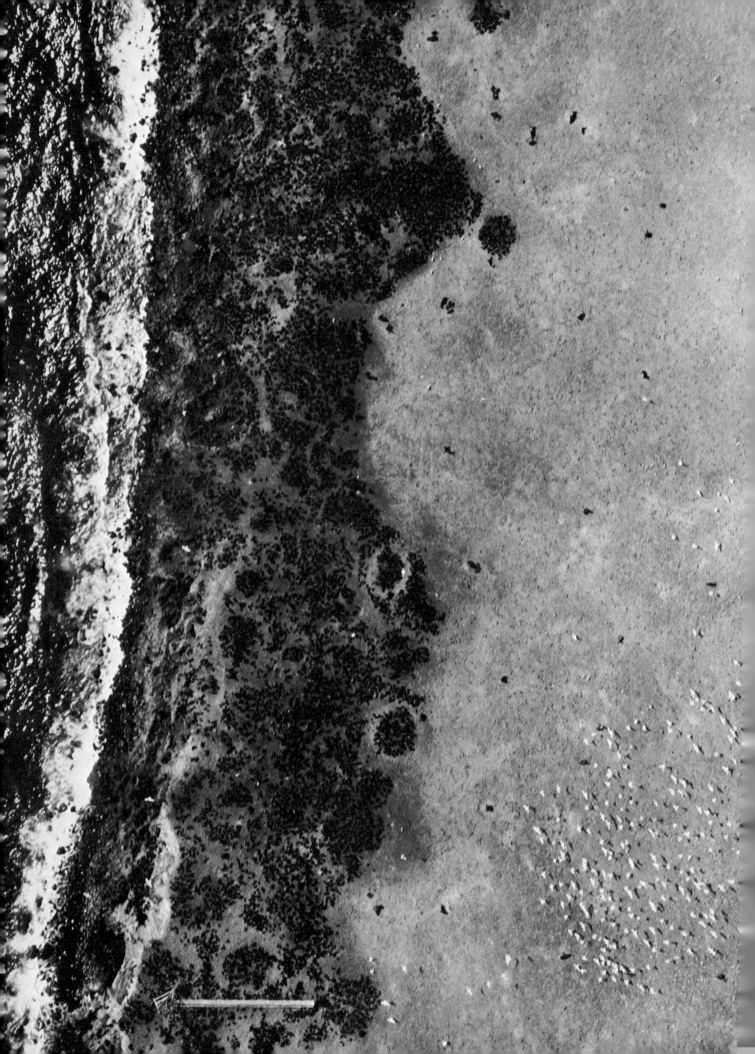

encroachment of a "sea" of ice throughout a long age.

The existence—in the present or the past—of a flowering plant species can be certified by the unique characteristics of its microscopic pollen grains. Ferns and their allies can likewise be recognized by their spores. Pollen- and spore-bearers which depend upon the wind to broadcast these minute reproductive particles yield enormous quantities of them. A few will ensure the survival of the species, but the vast majority are destined to become "fallout" of sorts. Where this wind-borne dust falls upon bog, muskeg, lake, or sea, it is ultimately assimilated into the varied detritus layering the floor of the watery area. Layer piles upon layer, each with its annual increment of mixed pollen and spores representing the region's plant cover. Sediments become compacted—bog muck to peat, lake and tidal-flat muds to shale—and in due course, if undisturbed, take their respective places in the sequence of geological time horizons. Through the eons of inevitable change, tidelands may be raised above the sea, bogs may dry out, and lakes fill with erosion debris to become meadowland or valley floor. But pollen grains and spores are all but indestructible when locked away from oxidizing air, under water or compacted into earth material.

These microscopic, organic particles have thus written significant chapters in the history of the land, a history with its living expression in the migrations and changes of whole populations of plants.

The greatest migration was, naturally, from that largest of genetic "reserve banks," the forested lands just out of reach of the ice sheet's most southerly advance. Lodgepole pine led the slow northward march of the vast forest of cone-bearers. Standing in their straight and rather somber ranks—perhaps thirty-five to fifty miles south of the glacier vanguard, which halted a few miles beyond where Puget Sound's farthest inland waters lie today—the shivering trees needed only the freshly opening, warming,

Fur seal rookery, or breeding ground, on the Pribilof Islands, Alaska, at the peak of the mating season in mid-July. The Bering Sea surf breaks on the left; the black dots in the middle are thousands of adult seals with their newborn pups. On the beach, an occasional "harem" shows clearly as a cluster of seals surrounded by a well-beaten path made by the bull patrolling his territory. A flock of white gulls rises from the bare tundra at right, where a few idle bulls are holding territory but no mates.

and drying ground. Seedling by seedling, they reclaimed the emergent land. Decade after decade and century upon century, the great afforestation followed the glaciers' accelerating retreat.

OF THE SEVERAL ice-free refugia which helped to repopulate the post-glacial Northwest Coast, probably none equaled in significance that of the Queen Charlotte Islands. Lying well offshore midway of the latitudes crossed by the Inside Passage to Alaska, this most ocean-bound of the coastal archipelagoes alone among them remained to a significant extent unconquered by the ice sheet.

The wide and deep waters of Dixon Entrance on the north, Hecate Strait on the east, and Queen Charlotte Sound to the southeast, floated the westering ice-bulk (six-sevenths submerged) around and past these islands. So great were the mass of the ice sheet and the thrust behind it, however, that as it fronted the Queen Charlottes along their eastern shores, it rode up-slope and over their moderately elevated lowlands. Nevertheless, the western mountain ramparts of the largest islands, Graham and Moresby, withstood the icy onslaught almost entirely.

Before the bridging land was drowned by the ancient sea, which also filled the lowest valley bottoms between hills and ridges of the westward range, the Queen Charlotte mass was populated by a rich variety of continental plants and animals. These flourished in a mild maritime climate and clothed the future archipelago with their abundance.

The islands have been isolated long enough now for evolution to have worked its changes on many of their living forms, especially the animals. Marten, weasel, and caribou have become species unique to the archipelago. Shrew, white-footed mouse, and black bear are now races distinct from the parent species of the continent. Such differentiation is strong evidence for the continuous existence of populations since preglacial times—populations of undoubted continental origin, cut off perhaps by the total glaciation of their sometime land bridge, never again to mingle with those of the mainland after the sea's postglacial inundation of Hecate Strait.

A number of plant species also have become distinctly endemic to the Queen Charlottes—for example, a saxifrage found in the mountains. But

*Kodiak, the chief city and port of Kodiak Island, Alaska, is surrounded by water
and Sitka spruce forest. The view is southeastward across Chiniak Bay.*

*Dawson Inlet, on the southwest coast of Graham, the northernmost and largest of the Queen Charlotte
Islands, shows the V profile of an unglaciated valley. This has been a fruitful area for botanical
explorers; it is one of the pockets of life spared by the Ice Age glacial advance.*

certain kinds have quite certainly returned from this ice-age refugium to begin repopulating the mainland opposite in areas known to have been completely denuded by the ice sheet, and to which these plants could not have come from over the high alpine Coast Range. They are plants which belong to cool-temperate, moist, maritime lowlands. It was essential that their diaspores, or reproductive structures, could be blown, carried, or floated across at least forty miles of open sea.

When the population densities of the chief forest trees in British Columbia were plotted recently, the thickest stands of Sitka spruce and western hemlock were found upon the Queen Charlotte Islands and the mainland directly across the strait. The hugest and oldest of these maritime spruces are living on the Queen Charlottes. The hemlock thins out, from the Hecate Strait area, along the coast to the south, re-appearing in abundance on certain areas of Vancouver Island. When the glaciers' retreat left them foothold, these and other migrants from the Queen Charlottes' haven of life fanned out to the north, south, and east to the foot of the Coast Range. In succeeding generations they met and mingled with populations moving up from western Washington and down from the Gulf of Alaska borderlands. The coastlands which had been left naked by the ice sheet were rapidly reclothed in their former forest green.

Another important "island" of life held out at nearly a thousand feet above the seaward edge of the Cordilleran ice sheet in the north central mountains of Vancouver Island, where the highest marks of glaciation are seen at 6,300 feet. What plant species rode out the glacial sea here is not yet fully known; but among the animals of this highland today is a marmot which is close to, but distinct from, a species of the nearby mainland. And the island has a ptarmigan which is at least a clearly marked race of its continental species. Vancouver was perhaps an island refuge unto itself, contributing less to the repopulation of the mainland than did the Queen Charlottes.

ISOLATION, evolution of new forms, migration, dispersal, survival, sometimes extinction—these are among the landmark factors by which science attempts to reconstruct the story of ever-changing life. Islands, whether of the open sea or of the coast-line, are by their nature ideal stages for observation and study of distinct episodes in the drama. Isolation of the "experiment stage" aids in controlled studies of evolution at work. And as with a "theater in the round," an observer can not only watch every entrance and exit but can see the direction of each actor's coming or going.

CHAPTER 12

ISLANDS OF THE CALIFORNIAS

Geography of a nearby but little known world—
a closeup of offshore islands and the life forms they support.

And then, straight out at sea, loom the islands, . . . all of which, standing in a line, are but several parts of another mountain range, under water still except for these higher summits.

—Bradford Torrey, FIELD-DAYS IN CALIFORNIA

THE GREEN BEAM of the Los Angeles Light, rotating from its seventy-three-foot tower on the end of the San Pedro Breakwater, drops quickly astern. The fishing boat leaves the calm of man-made Los Angeles Harbor and squares away into choppy swells under the night wind. Soon Point Fermin's light, marking the southeastern bluff of San Pedro Hill, fades beneath the stars as our vessel picks up cruising speed and bears west fifteen degrees north from San Pedro Channel.

Eight hours and seventy sea miles later, a lee shore lulls the rhythmic rise and dip of the vessel that has meant misery for some, a rockaby sleep for others. Passengers, on deck, line up at the port rail as word of the landfall spreads rapidly below. Now the long, high wall of tawny cliffs, seen dimly in the early morning fog, signals adventure for everyone.

Bearing northeast into Anacapa Passage, the little ship coasts quietly along the southeast face of Santa Cruz Island's eastern end. Fog still shrouds the clifftops, but it has lifted from the rock islets where California brown pelicans, cormorants, and other birds of the outer coast, with much flapping and diving, taking off and landing, are beginning their day. Gulls wheel gracefully around the boat, waiting for galley scraps to drop over the side. And as the overcast begins to dissolve, they catch the first of the sunlight on white wings. A fine June day is breaking upon offshore California.

While skipper and crew give every nerve to standing close inshore at just enough speed to offset the lazy shoreward swells, the passengers, who have chartered the vessel for an island-coasting weekend, probe the thinning haze with binoculars and cameras. For most—Californians or not—this is discovery. The history-minded ones may feel some kinship with the discoverers of more than four centuries ago. With familiar mainland features so completely cut off by fog (though not by distance), this bit of wild island shore seems at this moment as far from any known world as the whole California coast was to Cabrillo's company in 1542. Besides, the night-long cruise from San Pedro has beguiled our imaginations.

As the mist clears from Anacapa Passage and the Santa Barbara Channel, the boat rounds San Pedro Point—Santa Cruz's eastern tip. A serrated shape, blue and faint on the horizon, is the Santa Ynez Mountains cresting thirty miles to the north. The city of Santa Barbara lies hull down at the foot of the range, adding to the illusion of distance. As we prepare to land (here the act must be legitimized through prior permission of landowners, unless certain beachheads are strictly held to), we are filled with the singular enchantment of first setting foot upon an unknown shore. And every mind is shaping questions, every eye sharpened for the big and little differences in living things, rock formations, or whatever else it

A pair of California brown pelicans, nesting in futility on Anacapa Island. The tally for this major breeding ground in the 1970 season: one brown pelican hatched—thanks to DDT concentrated in the fish that pelicans eat.

Cormorants perched on an offshore rock of Islas Todos Santos, west of Ensenada, Baja California.

CHAPTER 12:   ISLANDS OF THE CALIFORNIAS

is, beyond the few miles of salt water, that sets these islands apart from the nearby mainland.

THE ISLAND WORLD of the Californias, although widely scattered over the Pacific, has a certain recognizable unity. Its sixteen separate islands (some close-knit groups are named as one) spread across six degrees of latitude, from 28° to 34°N, and stretch fully five hundred miles northwest to southeast between Point Conception and Punta Eugenia. Largest and farthest from the mainland is Guadalupe, its 98 square miles of volcanic mountain lying 157 miles off Baja's northwestern shore. Tiny San Martín, three miles out, is the closest; and the least is San Gerónimo, a fifth of a square mile of seabird perch six miles from the coast. All are outliers of the continent except Guadalupe, a true ocean island.

The geographical relationships of these islands to the continent and to each other are quickly seen on our chart, page 123. But their biological story—the unity they share, their differences one from another and from the mainland—is one which science is still patiently unraveling, interpreting, and piecing together. Although it may never be wholly understood, the story rounds out as it lengthens, through exploration and through studies in evolution, migration, and relict populations both insular and continental. As always in such matters, hypothesis and debate play important parts.

The California Islands fall, for convenience, into three groups (named in each group from west to east and north to south)—the Northern Channel Islands: San Miguel, Santa Rosa, Santa Cruz, Anacapa; the Southern Channel Islands: Santa Barbara, San Nicolas, Santa Catalina, San Clemente; and the Baja California Islands: Los Coronados, Todos Santos, San Martín, San Gerónimo, Guadalupe, San Benito, Cedros, Natividad. Their geological relationship to the continent was not clearly understood until after the fathometer had been developed. This echo-sounding device for measuring water depths gave a picture of the bottom in the island area and revealed that the platform on which these islands rest is a unique *continental borderland*.

The continental shelf, generally much narrower on the Pacific than on the Atlantic side of North America, narrows even more markedly south of Point

ISLANDS AND INLETS

Sur as its edge shifts from the hundred-fathom to the fifty-fathom line. It is believed that a sinking of the ocean bottom is responsible for this and for the continental borderland as well.

Beginning rather abruptly at Point Conception, the continental borderland widens to 160 miles in the Channel Islands area. It consists of a series of basins and ranges quite similar to those of the adjacent mainland. The Santa Barbara Channel is the submerged larger part of the Ventura Basin. Along the south side of the channel, the four Northern Channel Islands extend the line of the Transverse Range of the Santa Monicas westward. Geologists call this former outreach of the mainland the Cabrillo Peninsula. The four Southern Channel Islands and their submarine ridges trend northwest-southeast with the Peninsular Ranges. An erstwhile fifth member of the group is the Palos Verdes Hills, an island until it became joined to the edge of the Los Angeles Basin.

Along its seaward edge, curving south-by-east toward Baja's Punta Eugenia, the broad borderland platform falls away in a steep slope to twelve thousand-foot ocean depths. This was in some past time the edge of the continent. If the sea were to be drawn down to a level below the rim of the continental borderland, the uncovered land would still be one-fourth under water, beneath eleven large and very deep lakes—6,300 square miles of them. Three would be close to a thousand square miles each, and most would run deeper than any existing North American lake. At 2,880 feet, Santa Cruz Basin would exceed the continent's deepest freshwater body, 1,996-foot Crater Lake, by half.

These submarine basins and the islands and near-islands rising among them are strikingly similar to the alternating valleys and mountain ranges of the nearby mainland, even in relative depth to height. Summits of the San Bernardino Mountains reach over 10,000 feet above the contiguous basin floor. Santa Cruz Island's 2,167-foot highest peak rises nearly 9,000 feet above the Santa Cruz Basin. Moreover, the directional trend of ridges and troughs is the same on land and beneath the sea: closely parallel to the great arc of the Southern California coast.

The Channel Islands stand on platforms which level off at the hundred-fathom contour, suggesting the wave-cut terraces of an ancient sea level. The four northern islands share one platform; each of the four widely scattered southern islands has its own. One theory of the origin of these island-blocks and the basins around them is that they were subject to the same rising of fault-block mountain ranges and sinking of valley troughs as occurred on the adjacent land. The joints between rises and sinks are crustal faultlines. Such up-and-down movement, infinitely slow, is continuous. Those platforms or terraces now a hundred fathoms beneath the Pacific mark a time when crustal movement was slowed or halted long enough for the sea to gnaw far into the island masses, after which a further subsidence took place. This offshore sinking was constantly aided by the weight of great quantities of erosion material washed down from the mainland mountains and from the

The Islas Todos Santos appear to extend the geological formation of Punta Banda, Baja California.
Ensenada lies to the left (north) of the point.

islands themselves. Much of this material was once land that linked islands to continent as seagoing extensions of those Southern California ranges. Thus are great crustal pressures and processes expressed as grand strategy in the war between land and sea.

THE LONG SEPARATION and occasional joining of borderland and mainland is a story told not only by the visible forms of islands and rocks, and the fathomable contours of basins and channels, but also by the nature and patterns of island life, in both present and past times.

From the Cretaceous period down to the middle of the Miocene epoch, according to theory, the whole area of the present Channel group was one large island — Catalinia. Subject to eons of crustal rise and

fall, Catalinia became a combination of areas even before the final isolation of its separate islands. It was large enough to have had zones of varying climate; these, together with the periodic crustal shifts from high rises to submergence to dry land again, caused its plant and animal life to evolve into assemblages of locally differing forms. The endemics, or natives, of the islands in large part have descended from such forms; others stem from migrants across the channels.

Each island has some distinctive forms of life, and the island group as a whole has some that are different from those of the mainland. At the same time, all the islands have elements in common, and the group has strong biological ties with the continent — more evidence of alternating separation and connection during past ages. Significantly, some species show

121

more marked evolutionary change on the mainland. The only remaining natural populations of Torrey pine are at mainland Del Mar, San Diego County, and on Santa Rosa Island. Studies of genetic differences between the two seem to indicate that the island form is the older—going back to a time when all California enjoyed a moister, more temperate climate, like that of the islands today—and that the mainland form has changed, even deteriorated, in the face of dryness, encroaching brush, insects, and man. Subdivisions and smog are evolutionary factors not yet noticeable on Santa Rosa Island.

The ocean tempers climate, mediating between extremes and retarding change. However, while crustal movements were slowly forming the islands of Cabrillo's discovery and ours, a long-term change in climate was under way; it altered life greatly in the islands as well as a large part of the mainland. During the last ten million years, the climate has grown gradually drier, not only in the Californias but in the warm temperate belt of their latitudes around the earth. The trend has been interrupted periodically by returns to wetness, and by the exceptional reversal of the Pleistocene ice ages, but it has been marked nevertheless.

The Channel Islands lie exactly in the latitude of the Mojave and Colorado deserts. In these deserts east of the Transverse and Peninsular ranges are the salt-crusted beds of many lakes and rivers which have dried up in very recent geologic time. The offshore islands, although ocean-bound and often fog-swept, have suffered the same progressive desiccation.

In mean annual precipitation the range of the islands from north (San Miguel, about fourteen inches) to south (San Clemente, about ten inches) is virtually the same as that from the Los Angeles Basin to San Diego. The islands enjoy a higher average relative humidity, however; theirs is a distinctly oceanic or maritime climate. Only the southern end of San Clemente is near-desert, although the vegetation is characteristically xeric (dry type) on other islands' south-facing slopes where the angle of direct sun is combined in effect with scant soil and strong wind. Windiness is chief of all conditions adversely affecting the plant life of the islands.

One of the signs of the islands' gradually increasing dryness is the scarcity of seedlings of certain plants,

such as the island oak, a tree poppy, and ironwood. These plants seem to have almost lost the capacity to reproduce by seeding, under the present island climate. To interpret such signs, one must look to all conditions and factors, including introduced forms. Guadalupe Island, for instance, has been all but stripped of its endemics by goats. Brought there in the nineteenth century for a canned meat venture, the critters—and their flourishing progeny—have wiped out several plant species altogether. About the only leafage remaining above the grasses is on the branches of the closed-cone pines, out of the goats' reach. Tree seedlings too were devoured; the only trees now standing are those that had matured before the goats were turned loose.

How numerous Guadalupe's plant species may once have been is perhaps illustrated by tiny Outer Islet, two miles away, which one botanist has called "a goatless refugium." This volcanic speck has yielded five species not found on Guadalupe at all, though presumably they originally grew on the main island. Fortunately for the survival of these few, goats are not known to swim two miles of ocean.

Long-term changes aside, islands, with their equable climate and relative freedom from outside influences other than man, tend to be conservers of the life in residence. As environments they can be, on the other hand, extremely fragile. California's islands are too high to be obliterated by tidal waves, and they are far from any hurricane belt. But their life is vulnerable to several other forms of short-term, occasionally instant catastrophe. In 1952 a volcanic eruption that almost doubled the size of San Benedicto, a small island on the southern edge of our horizon, also buried most of its plant life. Paradoxically, this has opened new possibilities for ecological study—observing the re-introduction, establishment, and succession of both animals and plants on a remote, seabound speck of land. Science is opportunistic.

Nature disposes as it must, but man is not bound by any natural law to destroy for his short-term gain. Yet, we have seen the Farallon eggers at work, in the wake of sea otter hunters; sheep and cattle ranching and naval gunnery and bombing practice have greatly modified certain Channel Islands in a very few years, a loss to the quality of experience for several future

THE CALIFORNIA ISLANDS, SHOWING BASIN AND RANGE
TOPOGRAPHY OF THE CONTINENTAL BORDERLAND.

Shore party on a "desert island," the southeastern side of Santa Cruz in California's Channel Islands. The prickly pear cactus is evidence of aridity on this "rain shadow" exposure.

human generations; and alien goats have, within a century, virtually demolished the native flora of Guadalupe, which as the remotest of all these islands was potentially the most valuable to science.

Unique, always in some degree beautiful, hospitable to life, and preserving a measure of wildness, these islands of the Californias still offer us the long-term potential for enjoyment and benefit if we will save and cherish what remains to the dispositions of nature. There is the long-standing proposal to expand the minimal Channel Islands National Monument of Santa Barbara and the Anacapas into a full-fledged national park embracing at least the three major islands of the northern group—San Miguel, Santa Rosa, and Santa Cruz. And one can have no legitimate quarrel with the well-developed recreational facilities of Santa Catalina—Southern California needs them. Hopefully, such military necessities as still keep San Nicolas, San Clemente, and San Miguel in the limbo of limited access will

someday go the way of the dinosaur. For its part, Mexico has shown a willingness to minimize further exploitation of Baja's islands, of the sort that brought the Guadalupe fur seal to near-extinction.

THE CALIFORNIA ISLANDS belong to two neighbor nations. So long as the possibility exists for at least one group of islands to be preserved as a national park, could not similar status be conferred on others, even those of Baja? Mexico and the United States both have values at stake in their respective California Islands. The further step, then, would be the creation of an international island park—a great and unique oceanic preserve set aside for all time for the mutual enjoyment, adventuring, and scientific interest of our two peoples and all others. They would come, in the understanding of a common trust, to explore, study, restore the spirit, and find all those intangible, if not indeed inexpressible, values peculiar to islands.

The Santa Cruz Island pine is a relic of the Pleistocene epoch, clinging to island outposts and the mainland coast not far north of Point Conception.

A cactus of the genus **Cochemiea**, *which is limited to Baja. Each species is known only by its locality; this one grows on Isla Cedros alone.*

Overleaf: Isla de Cedros, twenty-three miles long and nearly four thousand feet high, forms the western rampart of Bahía de Sebastián Vizcaíno, about midway on the Baja peninsula. It was named for cedars that grow on its ridges, but not on the nearby mainland.

CHAPTER 13

THE INSIDE PASSAGE

*Scenic sea route from Puget Sound to the Alaskan Panhandle—
an awesome project of the Ice Age.*

IT STARTS from Alaskan Way on Seattle's Elliott Bay. It has carried sail and steam, frigates and ferry boats, though it once bore only the great cedar dugouts of the Northwest Coast Indians. It has been the road of chiefs and explorers, salmon fishermen, whalemen, and lumbermen, Alaskan governors and sourdoughs, settlers and "round-trippers." Every stretch of it has been the sea road from some point, island, or inlet to another, since man first plied any sort of craft along this coast—and that may have been several thousand years ago. For the first few generations of our own Northwest time, before airlines or Alaska Highways, it was the road north, the only road to our Alaska.

The Inside Passage is a two-way road. It also starts at Skagway's docks, or at any of the Panhandle ports, for the southing Alaskan. Since there can be no story of passage without direction, ours takes the outward-bound orientation of an undoubted majority of readers and travelers for whom Alaska spells not home but discovery and adventure. From Puget Sound to the Panhandle's near end, from a Seattle departure to a Ketchikan arrival, it is more than seven hundred fifty miles by the Inside Passage. To the end of the road at Skagway, up the Lynn Canal, it is nearly twelve hundred miles—miles enough to go halfway across the old forty-eight states. Now it is one of three ways to Alaska, the way of fishing vessels and freighters and leisurely pleasure craft, from private launches to large excursion liners.

This was John Muir's Alaska road in 1879, when even the near part of our newly acquired territory was still so much an unknown wilderness that great Glacier Bay itself awaited discovery. Surely no one has more compellingly related the special magic of the Inside Passage than Muir, describing in *Travels in Alaska* his first voyage north through the Alexander Archipelago:

DAY AFTER DAY, in the fine weather we enjoyed, we seemed to float, . . . tracing shining ways through fiord and sound, past forests and waterfalls, islands and mountains and far azure headlands, . . . an intricate web of land and water. . . . Here you glide into a narrow channel hemmed in by mountain walls, forested down to the water's edge, where there is no distant view, . . . the crowded spires of the spruces and hemlocks rising higher and higher on the steep green slopes; stripes of paler green where winter avalanches have cleared away the trees, allowing grasses and willows to spring up; zigzags of cascades appearing and disappearing among the bushes and trees; short, steep glens with brawling streams hidden beneath alder and dogwood, seen only where they emerge on the brown algae of the shore; and retreating hollows, with lingering snowbanks marking the fountains of ancient glaciers. The steamer is often so near the shore that you may distinctly see the cones clustered on the tops of the trees, and the ferns and bushes at their feet.

But new scenes are brought to view with magical rapidity. Rounding some bossy cape, the eye is called away into far-reaching vistas, bounded on either hand by headlands in charming array, one dipping gracefully behind another and growing fainter and more ethereal in the distance. The tranquil channel stretching river-like between, may

Juneau, Alaska, is a capital city connected with the outside world only by sea and air.
Glacier Highway runs about thirty miles north and passes Mendenhall Glacier. Juneau itself
is over the dark ridge to the left. The westward view extends to the Fairweather Range.

be stirred here and there by the silver plashing of up-springing salmon, or by flocks of white gulls floating like water-lilies among the sun spangles; while mellow, tempered sunshine is streaming over all, blending sky, land, and water in pale, misty blue. Then, while you are dreamily gazing into the depths of this leafy ocean land, the little steamer, . . . turning into some passage not visible until the moment of entering it, glides into a wide expanse — a sound filled with islands, . . . some of them so small the trees growing on them seem like single handfuls culled from the neighboring woods and set in the water to keep them fresh, while here and there at wide intervals you may notice bare rocks, just above the water, mere dots punctuating grand, outswelling sentences of islands.

While Muir the poet was absorbed in all this beauty, Muir the geologist was keenly aware of glacial origins in the unfolding landscapes. He saw that variation of the islands in contour and grouping resulted from "differences in the structure and composition of their rocks" and the unequal action of glaciers upon separate parts of the coast. He recognized both the massive effect of a major ice sheet's blanketing the region and the fact that its subsequent breakup into discrete glaciers produced marked variations in the general pattern:

THESE CAUSES have produced much of the bewildering variety of which nature is so fond, but none the less will the studious observer see the underlying harmony—the general trend of the islands in the direction of the flow of the main ice-mantle from the mountains of the Coast Range, more or less varied by subordinate foothill ridges and mountains. Furthermore, all the islands, great and small, as well as the headlands and promontories of the mainland, are seen to have a rounded, over-rubbed appearance produced by the over-sweeping ice-flood during the period of greatest glacial abundance.

Muir took an artist's delight in the harmonious arrangement of the tapering spruces and other trees of the small islands, making of each "a well-balanced bouquet." Finally he summed up the whole entrancing picture with a tribute to its origin:

THUS perfectly beautiful are these blessed evergreen islands, and their beauty is the beauty of youth, for though the freshness of their verdure must be ascribed to the bland moisture with which they are bathed from warm ocean-currents, the very existence of the islands, their features, finish, and peculiar distribution, are all immediately referable to ice-action during the great glacial winter just now drawing to a close.

And so, to sail the Inside Passage is to sail through coastal river valleys, long, narrow, deep, and open-ended, scooped out of the crust by ice and drowned by the ocean in the melt of ice returning to its source. Hills and ridges became islands. The ocean crept up many valleys lateral to the main ones, as well, creating fiords, inlets, or "canals," as they are called locally. In the heads of some, the shivering snouts of glaciers may be seen beneath the mists of a watery land.

THE INSIDE PASSAGE begins at Seattle, or at Tacoma or Olympia if you like, or at Bellingham, Victoria, or Vancouver—any port, large or small, in these interconnected waters where one may cast off for the voyage north. The many islands, inlets, and forested shores of Puget Sound and the Strait of Georgia, and the open seaway of Juan de Fuca Strait, give more than hints of what is to come. The Pacific Coastal Forest will meet the shoreline almost continuously along the entire passage; and the deep cleft between the Olympic Peninsula and Vancouver Island is but the first of several westward openings in the wall of islands through which the long ocean swells reach unopposed. Strait and sound are the southernmost and last grand excavation jobs of the Cordilleran Ice Sheet, the climax of glacier work that created every mile of the passage.

Vancouver, British Columbia's great seaport metropolis, is the last large-scale work of man to intrude upon these still essentially primitive shores. Beyond the docks and towers on the point where the Fraser River floods into the broad Georgia Strait, the Inside Passage is a natural water road tamed only by its island-given protection from the open sea. It is a thing of surging tides, long placid reaches, racing narrow passes, sweeping curves, short sharp bends, sudden rocky danger, and always the fringing forest.

From the Fraser's mouth the Strait of Georgia runs about a hundred miles long, and a score or so wide, to that maze of islets and constricted channels by

The Inside Passage and its many branching inlets offer an endless succession of scenes of forest, rock, and water. This is Shannon Falls on the east side of Howe Sound.

which Vancouver is barely severed from the mountainous mainland. The strait lures boatmen from the entire West Coast and beyond to some of the most enchanting saltwater experience known to veterans of power or sail. Some prefer the excitement of salmon derbies, others the sociability of numerous resort anchorages. And there are those who love most to explore the misty inlets zigzagging into the heart of the ice-capped Coast Range. One of these inlets—Jervis—leads into Princess Luisa Sound; together, they give sailors fifty exhilarating sea miles of a narrow run between glacier-carved stone walls reaching eight thousand feet skyward.

Voyagers pursuing the Inside Passage beyond Georgia Strait have a real reason for breathlessness. At the 50th parallel, hard along Vancouver Island's coast, vessels enter the eighty-mile channel of Discovery and Johnstone straits, whose width seldom reaches two miles. Where the two straits join, at Seymour Narrows, the passage suddenly pinches to less than half a mile, making a perilous tidal raceway with the flood boiling through at twelve knots. It is foolhardy not to anchor here, if need be, and wait for the twenty minutes of slack on which to run the mile and a half through to wider water. In a century of navigation the chief hazard of the Narrows' tide, submerged Ripple Rock, stove and sank more than two hundred vessels. Even though the twin-peaked rock has since been blasted away, tides are still a danger to reckon with.

In 1792 Vancouver's two little ships first ran this passage through, from the Strait of Georgia, northwestward to the open Pacific. The Royal Navy party had completed its thorough pioneer survey of Puget Sound and set out to explore the big strait leading north to fresh unknowns. Pushing ahead into the channels threading the tight, small island group, James Johnstone, master of the tender *Chatham*, made the exciting discovery of the sea passage named for him. Vancouver called the first reach before the Narrows after his flagship *Discovery*. Thus was the first great link of the Inside Passage opened to the era of sail.

The outward run to Queen Charlotte Strait is closely guarded on the southwest by Vancouver Island's moderate mountains. Sixty or seventy miles away the British Columbian Coast Range, crowned by 13,104-foot Mt. Waddington, overtops ice-field relicts of the once mighty glaciation that thrust seaward to cut the island's continental bonds.

Now at Vancouver's northwestern end, where the strait opens to the broad sound of the same royal name, ships turn north and expose portsides for a number of hours to Pacific swells and weather. With narrow Fitzhugh Sound the passage is again inside, and a series of channels takes us, it seems, straight into the heart of the mountainous land. At Boat Bluff one might see deer, bear, and other wild animals swimming across the channel. Countless waterfalls ribbon the cliffs with silver. Above them, mountains reach to five thousand feet and more.

After an exceedingly narrow exit from one salt "river" gorge, the relief of wide water follows for a few miles. Then comes forty-mile Grenville Channel, almost straight enough to see its length on a clear day—but not quite; it too narrows to a mile or less, near midway. Then above Grenville's exit into Chatham Sound the fresh water of one of British Columbia's chief rivers, the Skeena, spills into the salt. In its last thirty miles before meeting tidewater, this glacier-born stream is cutting deep into the bottom thousand feet of an outer Coast Range massif over seven thousand feet high. Here the Skeena races automobiles and locomotives out of the interior and through its chasm to the sea. The end of the line for both Provincial Highway 16 and the Canadian National Railway is the ice-free port of Prince Rupert. Reached by the railroad in 1914, this little city of about seven thousand clings to the northwest shore of small Kaien Island, whose two saltwater bridges tie it to the peninsular mainland on Chatham Sound.

The next leg of the passage, from Prince Rupert across the international boundary to Ketchikan, in part follows an historic emigration route to the north which led to the founding of Metlakatla, a Tsimshian Indian community. The Tsimshian are a group of tribes of the Skeena and Nass river valleys and the coast between, including its offshore islands.

Air passengers taking the fifteen-minute connecting seaplane hop across and up the channel to Ketchikan soon find out why the new age of travel, like the old, comes by water to Alaska's southernmost city. Ketchikan was built on the side of a steep mountain or—more correctly—on the foot, where it plunges

Late afternoon sun over the Inside Passage, near Juneau.

into the tide. The Inside Passage reaches it from the southeast by way of Revillagigedo Channel, where the Tongass Narrows forms a deep harbor admitting ocean vessels to dockside despite a tidal range of 10 to 15 feet twice daily, with higher highs of 16 to 18 feet not infrequent. The rise and fall of the tide are nothing, however, compared with the day-to-night altitude change of a large number of Ketchikan's six thousand people. From its attenuated longshore base, the city climbs sharply up the slope of three-thousand-foot Deer Mountain, its spruce and cedar homes reached by strenuous stairways of wood. With the mountainside forest crowning its homes, Ketchikan seems to the arriving visitor like a city of tree houses at the tops of long ladders.

Leaving Ketchikan, our route continues up Tongass Narrows to Clarence Strait. To seaward is Prince of Wales Island, 135 miles long, southernmost and largest member of the Panhandle's Alexander Archipelago. Haida Indians people the southern end of this heavily timbered island—descendants of a band that migrated from the Queen Charlotte Islands on the south before white men came.

So intricate is the web of channels, and woven about so many islands, that the Inside Passage is a thing of multiple choices. Making his own decision would seem to be the prerogative of each map compiler attempting to mark the main route. No two charts agree on all channels, and neither do the shipping firms. Wrangell and Petersburg may both be reached, for example, by a series of passes to eastward barely severing their respective islands from the mainland. A favorite route to Petersburg, however, is tortuous and rock-studded Wrangell Narrows between Mitkof and Kupreanof islands. It is like taking a road through forest-clad mountains, with Petersburg coming into view around the last bend.

Out of this port, into Frederick Sound, and north through broad Stephens Passage, it is a clear run past Admiralty Island and on to Juneau.

Admiralty Island is a wilderness of 1,664 square miles or over a million acres, managed by the U.S. Forest Service for recreation. Like most of southeastern Alaska, it is on the Tongass National Forest, but its yield is presently in the restoration of the human body and spirit, not yet in board feet of lumber. Hiking trails and boating streams are its

roads. There are many lakes, and mountains nearly five thousand feet high. Some Indian villages cling to the shores of little bays and inlets of its deeply indented coastline. But for the most part, upriver where the clear cold water tumbles out of the central ranges, the island is home to salmon, to the stately brown bear, and to the Sitka black-tailed deer. There are neither moose nor mountain sheep and goats— these are animals of the mainland.

Opposite Admiralty, near the midpoint of Stephens Passage on the east side, lies Holkham Bay. Excursion boats enter here for side trips into Tracy and Endicott arms, twin fiords with a single mouth opening on the passage. Between mile-high walls they penetrate deeply into the Coast Range, which sends majestic glaciers down to meet them—Dawes Glacier into Endicott Arm, Sawyer and Denali into Tracy Arm. The stout little excursion liners ply the length of the fiords, threading flotillas of icebergs, to give tourists the thrill of watching bergs thunder off the ice walls—spectacle of wild nature's sublime beauty and awesome power combined.

Another of the great fiords visited on some excursion runs is Taku Inlet, into which breaks a broad tongue of Taku, one of Alaska's largest glaciers. It is, altogether, a vast, sprawling ice field blanketing the highlands north of Juneau. Just beyond the wide mouth of the inlet, the Inside Passage continues up narrow Gastineau Channel past the capital city, which lies on the channel's constricted midpoint.

A thousand miles from Seattle, Juneau hugs a small strip of land between high tides and high mountains. A bridge across the channel links it to Douglas on the island opposite. Together the two cities, called the Gastineau Channel Community, number around eleven thousand Alaskans. When Joe Juneau discovered gold here in 1880, a boomtown sprang up. Twenty years later it was the territorial capital. A mild climate, all-year port, and plentiful resources of timber, mines, and fisheries brought it many business, industrial, and government establishments.

Taking off from the junction of Stephens Passage and Chatham Strait and pointing a few degrees west of due north, Lynn Canal is the last leg of the Inside Passage. For the first time the passage is not a way winding among islands or between island and mainland, but a thrust deep into the continent itself. The

Gastineau Channel runs northwestward between Juneau, on the right, and Douglas Island and town, on the left. The Alaskan capital's airport lies beyond, at the extreme left. Lynn Canal is at the top of the photo and the mountains on the other side extend between the canal and Glacier Bay.

canal extends Chatham Strait, and together they form a broad, remarkably direct, and easily navigated seaway from the open Pacific to southeastern Alaska's only rail and highway terminus—Skagway, threshold of the interior.

A fifteen-mile run across Chilkoot Inlet and north up slender Taiya Inlet to the mouth of the Skagway River, and our voyage on the Inside Passage is done. The 450-mile threading of the Panhandle maze has led at last to the head of navigation and principal gateway to mainland Alaska.

Along most of its length, the tidal waters of the Inside Passage flow fifty to eighty—at Skagway a hundred—miles distant from the outer ocean shore. Deep in certain arms, tides meet rivers at still farther reach from the sea. A broad, mountainous rim of the continent lies between. This edge, from Puget Sound to Lynn Canal and Glacier Bay, is a major arena of the ancient land-sea battle.

Sailing the Inside Passage is running ancient stream channels, river valleys, glacier gorges, even mountain passes. Not a sea voyage, not in fact coasting, it is travel across country, a country of many somewhat parallel mountain ranges. But first the ocean had to drive sea roads, at sea level, through the valleys and gorges between ranges, and over the passes. All this was the work of many ages.

FROM DEEP WITHIN the crust rock rose, and the structure of this land was roughed out. Overlying rocks gradually eroded away. The new material was grained in accord with the long trend of the continent's edge as it paralleled great arcs of faulting concentric with the curve of the Alaskan Gulf coast, the Alaska Range, the Aleutian Islands, and their deep-sea trench. In the Panhandle, the most prominent feature related to this arcuate band of ridges and troughs is the 230-mile channel formed by the linking of Lynn Canal and Chatham Strait. Deep and rather wide where it opens to the sea, this north-south slash runs diagonal to the Panhandle for two-thirds of its length. Significantly, the rocks and their structures on the west side of this trough do not match those of the east side. Geologists take this to suggest a major crustal break or fault extending from Skagway northwestward into the mainland and then to the west to meet the great curve along the Alaska

Range that parallels the gulf with glaciered ramparts.

The end of the Inside Passage at the head of Lynn Canal thus appears to mark a great forking of southeastern Alaska into two giant prongs. The one west of the trough is rooted in the St. Elias Mountains and reaches south along the Fairweather Range and the outer islands to the tip of Baranof—Cape Ommaney—at the ocean entrance to Chatham Strait. The main thrust of the eastern prong is the great Coast Range batholith, running from Yukon Territory some twelve hundred miles southeastward with the Alaska–British Columbia boundary peaks on its crest, and ending at the Fraser River. This huge, chiefly granodiorite mass is believed to be the largest such body of intrusive rocks on the continent. The Inside Passage follows its western side, where its rocks are exposed to the coastline or at no great distance inland, from Vancouver to Skagway. There, Lynn Canal cuts into the flank of the batholith, the last of many fiords deeply gashing the Coast Range.

Ages of slow geological change contrived (as though for us!) the possibility of that splendid scenic voyage along shores of an inner coastline of the greatest ocean. The story involves the enormous complexity of many different rocks and their origins, the sinking and rising, folding and faulting of the crust, deposition and erosion, igneous intrusion, volcanic eruption, advance and retreat of the sea—a knotty sequence of causes and effects that readied giant structures for the fine glacier-carving of present landscapes.

The great glaciation was the overwhelming event of the Pleistocene epoch.

For nearly a million years the monstrous complex of glaciers held its grip on the deep-buried land, relaxing only for occasional spells of interglacial warmth. In maximum periods the ice sheet, ever flowing downward along intermountain corridors of the continent's uplifted edge, rode far out over the ocean. Its main seaward avenues were such broad openings as Dixon Entrance and Queen Charlotte Sound. Only the highlands of the Queen Charlottes, lying between those wide arms of the Pacific, and of Vancouver Island, south of the sound, escaped the overriding ice; and even they bore small glaciers of their own. All the land now forming southeastern Alaska's archipelago, and the other fringing island groups of the British Columbia coast, were overcome by the great ice sheet.

Ice became the chief geological force shaping this coastland during the most recent chapter of its history. Our present chapter tells the story of the last twelve thousand years—the postglacial, or perhaps only another interglacial, epoch in which we may briefly enjoy this landscape.

Twelve thousand years ago, or less, the last general but uneven retreat of Great Ice Age glaciers was under way. As glaciers retreated and ocean crept in, former troughs and valleys became the deepwater channels that ships ply today. Such are the seaways of the Inside Passage and other inter-island routes of British Columbia and the Panhandle, and the intricate waterways of Puget Sound.

One might reflect from the boat deck: How could there have been a time, ever—and a quite recent time, at that—when this landscape wore the face of icy barrenness? All things are relative, one to another. For the earth, for rock, for the building and weathering processes that shape the crust, it was a very little while ago. But for eager, impatient life, it took infinitely long, even with the help of those strategic refugia, to win back this channeled no-man's-land.

T HE INSIDE PASSAGE is a winding corridor through time. Age unimaginable may be lightly grasped in microscale. Think of those ports of departure and of call, the few widely spaced coastal and island settlements, as ticked off in the last few seconds. Indian time, marked by abandoned sites and some living communities, was the moment before this one. The seemingly endless forest, passed through as by a river, is a few hours old. Yesterday the ocean filled the channels beneath our keel which glaciers had, during the week just gone, gouged out of rock formations assembled here a year or so ago. How much time was needed to build the several kinds of rock out of their various mineral constituents? On the scale suggested, the combining of elements, the crustal processes that forged, compressed, split apart, made molten, metamorphosed, hardened, crystallized, shattered, and recombined the molecular matter of rock—these had taken numberless centuries. The beginning of all of it is hard to grasp on any scale of time.

THE INSIDE PASSAGE

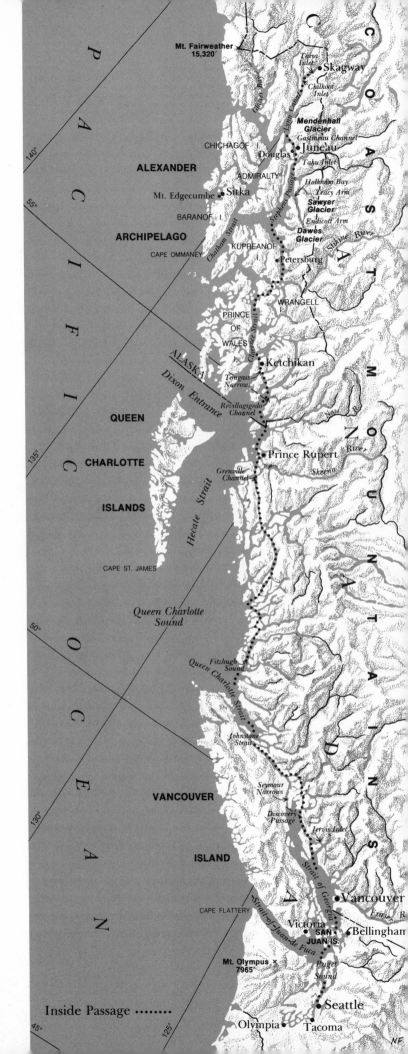

CHAPTER 14

WATERS OF THE GOLDEN GATE

San Francisco Bay—its geologic origin; its past in Indian, Spanish and gold rush times; its present; and man's concern for its future.

Although in my travels I saw very good sites and beautiful country, I saw none which pleased me so much as this. And I think that if it could be well settled like Europe, there would not be anything more beautiful in all the world, for it has . . . all the conveniences desired, by land as well as by sea, with that harbor so remarkable and so spacious, in which may be established shipyards, docks, and anything that might be wished. . . .

— Pedro Font, COMPLETE DIARY

SAN FRANCISCO BAY is the only major ocean inlet of the two thousand air miles of coastline between the Strait of Juan de Fuca and the Sea of Cortés. With the Golden Gate it is the estuary for the one large river system flowing to the Pacific between the Columbia and the Colorado. It has become the key to a local and regional scheme of nature, and has its place in the larger coastland world as well. The Bay Region today is recognized as an area of transition: coastlands to the north are cool and moist, to the south warmer and drier. A few plants and animals literally end their ranges at the Golden Gate.

The bay we know represents a very recent stage in the geological evolution of its regional coastland. Where the pocket-size "sea" now placidly rests, the ocean once rolled eastward to a shore beyond the present delta and inner coast range area. In that Miocene time, fifteen million years ago, an unbroken ridge from north of the Golden Gate to south of Palo Alto formed one of several offshore islands. Lava-spewing volcanoes studded the area, but by the epoch's end all mountains had been eroded away almost to sea level.

Then a dramatic sequence occurred: upheaval, faulting, folding, earthquakes, and more volcanic activity brought in train a jumbled rising and sinking of coastlands and a retreat of the sea. Erosion again leveled the land and the sea returned, after which a long period of volcanism ensued, especially to north of the bay. At the end of a relatively quiet Pliocene epoch, about a million years ago, there was a more turbulent outbreak of crustal violence than the previous one, and the ocean was pushed farther west than it is now.

After this came the Pleistocene, with its sea-level changes, and a new wave of all the mountain-building forces in full tilt. As fast as mountains rose, streams deepened their channels. The Great Valley riverflow simply sawed its way through the outer range to form a gap, the Golden Gate, where the ocean flooded in, during its last great interglacial rise, to fill the depressed basin. Thus, perhaps less than half a million years ago, San Francisco Bay was born.

However large and dramatic the landform changes that preceded the bay's so recent appearance, they were nonetheless slow enough to allow the coming and going of living communities in continuous succession. These migrated and evolved, increased and dwindled, changed face and species, in response less to local shifts of the movable stage than to far-flung changes of climate. Bay area fossil beds yield palm trees; they were not wiped out by sea flood or mountain rise but by a gradual cooling that brought more

San Francisco Bay—midpoint and crossroads. Ships come in through the Golden Gate to confront "the Rock," Alcatraz Island. The bay's finest views are when the sky is piled high with cumulus clouds, with seabirds' dark forms against them.

temperate climate plant types in to replace them.

Nothing is more revealing of change, as the map shows, than the story of the bay's shoreline. Perhaps nowhere else on the Pacific Coast has change been as exhaustively studied and documented, decried, celebrated, projected, and often deliberately hastened or hopefully thwarted. And nowhere but on this bay's shores has man become with such haste the conspicuous chief changer.

There are places where man has grown disproportionately big with dramatically visible effect, by virtue of his numbers and the natures of those areas. Manhattan Island and San Francisco Bay both come to mind: neither was a place to hide man's works, had there been the desire.

New York City, an old and absolute artifact of stone upon stone with nothing in view to challenge it, has long been accepted as a geometric landscape. But San Francisco Bay wears the look of nature surprised and caught, though not yet altogether violated. Its two concentrations of tall buildings, San Francisco and Oakland, and even its great bridges, are not out of keeping with its expanses of water, gateway headlands, and gracious girding of moderate heights. Nature and man appear on the whole in balance, except perhaps to the absolutist, as though human ecology were here imposed upon a land destined to receive and nurture it.

Any natural balance is precarious, and the more so if happenings run counter to nature. The nearly four million people of the San Francisco Bay metropolitan area are on notice that their ecology has seriously impaired its own natural support—the bay itself—and could in fact destroy its viability. A so-so balance of the larger aspects is not enough; every small part must be in harmony with every other part. Some harmonies are still sounding in the bay, but they could die on deaf ears; others must be carefully restored or all will go out of tune for good.

Iᴺᴰɪᴀɴ ᴀɴᴅ ɪʙᴇʀɪᴀɴ ways of life, in the guises under which they met on bayshores at San Diego, Monterey, and inside the Golden Gate, were largely of the make-do and "nature will give if you scratch her" kind. All bay and ocean shores occupied by the few thousand Costanoans—from the delta around the east and south bay shores, the San Francisco Penin-

sula, and the ocean side south to Monterey Bay and Big Sur River—became heaped with shell, chiefly mussel. Lower shellmound levels are at least three thousand years old; in the bay, some have been found below the tide line. Only the islands off Santa Barbara vie with San Francisco Bay in the extent of these aboriginal garbage dumps, which have yielded so much data about the cultures that produced them.

The Costanoans, like other California Indians, burned large areas of oak savanna and hillside, clearing underbrush to give more ground for annuals with edible seeds, and making it easier to gather acorns. Fire was great for flushing rabbits and other game. Winter was salmon-fishing time, when the water was high. Curiously, in this bay which now produces a third of the world's sun-evaporated salt, the Indians got theirs from seaweed. Indian economy partook of natural ecology. Fire belonged to both. The mounding of shell was a form of geological deposition. All in all, the Costanoans, and the Miwok and Wintun of the northern bay and delta shores, scarcely disturbed nature's harmony.

In their time, the padres—Serra, Crespi, Font— and their leathern captains—Portolá, Fages, De Anza—and navigators such as Ayala, all attuned to the harmonies they knew, envisioned here the concord of a land "well settled like Europe." A wilderness won by hard months and half a world of travel could charm, especially when nature presented familiar Mediterranean forms; but to homesick men, how perfect this land would be when peopled with their own, transplanted with customs, institutions, and above all, their homes! Indeed (the purist view aside), can it be said that the Iberian life style of two centuries ago—the imprint on San Francisco Bay waters and shore of a pastoral, maritime, and churchly culture stemming from a similar land and climate, uncomplicated by modern technology—would ever have destroyed all natural harmony? Change it brought, yes; but, by a kind of ecological succession, the Spanish way altered this coastal land only in degree more, and faster, than the Indian.

Time was unhurried for man and nature. The Indian lived in a placid continuum without goals of "progress." The Spaniard's coming meant disruption, but no quick end. In haste to enroll Indian souls, the Spanish were yet deliberate in their intent to

The bay beyond bridges, tall buildings, and anchor chains: the "baylands," or tidal wetlands, or creek, salt marsh, and mudflat. These belong to a million birds and a billion lesser creatures on which they feed. This is South Bay, and is similar to San Pablo Bay in the north, with its equally extensive sloughs.

create a *gente de razon* in a new pastoral setting. Their slow thrust was gentle upon hills and valleys, though not upon the *Indios,* thanks to imported diseases, in large part. The *Californios,* themselves, did not greatly increase, though their cattle did, at the expense of elk, antelope, and native grasses. California and the Bay Region merely adopted the foreigners and made them their own. This was a big land.

This was a large bay. With tidewater and wetlands, it covered nearly seven hundred square miles. A necklace of mussel shell, some pitiful *rancherias,* three or four missions, a presidio, scattered adobes—the bay's shores swallowed them easily, and its tides felt the occasional Spanish keel no more than the Costanoan tule rafts. The Europeans' skills were applied to simple architecture and water supply, subsistence farming, wine making, boat building—things of light impact upon the environment. The few mercury and other mines they dug remained mostly recondite affairs of the adjacent mountains. Rarely, brush-burning coincident with temperature inversion caused a faint portent of smog; but an occasional tannery, tallow-works, or limekiln was a scant polluter of air

or bay and river waters. Shrimp and oyster, salmon and rockfish, and the myriad waterfowl of tule and mudflat were pure, abundant food.

And so flowed the time and tide of San Francisco Bay. It was a clean tide that nourished the teeming life of the broad South Bay; that mixed with mountain water in Carquinez Strait, Suisun Bay, and the delta. And it was an aimless, quiet time, comfortable to live in for mallard, marsh hawk, and man.

ANOTHER TIME began for San Francisco Bay in the mid-nineteenth century. A different breed swarmed in: hurrying, exploiting men. Gold-fevered, destiny-driven across the continent and over the seas, they put a sudden stop to all past time, telescoping their own hectic present into a hopeful but heedless future. They cut the Indians' span of days and pushed the dons into crumbling rancho retreats. They brought fearful energy with them, and turned it loose in all directions.

The bay was a useful base: for seizing the land, for assaulting the gold-rich Sierran slopes. To build towns, then cities, overnight, the argonauts stripped

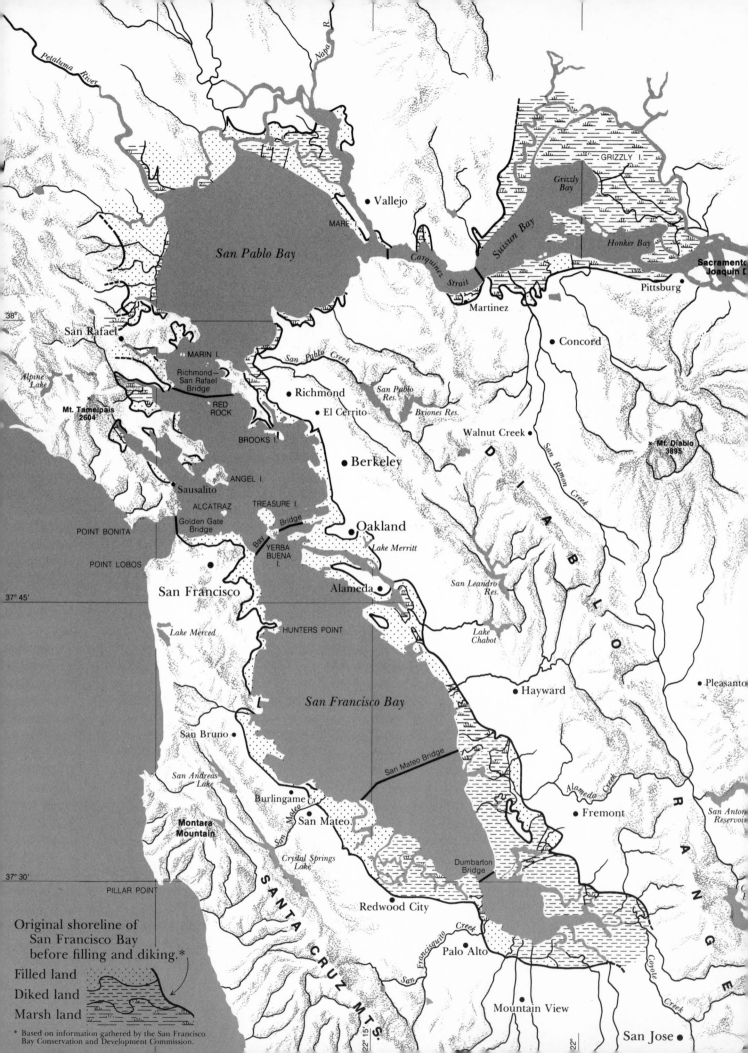

Petaluma River

Napa R.

Vallejo

MARE I.

GRIZZLY I.

Grizzly Bay

Suisun Bay

Honker Bay

San Pablo Bay

Carquinez Strait

Martinez

Sacramento
Joaquin

Pittsburg

38°

San Rafael

MARIN I.

Richmond—
San Rafael
Bridge

San Pablo Creek

Richmond

San Pablo
Res.

Briones Res.

Concord

*Alpine
Lake*

Mt. Tamalpais
2604

RED
ROCK

El Cerrito

Walnut Creek

× Mt. Diablo
3895

BROOKS I.

Berkeley

D
I
A
B
L
O

San Ramon Creek

ANGEL I.

Sausalito

ALCATRAZ

TREASURE I.

Bay

Bridge

Oakland

Lake Merritt

POINT BONITA

Golden Gate
Bridge

YERBA
BUENA
I.

San Leandro
Res.

POINT LOBOS

San Francisco

Alameda

*Lake
Chabot*

37° 45'

Lake Merced

HUNTERS POINT

Hayward

Pleasanton

San Francisco Bay

San Bruno

San Mateo Bridge

*San Andreas
Lake*

**Montara
Mountain**

Burlingame

San Mateo

Alameda Creek

Fremont

San Antonio
Reservoir

*Crystal Springs
Lake*

Dumbarton
Bridge

37° 30'

PILLAR POINT

SANTA CRUZ MTS.

Redwood City

San Francisquito Creek

R
A
N
G
E

Original shoreline of
San Francisco Bay
before filling and diking.*

Palo Alto

Coyote Creek

Filled land

Diked land

Marsh land

Mountain View

San Jose

22° 15'

* Based on information gathered by the San Francisco
Bay Conservation and Development Commission.

*The most abundant harvest in the world, in yield per acre of food
for animal consumption, comes from the cord grass of the baylands.*

the bayshores of redwood and reached up the sea-coast for more and yet more timber. They began filling tidal creeks and coves to make more flat land for their new bayside homes, hotels, and stores, and to bury the mud-bound hulls abandoned for the gold-fields. First they hacked the feet of San Francisco's hills, later dredging sand and muck from the bay bottom. The modern phase of the fill process, which has shrunk the bay by more than 40 percent, has also served for massive urban waste disposal.

For a dozen decades there was no legal let, and little if any ethical hindrance, to the trammeling and general abuse of bay waters and shoreline. The state early yielded paramount rights to local public and private interests. In the use of tideland and shore, no county, city, or private owner was constrained by regard for the rights or needs of other users. The net result of a mindless, ruleless free-for-all is history, an unhappy story well detailed in books and reports (see Bibliography). A glance at the map comparing the bay shorelines of 1850 and the present reveals the large geographic effect of man's impact on this unique body of water. The ecological loss and its implications are less quickly grasped. And Bay Area people are loath to face the fact that to enlarge their

own habitat by usurping what belongs to other bay dwellers is to jeopardize both man and nature. Once it could be said, "they know not what they do," but that excuse is no longer a defense.

The bay's wetlands—salt marsh and tidal flat—comprise the most important resting and feeding grounds for waterfowl in the midsection of the Pacific Flyway from the arctic to South America. Seventy percent of the coastal migrants stop at this vital "half-way house," where some birds also breed and nest. A hundred kinds of water birds are at home here during all or part of their lives. Counts have ranged up to twenty thousand birds per shoreline mile. Possibly a million waterfowl—ducks mostly—winter on the baylands. It gives one pause to weigh such wild-life needs against the fact that since 1850 almost half the bay's natural surface of open water and tidal wet-lands has been lost to diking and filling; bordering marshlands have been cut to seventy-five square miles from a former three hundred. A loss of habitat, here or anywhere, means the shrinking of wildlife populations, and that is everyone's loss.

Ours is a day of "systems," their study, application and control. We hear a lot about systems engineering. Bodies of water like San Francisco Bay have long been seen as systems, but insight has been limited to understanding currents, tides, sedimentation, and related geophysical and hydrological phenomena, in order to solve problems of construction, transport, defense—human needs and convenience, often immediate or short-term. The idea that such natural entities are life-support systems—in which the well-being and even the survival of cord grass, mud snail, egret, and man are forever interlocked—is new in our time. It is an idea now taking hold with the speed of great urgency. It must grow still faster wings.

So a new era begins for San Francisco Bay in this second half of our century, one for learning that the bay's value to us as a natural ecosystem—a web of complexly interrelated life in which we are inescapably enmeshed—greatly exceeds all others. It is the time for decisive action to preserve this value, to strictly limit and hopefully end further filling of bay marshes and mudflats, to end the loss of living waters and shortening of the shoreline. This time is here because a few people saw it as past due and then went about making it happen.

Biologists understand the "web of life" idea and how, through research, to find its applications to this area. One college professor, with his students over the years, has sought and charted the few surviving remnants of the original bay shore, the true biological as well as tidal shoreline as it existed when only nature was shifting and changing it, with special regard to bird life. Others have studied minutely the ecology of plants, fishes, or invertebrates. Whatever their bent, these scientists are devoted to understanding the whole spectrum of life in this delicately balanced environment and sharing their insight.

The bay's first conservationists, such biologists furnished inspiration and facts for dedicated citizen groups, like the Save San Francisco Bay Association, which, in turn, aroused the public and fostered a Bay Conservation and Development Commission. As a temporary body, the BCDC investigated all aspects of the bay and made policy proposals. Now with tenure and teeth, after a legislative battle to continue it, this state body has regulatory power. Its chief target is the control of filling. Public and private corporate bodies still seek permits to fill or dike bay shorelands; a few are granted, but only when judged to be in the larger public interest. The largest

and paramount interest is the safeguarding of San Francisco Bay's remaining natural environment.

THE BAY SHORELINE, like that of the ocean outside the Golden Gate, is a band of concentrated living matter. It has often been asked, with regard to the bay: are birds more important than people? —and what good are mudflats and salt marshes?

Consider cord grass, for example. Acre for acre, this densely growing salt marsh plant yields seven times the food value of wheat. We do not eat cord grass, but it supports a vast assemblage of life both in the marshes and in the mudflats at the next level below, which are alternately exposed and covered twice daily by the tides. Ducks, geese, and other birds feed directly on the marsh plants and on the animals of brackish water that live among their roots. As cord grass and other marsh plants die, their products of decay are washed down to nourish—as plankton also does—myriad mudflat forms, including shrimps and clams, and indirectly those that in turn feed on them: diving ducks, striped bass, and man.

Mudflats are an important source of oxygen: algae, exposed alternately to water and sunlight, free the vital gas and give it to both water and air. Marshes, too, have a significant role in purifying the air: many marsh plants convert carbon monoxide into harmless carbon dioxide—reason enough in a populated area demanding restoration and increase, not destruction, of salt marshes. Yet, according to a BCDC report, "three quarters of all the marshland that ever existed around San Francisco Bay has been filled or diked off." And research on the value of these most productive of natural communities has only begun.

Finally, and not least important, are the aesthetic values of the bay's marshes and mudflats. At their unspoiled best, they are clean and wholesome places, sweet, salt-smelling in a fresh and heady way when the wind blows. They die and stink only when smothered with sewage and garbage. Alive and untrammeled, the marshlands give open space where it is often possible to glide quietly by canoe along winding tidal creeks, and listen to the lilting cry of red-winged blackbirds as they explode into brief flight among the grasses and tules. One cannot get this close to so much vibrant life without feeling a part of it. There is more than shoreline to reward the search.

The San Francisco Marina, between the Golden Gate and the larger slips of the Embarcadero.

Downtown San Francisco, with Telegraph Hill and the Bay Bridge at the left, viewed from the Marin headlands.

*Overleaf: The central part of San Francisco Bay, viewed from 2,500-foot Mt. Tamalpais,
northwest of the Golden Gate. Mt. Diablo, 3,849 feet high, rises beyond the East Bay hills
to the left. The town below, right, is Mill Valley, extending toward Richardson Bay and
Sausalito. The tall white buildings of downtown San Francisco appear in the upper right.*

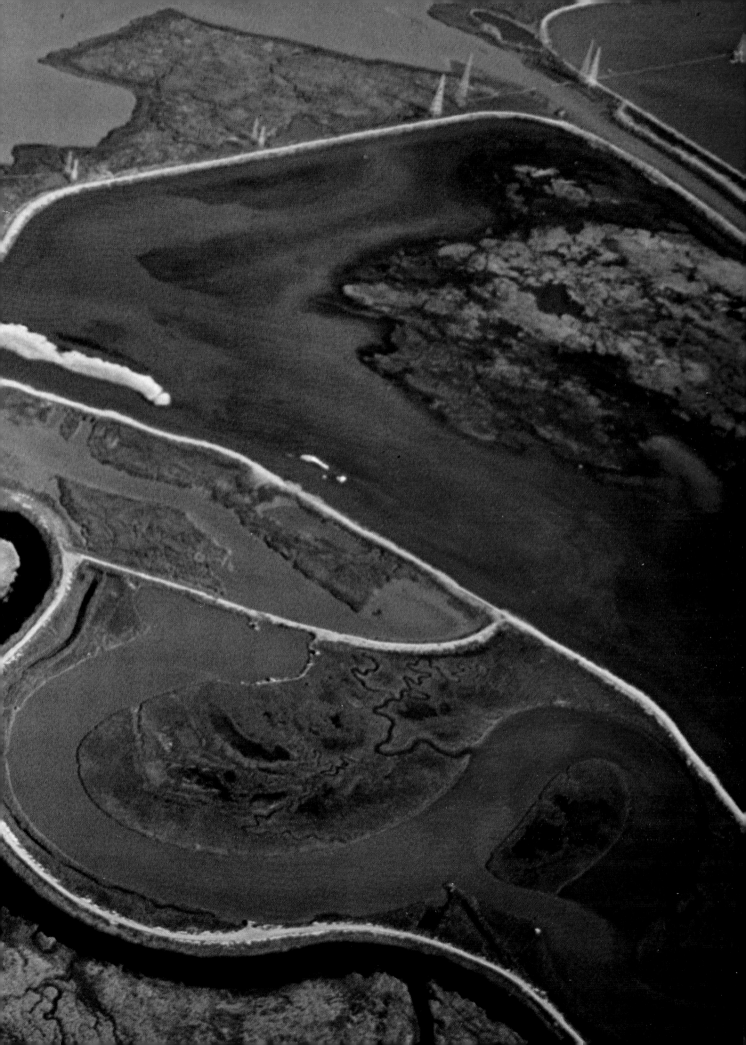

A camp on the beach at Bahía Concepción, Sea of Cortés.

Preceding page: From the air, the salt pans of the South Bay
form an intriguing, multicolored mosaic. Over forty thousand acres
of evaporating basins supply the world's principal salt extraction
industry, located here because of the unique combination of long, sunny
summer (the South Bay has little fog), tidal flats with an impermeable
clay bottom, and the combination of industrial know-how, transportation,
and markets.

150

*Young blue-footed boobies. Many of the islands of the Sea of Cortés are
fertile waterfowl breeding grounds and need the protection of sanctuary status.*

*Close to the Baja shore in the northern end of the Sea of Cortés, Las Islas Encantadas,
"the Enchanted Isles," are an interesting backdrop for a desert garden near the beach.*

CHAPTER 15

THE SEA OF CORTES

*The Gulf of California—its seismic birth,
its isles and tides; some tales of its exploration.*

Before my eyes lay the Vermilion Sea. . . . This Vermilion Sea, which I love because to think of it fills my soul with its mysteries, . . . warns us of earthquakes, for its waters, quivering, rise and fall before great shocks come. Those of us on the shore then rush for high land to avoid tidal waves. Those on our hills, seeing the Vermilion Sea troubled, lie down flat, for when its surface vibrates the land as well may be tossed up and down.

—Antonio de Fierro Blanco, THE JOURNEY OF THE FLAME

THE VERMILION SEA (Sea of Cortes), filling a great trough which apparently extends the San Andreas Fault rift southward from California, deepening and widening as it goes, owes its origin to mighty and continuing crustal movements. Generations living by its shores and plying its waters, from an unknown past down to the vivid present, have felt the tremble of both sea and land. Legend and history merge. It is intriguing to recall, from Fierro Blanco's wondrous historical novel, what the Indians of San Francisco Bay told the narrator, Juan Colorado, as he ended the journey of the Californias that had begun at Baja's tip:

THESE INDIANS said that their long and wide bay was very new, and had been formed by a great earthquake. Many of their tribe, who had lived in the green meadows now below this bay, were drowned when a river and the ocean covered them. To prove their truth, they took me out on the bay in their fishing boats, and tied them, while they fished, to the tops of tall trees formerly growing in these submerged meadows. These trees were so far below salt water that to touch even their tops one must reach down from the boats.

Where, indeed, does legend fade and history begin? While current knowledge of the bay's formation—recent as it was—puts the Indians' tall trees in tall-tale limbo, it is interesting nonetheless that California's greatest fault rift forms a linkage of sorts between the troughs of the two inlets—bay and gulf—over at least six hundred miles of mountainous land.

Pursuit of this thought leads us to a scientifically respectable notion concerning the origin of the Gulf of California: In the closing period of the Mesozoic era, around a hundred million years ago, Baja California lay snugly against the continent with no gulf intervening. Cabo San Lucas adjoined Cabo Corrientes. Perhaps the beginnings of a crustal rift were present, along the line of the San Andreas Fault as we know it, and extending southeastward along what is now the Sonora-Nayarit coast—a weakness ready to yield to sufficient tectonic force. When this happened, the huge mass of outer crust began ever so slowly to creep northwestward, the two southern capes parting. The northern end of the mass continued to hug the continent as it moved; the southern end pulled away gradually, opening the Gulf of California mouth and isolating the Baja peninsula. The mass is still moving in the same northerly direction, averaging about two inches a year between certain measuring points in the area north of San Francisco

*Sea of Cortés islands: Ventana (foreground), Smith, and
Angel de la Guarda (on the horizon).*

153

Bay. The hundred-million-year journey has taken this coastal land mass three hundred miles—the distance between Cabo San Lucas and Cabo Corrientes.

The mechanism of the postulated movement has been described as a "subcrustal convection current." Recalling that the ocean-floor layer, which extends under continents, is more fluid than the outer crust of "floating" blocks, we see this moving force or mechanism as a kind of underground conveyor belt carrying the block along at its infinitely slow pace.

This theory of the opening up of Cortés's Sea finds support in recent seismic work which reveals the crust of its bottom to be oceanic. And there are great deeps in the southern half of the gulf—one, in the center between latitudes 25° and 26°, has been sounded at 10,740 feet.

Quite certainly, there has also been vertical fault movement, with the peninsula uplifted and the gulf downfaulted. In the long course of this happening, Baja California shook loose the string of offshore islands, like ships anchored in a roadstead of the Vermilion Sea. Some, as they were launched from the mainland, listed crazily. Their many-colored strata dip sharply into the sea, while on the nearby Baja shore the same formations stay high, dry, and properly horizontal.

The geological history of the gulf islands—thirty or so large islands and many more small ones—tells of various origins and ages. Some are fault-blocks, cut off from the peninsular main by the sinking of the sea floor to create the channels between; others were isolated by the erosion of the connecting land. A few are volcanic, the result of Pleistocene and more recent eruptions.

Reading geological history in textbooks can be dull, but not so in nature. The gulf and its islands and long mountainous coastlines are a big, bold-type, full-color volume in the Earth History series. They are rock—scorified in volcanic blast furnaces, crystallized out of magmas, limed by the shells of a Miocene sea; they are water—a spur of the ocean marvelously blue, calm, and clear, until swept into channeled tides or lashed by sudden winds; they are sky—a vaulting splendor of sunrises, stars, and space; they are life— swimming, flying, blooming, and wild.

There is something in names. "Gulf of California" belongs to textbooks, tide tables, sailing directions, charts, atlases, and all prosaic matter. "Sea of Cortés" is flavored with discovery, exploration, the far frontier of New Spain, black-robed padres and their mission realm, easting Manila Galleons on the run between the San Lucas and Corrientes capes.

Vermilion Sea? The name springs from the vibrant reality. There are rocks like glowing embers and walls like firebrick, down inside the cape. Tides of the spring once ran red, in the upper gulf, with all the silt of southwestern plateaus, before the great Colorado was dammed. Who named it? Someone enchanted, it might have been, when a flaming sunrise lacquered all the quiet water of his anchorage cove. The name belonged to the times, apparently, in Fierro Blanco's account of 1810 Baja life, and to the twelve-year-old hero it was "our" Vermilion Sea, and "our" Scarlet Gulf. One pictures Bahía de la Paz running red as the pearl divers regale wide-eyed Juan Colorado with the stories of their comrades being chomped in two by thirty-foot mantas.

Perhaps the answer is here after all, in the aged narrator's recall of the time in La Paz when he was "filled with sea lore and sailors' tales" on his first visit to "my Vermilion Sea, that vast Gulf of Cortés which rises in a still greater river [the Colorado]. . . . At each tide this river thrusts up a curling wave twenty feet high, to drown man or boat which, seeking to explore its unknown reaches, offends its virginity. On its banks are springs of cold crimson water, burning the flesh it touches; and from this coloring comes that name I love—the Vermilion Sea."

In 1532 Hernán Cortés's men first saw its shores, but only on the east, and they went away unaware of the peninsula beyond. The conquistador, still curious as to the "mysteries of the north," sent another crew the next year. This, through mutiny and the murder of its captain, fell to the command of the unlucky Fortún Jiménez, finally reaching Bahía de la Paz, where the Indians further reduced it by twenty men, including Jiménez. The survivors got back to Cortés with tales of the pearly wealth to be had for a little skin diving—Indian skins, no doubt. Next, in May, 1535, it was three ships with Cortés himself in command that crossed to the bay of pearls, but the bay was not yet in the mood to yield its fortune. The toll: twenty-three men dead of starvation; one ship wrecked returning for help. It was Cortés's first and last trip across his namesake sea, but it confirmed the presence of a new land on the other side. This was soon named California—later, Baja California. And California, people knew, was an island.

For the next hundred years, expedition followed expedition to Cortés's Sea and the California "island," but with no great gain in either knowledge or wealth. Ulloa bucked the baffling tides to reach the Colorado delta in 1539, proving California was no island after all; but the fact was mislaid during the next century and a half, even though Alarcón had confirmed it in 1540 by sailing far up the great red river in his attempt to join Coronado on the road to Cíbola.

Meanwhile, the Jesuits were pushing their missionary empire northwestward up the Sinaloa coast and into the Sonoran Desert. New Spain was looking again to the hostile peninsula: the pearls still beckoned, and a California haven for the incoming Manila Galleons had long been needed. In 1683, Admiral Atondo y Antillón sailed for La Paz with the greatest of the Black Robes, Eusebio Francisco Kino, and other padres, aboard. They entered the bay with its fringe of palm trees, built a chapel and fort, and began to cultivate the Indians. But a cruel act by Atondo ended all friendship, and with it the hopeful colony.

Later the same year Atondo and Kino began another settlement, San Bruno, farther north under the craggy Sierra de la Giganta. This one lasted nearly two years and was a base for much exploration of the peninsular south. But the Spanish had not yet learned how to live in, and off, this bone-spare land. With people scurvied and starving, Atondo conceded defeat, and the colonists sailed back to the mainland, Kino carrying with him a resolve that someday this land across the Sea of Cortés would flourish with its people in the fold of his society's patron.

Beginning in 1697, the effort of a devoted succession of Black Robes to fulfill that hope is a ringing part of the human history of the Californias. Its first and truest heroes are Padre Kino's inspired and saintly protegé, Juan María de Salvatierra, the stalwart and energetic Juan de Ugarte, and the spirited Francisco María Pícolo. These men and a whole host of their colleagues and successors were giants in the land. They were to Baja what Kino was to Pimería Alta to the east; what Serra, Crespi, and Lasuen were, in their time, to Alta California. They were

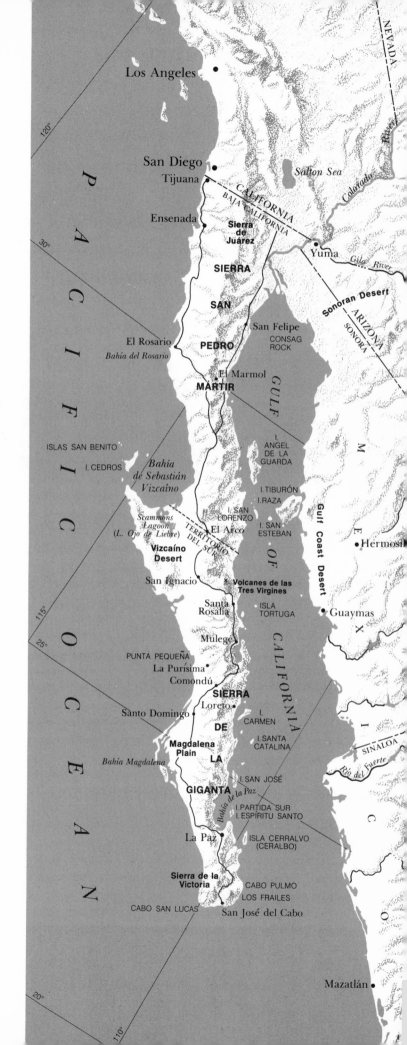

The epitome of a "desert island" landscape: Puerto Refugio, situated at the north end of uninhabited Isla Angel de la Guarda along the northeastern shore of Baja.

ecologists of sorts, learning the land and how to live with it, not unravel it. They created many an oasis around their mission compounds, some of which still enrich the desert landscape.

Kino remained in the Baja story long enough to prove, once more and for good, that California was a peninsula, not an island, and he did so through observation worthy of a scientist. With Atondo, in 1684, Kino had reached the Pacific shore, feeling, so it is recorded, "like a Balboa." Among shells the local Indians prized were some exceptional blue ones —abalone. Kino remembered these for years after, until he saw the same kind again, far inland, adorning some Northern Pimas. Indians did not cross the gulf, he knew, and no such shells were native to it. With the truth now dawning in his scientist mind, Kino resolved some day to solve the "island" question.

In March, 1701, Kino and Salvatierra, who had kept in touch by letter across the gulf after the founding of Baja's first permanent mission at Loreto, set out together from the Sonora side in the hope of finding a land route to Baja. Although they were thwarted by the waterless dunes stretching for miles

to the east of the Colorado delta, their peninsula theory was confirmed. Near the head of the gulf, the padres climbed a peak at sunset. As Peter Masten Dunne stated in his *Black Robes in Lower California:*

. . . From [this] crest the fathers were rewarded with the view and the knowledge they had been looking for. . . . They descried the northern limits of the Gulf of California floating on a crimson sea. They saw how the tall sierras of Lower California bent east and commingled with lower hills and plains which curved south to form the northern frame of the gulf. California was plainly a peninsula. . . . [They] were firmly convinced. Reported Kino: "The sun set, and from the peak we saw with all clarity all the sea below, toward the south, and the place on the beach to which we had descended. We saw that the half arch of sierras of California whose end had been concealed from us by the spur of the mountains kept getting constantly closer together and joining with other hills and peaks of New Spain."

A more than careful observer, Kino was not fully satisfied until the next year, when he (as Dunne

Brown pelicans and California sea lions in the Sea of Cortés.

The dolphin is the frequent escort of boats in the Gulf of California.

*Elegant terns in a rookery on Isla Raza; thousands of them
are crowded into an area of less than half a square mile.*

writes) "put the discovery beyond the shadow of a doubt. He rode northwest to the junction of the Gila and Colorado, followed the latter down stream, and then threaded down its eastern bank to the estuary which swings west at the head of the gulf. He now stood west of the sea, he saw the lands across the estuary, and he watched the sun rise over the waters of the Gulf of California. It was fixed and certain: California was not an island." And Kino took his place among the great explorers of our continent.

Cortés's sea is still there for discovering and exploring. The Vermilion Sea is there, for seeking adventure and wonder and beauty. Perhaps the surest hope for the preservation of the future Baja experience lies in the determination of some internationally cooperating scientists, with the help of concerned laymen, to see wildness perpetuated in both peninsula and sea.

Baja and its waters have beckoned and challenged natural scientists of every stripe for generations. Once the area demanded hard legwork and harder sailing. Now every mountaintop can be reached by helicopter, every cove and island by motor launch or seaplane. Can wilderness be saved, here?

The islands of the Vermilion Sea comprise one of the great bird breeding-grounds of the Western Hemisphere. The Mexican government, through a strongly headed Department of Wildlife, has set aside small Isla Raza as the gulf's first official migratory waterfowl sanctuary, thus guarding major rookeries of gulls and terns. Other animals and plants, several of them unique, live on the islands as, in the words of one biologist, "end products of many millions of years of evolution." Isla Santa Catalina, for instance, is the only habitat of a curious little rattlesnake with no rattles, recently discovered. Here too is the largest stand of a giant barrel cactus, ten feet in height.

The "Siamese twin" islands, Partida Sur and Espíritu Santo, which form the outer rim of Bahía de la Paz, are the final home of a black jackrabbit. The species, now in a precarious state, defies the rules of protective coloration: there is nothing black to blend with in its small environment. To the north, near Raza, another Isla Partida (actually a pair of islets) became famous among birdmen earlier in the century when the second, and principal, least-petrel breed-

ing colony was discovered here; the other is on Islas San Benitos on Baja's Pacific side.

The gulf's larger islands—Cerralvo (or Ceralbo); San José; Carmen; Angel de la Guarda, high in the north and over forty miles long; and on the east side, the biggest of all, Tiburón, once notorious for the cannibal Seri tribe—all have their particular fascinations for particular kinds of explorers.

In the Midriff area, where these last two named almost close off the northern third from the rest of the gulf, the big islands, along with small San Esteban and the San Lorenzo group, are joined in barricade duty by the most feared phenomenon in all the Vermilion Sea: the fantastic tidal raceway and maelstrom of Sal Si Puedes Channel. The early navigators had reason to name it "Get Out If You Can."

This is the infamous bottleneck between the wider and much deeper southern two-thirds of the gulf and the shallow northern third. On the rising tide the Pacific pours a great head of water into the funnel of the gulf. When this slams into the baffle of islands and suddenly pinched-off channels, it does all kinds of fearful things. Water may boil straight up from the deep, heaping a great churning mound above the general level. And there is the sometime whirlpool, whose fame as a swallower of ships is perhaps more of legend than of actuality.

Passing all this, the voyager enters another world, a strangely lifeless one. The peninsular coastland between San Felipe and Bahía de los Angeles is said to be the most barren and forbidding of Baja's deserts. And of the last of the isles of the Vermilion Sea, a three-hundred-foot rock east of San Felipe, a naturalist has written: "Consag is absolutely dead." He meant, certainly, in the geological sense; for on its top he noted, at the same time, many kinds of birds, their nests, and eggs.

Nothing in nature is quite dead, if we grant that life exists in change. Geological change is one expression of a living earth. A Consag Rock or an Isla Cerralvo will one day disappear, as dry land, as home of bird and lizard and cactus. But other islands will take their place, and birds will nest on them—provided, of course, they too have not disappeared as a result of some ecological carelessness or abuse of the normal processes of evolution. One may hope that the Vermilion Sea will never be called a "Dead Sea."

PART THREE:

FOREST NORTH
TO
DESERT SOUTH

The climate belts of the Pacific Coast ring their changes through successive types of vegetation: rain and fog forests of the north; sunny pine and oak woodlands of the mid-region (as these Bishop pines of Northern California); chaparral and scrub of the southland; and sparse coastal desert plants of Baja California.

CHAPTER 16

CLIMATES BORN OF THE SEA

The full spectrum of weather in the Pacific —
arctic, maritime, Mediterranean, desert, and tropical.

THERE ARE DAYS when the weather almost anywhere along the temperate West Coast seems
to stand still. It may be more or less sunny,
quite clear or partly cloudy, with light breezes idly
fingering dune grass or nudging the outermost
branchlets of some pines at cliff's edge. For a spell
nothing happens to show any marked climatic pattern or significant trend. At times like these when the
air has nothing much to say, it is not hard to read in
the land itself and especially in its plant cover what
sort of climate the region has—wet or dry, cold or
hot, with or without fog or strong prevailing winds.

Around the Gulf of Alaska, a cool to cold maritime
province with abundant precipitation is boldly pro-
claimed by the low snowline, vast ice fields sending
live glaciers down, sometimes to tidewater, and the
coastal coniferous forest which, although moisture-
loving, finds these latitudes too cold for its maximum
growth. In contrast, Alaska's Bering Sea coastlands,
while periodically milder during past epochs, have
long been too dry and frigid for glacier-building—a
light, powdery snowfall is as drifting sand. Nor does
their permafrost provide home ground for conifers.

Looking southward from the gulf—upon the
Panhandle's myriad islands, the Queen Charlottes,
the British Columbian forelands, Vancouver Island,
Puget Sound, and especially the Olympic Peninsula—
one reads in the grandest of all temperate forests the
sure sign of enormous rainfall. This wetness, coupled
with increasing mildness southward and ultimately a
year-round growing season, brings the great conifers
to their densest and loftiest growth, between the

Olympic Mountains and the sea. Here stands the
most splendid rain forest outside the tropics, climactic outcome of ten or twelve favorable millennia
since the last major glacial retreat. With the help of
deep, rich alluvial and volcanic soils, the prodigious
rains nurture on this lowland a bulk and weight of
living matter which is, per acre, probably the greatest
on earth. North America's heaviest mean annual
rainfall strikes this seaward slope: over 100 inches
along a north-south belt, 150 and possibly 200 inches
at some stations. Yet across the peninsula nineteen
thousand acres of farmland must be irrigated! There
the Dungeness Valley, between the town of Sequim
and Puget Sound, lies as a near-desert in the rain
shadow of our wettest mountains, its precipitation
averaging sixteen to twenty inches a year, close to
that of Southern California.

In Northern California, within a coastal belt from
above the Oregon line southward four hundred miles
to the Santa Cruz Mountains, another climatic factor
comes into the picture. In fall, winter, and spring,
rain is fairly heavy in the north end of this belt,
moderate in the central part, and light in the south.
But the area is not without significant dry-season
moisture: it is the belt of summer fog. The tallest of
trees identifies it—the coast redwood. This forest tree
of coastal river valleys and lower slopes needs no
excess of water but likes it spread throughout the
year. In the early and middle months of the long mid-
year rainless spell, redwoods capture fog droplets in
their lofty tops, enough to carry them past the later
weeks of drought and hottest sun into the time of fall

Summer fog over the ocean north of the Golden Gate.

163

rains. Besides its moisture, a boon to the redwoods is the fog's umbrella of shade. In its fraying edge the fog touches lands far to the south—Baja's coast has enough of it to hang moss on cactus—but the true fog belt is defined by the redwoods.

A token of change from the cool, moist climate of the Northwest Coast region to the central coast's Mediterranean type is given by certain pines. The marks of a longer, drier, hotter summer begin to show in the foothills of southwestern Oregon, where the golden grass and wide-spaced Garry or Oregon white oaks look so Californian. Here the northernmost closed-cone pine begins—the knobcone, whose cones cling tightly in whorls around trunk and branch until a summer fire opens them to let the many seeds drop. The cones of this and two other pines of the closed-cone group, the bishop and Monterey of the California coast, may also open in hot weather.

However still the day, trees and shrubs pressed flat against slopes and bluffs or leaning sharply landward with branches pruned to little or nothing on the ocean side, and dunes marching up from the strand in the same direction, announce a prevailing onshore wind. On the northern beaches, great windrows of sea wrack and driftwood stand all summer as reminders of furious winter storms.

South of the Golden Gate, the vast Pacific Coastal Forest yields rapidly to increasing dryness. Redwood and Douglas-fir cling to the Santa Cruz Mountains; but beyond the peninsular groves of Monterey pine, Point Lobos' cypress, and the last redwoods south of the Big Sur River, the vegetation proclaims an arid country. Except for the pines of Cambria and the San Luis Range, and oak canyons nearing the sea, it is now a land of grass and scrub and chaparral, of much sunshine and little rain.

Where the chaparral's huge acreage stops in northern Baja, the Mediterranean climate belt ends also. Both fade out on the western slopes of the Sierra San Pedro Mártir. On the coast, fog dampens the scrub and cactus mixture, festooning both sage and cholla with lichen. At mid-slope, chaparral merges into an oak belt, which in turn gives way to pine. Above the forest elevation, the granite crest is snow-capped in winter. From east of the range and the Gulf of California, the extremely arid Sonoran Desert sweeps across the Baja peninsula south of San

Pedro Mártir to the Pacific. Desert climate replaces Mediterranean.

Transitions from one climate belt or zone to another are seldom sharp. From the Los Angeles Basin to northwestern Baja, aridity and warmth increase gradually through an intermediate zone, sometimes described as having a dry-summer steppe climate. Baja's long central section, from latitude 30° through six degrees south to La Paz, gives us the absolute antithesis of the northern end of our coastal region on the Gulf of Alaska. The heart of it is the Vizcaíno-Magdalena desert plain with its marvelously strange plant life. Even this far south, the coast is cooled and moistened by fog, and perhaps a few drops of rain every winter or two. Paradoxically, its vegetation is sparsest where it is nearest to the ocean; there, constant onshore winds counteract the benefit of a little moisture.

At Punta Eugenia, midway of the peninsula on the west, the tropical climate zone begins with the mangrove as its indicator. Where this tree of the salt tide grows, it is fair to claim a tropical shore, even though lagoons and tidal creeks wet the edge of a sere subtropical desert.

Five degrees farther south, the Tropic of Cancer crosses the Sierra de la Victoria, placing most of the Cabo San Lucas region within the tropical zone. Climate confirms the ecliptic by giving this rugged outthrust of land tropical hurricanes and cyclonic windstorms—the dread *chubascos*—and the first regular summer rains encountered on the Pacific Coast south of the Northwest region. Plants typical of the peninsula's desert heart grow larger and more abundantly in the cape lowlands; their often dense and confusing tangle, called *tropical thorn scrub*, thins out on the march from alluvial valleys and arroyo bottoms toward rocky higher country. Five to seven thousand feet up in the Sierra, pine, oak, and madroño mix; wildlife here is much like that of similar woodlands many hundred miles to the north.

Thus the various effects of climate and weather appear on the face of the land. Less dramatic than the sudden work of storms but equally familiar to coastlanders are the gradual changes the seasons bring. Not many days after the first good soaking rains of fall, a magic transformation comes: hills, valleys, and coastal prairies from Oregon to Southern

California turn bright green. Faintly at first, then with a quick saturation, the new grass colors thousands of open acres; but in late spring a tawny tinge spells the beginning of the long dry months. And in the ranges between coast and desert, with less than ten inches of rain a year, deep-cut chasms and gravelly outwashes tell of occasional torrents. The signs of drought, at least in the southern third of the coastal region, are so plentiful over large areas and so persistent through most of the year, they are rightly taken for granted as normal. Each little leathery leaf of every coast live oak is a token of the usual state of dryness.

THE WET NORTHWEST, the dry southwest; the wet winter, the dry summer—these are the major contrasts of the Pacific Coast climate pattern, which stems from the sea and unfolds upon the land. The agent of seasonal shift and change is atmospheric pressure. This force is divided, or polarized, as high and low pressure—specifically the Eastern Pacific High and the Aleutian Low. These oceanic air pressure zones are like giant clock springs, oppositely wound, activating the gear-trains of the winds and weather cycles through time and space across the border between ocean and continent. With the High in the dominant role, they control air circulation. A glance back to chapter 3 will recall the broad picture of the Eastern Pacific's winds and pressure systems. Some of the detail should now be filled in—the detail of climate and weather which has so much to do with the variety and distribution of living things along our coast.

The chief role of the Eastern Pacific High (its most common name) is that of stabilizing and more or less evening the climate. It is strongest in July when it centers northeast of Hawaii in San Francisco's latitude. There it sits, for months on end, like a policeman in a traffic island, directing the winds and mobile low-pressure systems around and away from its zone, which is the entire northeastern Pacific. In summer there is virtually no Aleutian Low; when one occurs it gives the High a wide berth, moving over the continent well to the north of the Canadian border.

Bringing moisture from a cool sea, the prevailing westerlies that spin clockwise off the High's northeast side cool and humidify the coast from late spring

into fall. By October the High has shrunk, especially in its northern reaches, where its air has begun to be drawn off by a series of migrant lows. These form in the Bering Sea and adjacent Alaska at this season, move out over the Aleutians and southwestern Alaska, and appear on weather maps as an enlarged and persistent Aleutian Low. Weakening, the Eastern Pacific High shifts its center closer to the North American coast, or a few degrees southeastward, where by November it has become further drained by the equatorial low-pressure belt. The lows of the Aleutian system are traveling eastward one after another, causing general instability and—in the zone of contact with the wobbling High—storms, as pressure fluctuates from day to day through the winter months.

In spring, the pattern makes a gradual return to that of summer, when pressure is again higher over the ocean than the continent. Thinking in terms of the air masses set in motion by changes in atmospheric pressure and changed by what they encounter along the way, it will be interesting to note some of the results of these events upon the Pacific Coast.

In summer cold air hovers dry and stable over the polar regions, held at bay by the strong Pacific High. As that weakens in winter, the Polar Pacific air mass moves southeastward across the Alaskan Gulf and down the coast. There it is warmed and moistened by the North Pacific and drawn into the Aleutian Low pressure system. If the changed air mass now moves in over the coasts of British Columbia, Oregon, and Washington, it may override a long low wedge of cold air hanging close to the coastal mountainsides, which in winter are colder than the sea. The sudden chilling of the maritime air brings copious showers or snow—watery nourishment for the great coniferous forests of the Northwest Coast.

In California, the usual winter rains strike from the southwest, south, or southeast, even though a stormy air mass is bearing down from the north. What happens is this: the winter-weakened Eastern Pacific High allows Tropical Pacific air—moist, relatively warm and stable—to move northward along the coast from its source off Baja and Southern California and meet the stormy southbound polar front or, sometimes, cold continental air lying low upon the Coast Ranges. Then, sweeping above the colder air and thus being chilled, the Tropical Pacific air

The groves and small stands of Monterey pine, and the Monterey cypress, mark a climate belt which is transitional between the moist, forest-clad Northwest region, and the semiarid to desert regions of Southern California and Baja.

mass condenses into moderate but steady and widespread rainfall.

Nature in the Northwest does not—in a poet's terms—know the particular joy of relief that comes with the first seasonal rain in an arid land. Coastal northwesterners see little enough surcease of overcast skies and too much certainty of at least moderate rains every month, with more than plenty all winter. They point with pride, of course, to their year-round green, as Southern Californians do to their perennial sunshine, but each attraction has its foil: northerners rejoice when sun brightens the misty air; southerners are relieved when the first real downpour breaks the long summer drought.

The pattern varies. From the entrance of Juan de Fuca Strait to Point Conception, where coastal Southern California begins, cool sea fogs cross the shoreline on many a day from late June or July until September or even October. There is a warm weather lag, so that truly balmy days come to the coast around the time of the autumn equinox. Then the Pacific High begins to lose its force and the prevailing westerlies slacken. With rising lighter and warmer air, the heat felt inland since early summer is wafted out to the beaches. Like late spring, early to mid-autumn is a favored time on the Pacific strand. All nature seems to lie still and bask in a faintly hazy sun. The coastlands become dry, but they are never as dry as the inland areas.

The variation is from year to year. One year this equinoctial lull may persist through an Indian summer on into a crisply cool November or, rarely, even December, with no drop of rain. Delight then turns to apprehension in the prolonged dryness. Another year will bring a soft September rain before a later Indian summer. Now and then a freakish August or September throws in dry thunder and lightning to confuse the pattern. In such a year the Coast Ranges, tindered over with crackling scrub, woodland, and grass, may suddenly spout the plumes of dozens of lightning fires, like so many little smoking volcanoes.

Dryness is the price of the long rainless summer and a serene autumn. But—human values aside—nature adjusted long ago to this condition. Nevertheless, we like to feel that all nature, too, is glad when at last the long drought ends.

One day, change is subtly in the air, in elderly bones, or wherever else it may be felt. Rain is in the offing. And it will be welcomed—south of the Columbia at least. Indian summer, variably long but always bringing too few beach weekends and patio evenings, is unhappily synonymous with "fire season" in Oregon and California. For stockmen, farmers, and especially foresters charged with the protection of timber, watershed, and range, the most prayed-for signs of the year are that drop in temperature, rise in humidity, and overdrift of the first thin cloud cover. If the rain is overdue, if the previous winter was short so that streams dried early and reservoirs are rimmed with cracked mud far below the normal water line, if thousands of acres of grass, chaparral, and good stumpage are afire—then the first real rain is sheer salvation, a certainty of rebirth for the withered land.

An early fall rain on the coast may be a brief and gentle drizzle from the ocean, like a fog too heavy to stay airborne. A late rain bears from the land beneath a dark stratus overhang, softly at first. Then the wind rises, and larger drops pound southerly windowpanes that lately caught the wintering sun. Now heavy, it may slant in for hours or even days. An occasional letup, even a partial clearing, may come before the storm is over.

To call the late fall rain a "storm" is to refer to its origin in the North Pacific low pressure system, whether or not it packs a punch. If it does, forecasters may say "small craft" or "storm" warnings have been posted from Cape Mendocino or Humboldt Bay northward, and all the Northwest Coast stands to take a fair lashing. As the season advances into midwinter the flags go up farther and farther south —at the Golden Gate, Monterey and Morro bays, Point Conception. Beyond this the weather pattern changes as the coastline trends more easterly than southerly, almost to San Diego. Now, too, as the Aleutian Low disturbs north coast atmosphere with mounting force and frequency, storms come in series or "family" groups. One, two, three—they follow on each other's heels, often with little clearing between.

When the storm is finally spent, clearing brings one of the year's grand sky shows. Reasserting itself for a spell, the Pacific High once more sends cooler, drier air toward the shore from which it drives the warmer, still moisture-laden air upward and east-

FOREST NORTH, DESERT SOUTH

ward. Now the rainstorm is rolled up into huge, solid-looking white mountains of cumulus and borne away to the east beyond the Coast Ranges. These clouds are a splendid sight from a coastal summit—piled up against the Sierra Nevada, or the Cascades, giving the distant range a new skyward dimension as well as a blanket of new snow.

After the first storms the Pacific slope may lie for days or weeks in the numbing grip of almost static high pressure. In the cold of night and early morning, moisture rising from wet earth condenses at once in the bottom layer of the heavy atmosphere, causing the most unpleasant and hazardous of fogs. Called "tule fog" for the delta and bayshore regions in central California where it is most notorious, it "socks in" airports and grounds flights, makes highway traffic crawl through "pea soup," and fills newspapers with stories of collisions afloat and ashore. Relief comes after several days, either from a new cycle of Pacific storms or from an influx of cold, clear Polar Continental air sweeping down from the northeast or north. The latter clears the air and brings the coast its most frigid weather, with frost sparkling in early morning sunlight. Or the normal spate of cool air may blow in freshly from the Pacific in the familiar high pressure pattern.

So broad is the Pacific Coast winter variation between extremes of wet and dry, warm and cold, short and long, that is is hard to say what combination is normal. In general, however, temperature and moisture change together: warm and wet, or cold and dry.

Mid-December 1965, for instance, found California's central coast region glistening with early morning frost and going through day after day of bright sun without really warming up. At the very same time Los Angeles and San Diego, with normally half the annual rainfall of the central coast, were suffering a relentless deluge that followed a spell of eighty-degree heat. Several persons drowned in cars caught in arroyos ordinarily dry all year. Canyon rims and hillsides slumped and slid, especially where sites had been bulldozed not long before with no regard to geological structure or water-holding ground cover. Some costly new homes were totally destroyed. Great mudflows swept down canyon streets, engulfing houses in their paths. Then, after a short spell of fine weather, the mercury fell again as another round of storms set in with more heavy rains. There were floods in the desert, and the snowline dropped to fifteen hundred feet on the ranges ringing the Los Angeles Basin. Southern Californians could honestly make their customary claim that the bad weather was "unusual."

Unusual too were the rains of December 1964 that hit northwestern California and caused the most disastrous floods of recent times. Lumbermen claimed that the downpour of the few days before Christmas was the heaviest "in a thousand years." It would have been bad public relations, of course, for the owners and managers of much of the redwood region to admit that clear-cutting on watershed slopes had destroyed the ground cover. But with the plants uprooted, there was nothing to hold back the definitely uncommon quantity of rainwater; so every small stream became a raging torrent, and the Eel and other rivers rose to fill their valleys with the worst floods yet known to the region. Massive new freeway bridges were battered to rubble by huge logs; lumber mills and whole towns just disappeared, their wreckage swept toward the sea. It was many months before normal living and communications were restored. Those who did not or would not understand the relationships of climate and land cried loudly for a "flood control system" of multiple dams on the creeks and rivers. Since the disaster, some homework has perhaps been done on the ecological facts of life. A time for better understanding of nature's not so mysterious ways is of necessity hastening upon us.

THE CLIMATE of the Pacific Coast is frequently lauded as near-perfect, as close to ideal as a climate can be. Nature has found it suitable for the evolution here of one of the richest, most varied assemblages of plants and animals now existing anywhere in the earth's temperate zones.

Surely man has lived long enough in this region to have learned how to accommodate all aspects of his living to the usually gentle demands of a remarkably even-tempered climate. Such human problems as relate to climate and weather can be solved through a readiness to make reasonable adjustments to the environment, forego unreasonable demands upon it, and willingly accept *what is*. And this environment *is* one of the most favorable on earth.

Totem poles of Indians on the Kenai Peninsula, Alaska.

*All over southeastern Alaska, the forested slopes and shores of inlets such as this,
in northwestern Baranof Island, are under imminent threat of being opened for timber sales
by the U.S. Forest Service for clearcut logging, such as appears on the slope at the left.
These forests are about two-thirds Sitka spruce, one-third western hemlock.*

171

CHAPTER 17

TREES OF THE TOTEM CULTURE

Forest giants of the Pacific Northwest—
their importance in the life and economy of the Indians.

The history of man seems inextricably bound up with the history of trees and the rain that sustains them both.

—N. J. Berrill, MAN'S EMERGING MIND

DURING INDIAN TIME on this edge of land, before another world swept in under sail, the several Northwest Coast peoples had achieved a vigorous, competitive, materialistic, art-producing culture—an affluent society. Water and wood, the sea and the forest, were the insubstantial, impermanent bases of both economic and cultural life for a rude but viable civilization, in a world of islands, inlets, rivers, and rain, from beyond Yakutat Bay to the Columbia; its influence and patterns were felt among shore-dwelling groups as far south as Trinidad Bay and the Klamath.

This civilization grew to whatever unity it had, not by political bonds of the white man's sort but out of a distinctive life style. Language was the cement of tribal groupings. Northernmost was the Tlingit, whose fourteen tribes held most of southeastern Alaska. The Queen Charlotte Islands and nearby waters were the "sea kingdom" of the Haida, renowned for great canoes and carved slate. In British Columbia's channeled coastlands lived the Coast Tsimshian, Kwakiutl, Bella Coola, and others. The seaward side of Vancouver Island was home base for the Northwest's hardiest and most expert whalers, the Nootka. Indeed, this group, which includes the Makah of Washington's Cape Flattery, and certain other groups of the Olympic Peninsula, were the

only ones whose men hunted whales at sea. This required great canoes and greater seamanship.

The seaways of Juan de Fuca and Georgia straits, Puget Sound, and Grays Harbor were Coast Salish country. The Chinook held the Columbia from the Dalles to the sea, and the Tillamook a coastal strip to the south. Various smaller groups hung on to the Oregon and California coast, as far south as the Yurok region of the lower Klamath River.

The Northwest Coast culture grew to its height and complexity because the peoples who anciently came to these shores brought with them the intelligence and skills to take full advantage of an exceedingly bountiful nature. Theirs was not the "settled agriculture" route toward civilization. As completely a "hunting and gathering" people as the abject primitives of Baja California, so far removed in space and material advantage, the Northwest Coast Indians in their heyday enjoyed a paradise of natural resources so plentiful they could never be diminished, at least by Indian use. For all of time, they must have believed, the fat salmon would run upriver from that sea where whale and otter abounded and shellfish throve at tide's edge; berries would ripen in the forest and the great trees crowd to the shoreline, perpetually yielding canoe and totem pole.

One may fall easily into the view of the vast Pacific Coastal Forest as environmental determinant of that culture complex; the teleological thought is bound to rise as one plots the range of this forest around the northeastern Pacific rim. But the right conclusions may simply be that, with waterways everywhere

In the rain forest of the Pacific Northwest, a Sitka spruce, long dead, becomes a life-support system involving shelf fungi and a host of organisms; an Alaska cypress reaches toward vigorous maturity. In former days, it might have become a canoe or totem pole.

173

and land travel all but impossible, boats were needed; with long cold winters and very heavy rainfall, snug houses were needed; that the abundance of easily worked timber for these and many other uses made life a matter of easy problem-solving for good minds and hands. In any event, Indian culture and coastal forest grew together, for a long time. And a triumvirate of noble trees appears to rule in both.

O N KODIAK's northern end, as we have seen, and on Cook Inlet's circling shores, stand the dark ranks of Sitka spruce. They appear on the Kenai Peninsula, and follow the Panhandle to the British Columbia Coast Range, gaining altitude on one flank while hugging sea level on the other. The Queen Charlottes know the Sitkas as big, and they thrive on Vancouver Island's ocean side. A gathering of rivers meets Puget Sound tidewater in the somberly graceful presence of Sitka spruce. In the rain forest along the Pacific shore of the Olympic Peninsula they attain their greatest stature and glory, deployed to a depth of thirty miles up the short coastal rivers where ground and air are perennially moist. From northern Oregon the Sitkas reach southward to their final stand on California's Mendocino coast, keeping to the tidelands and especially the mouths of streams.

Remarkably parallel to Sitka spruce in its range on the Northwest Coast, but reaching much farther inland from British Columbia to Oregon, western hemlock is the most abundant tree of the Pacific coastal forest. Starting from sea level, this hemlock, like the spruce, thrives on the moisture of lowlands and seaward slopes, but it goes higher into regions of summer sunshine. It extends eastward along the Canadian border to the upper Columbia basin, from which it reaches to a height of five thousand feet on the Selkirk and Gold ranges.

A handsome tree, the western hemlock sends to the sky a slim leader shoot that arcs gracefully in the wind. Its seedlings do well in denser shade than most others can tolerate, enabling it to dominate large forest areas whenever the mature trees can reach the light. Although it has become extremely important for many industrial uses, this competitive edge has produced an abundance of western hemlock that augurs well for the future generations of the species.

Few in numbers compared with the first two, west-

ern red cedar is nevertheless the giant of the towering trio, considering not merely its size but its role in the life and times of the Northwest Coast Indians. Commonly it is known as "canoe cedar," a name well earned on sea and river waters of this forest region. Not a true cedar but an arborvitae, it was the veritable tree of life for the early peoples of our northern Pacific shore. Coming into its own on the southern islands and mainland of Alaska's Panhandle, the canoe cedar raises its great fluted and conically tapering boles in the wet lowland forests of the Queen Charlottes, Vancouver Island, the British Columbian inlets, Puget Sound and the Olympic Peninsula, and coastal Oregon and California south to Cape Mendocino. Found also on the slopes of the Cascades and up the Fraser, it reaches to the far inland mountains of British Columbia and south into Idaho. There, in 1805, Lewis and Clark discovered it, and from it made the five pirogues, or dugout canoes, in which they completed their historic journey down the Columbia to the Pacific Ocean.

The greatest western red cedars are found on Vancouver Island and the Queen Charlottes; their respective tribesmen, the Nootka and the Haida, built the most splendid and seaworthy of all Northwest Coast canoes. The most important part of the coastal range of this tree is precisely the region of the highest development of Northwest Coast culture. This tree was the chief material resource, after food, for this Indian way of life.

T O LIVE beside a river, along a sea channel, on a peninsular or island shore; to see towering overhead the tree giants which gave cradle, grave-house, and many objects of daily use between birth and death—such was the pattern of Indian generations, the context in which one succeeded another for centuries. The pattern grew intricate as the culture bloomed; but the context remained simple, an elemental one of water and wood.

The waters of ocean and river were the chief sources of food. Salmon came up from the Pacific in numbers past counting; and there were herring and smelt, halibut and cod, and the lower orders of sea food in abundance and variety. Hunting the marine mammals—seal, sea lion, sea otter—brought in meat and valuable skins, but it was also an exercise in skill, prestige, and ceremony. Land animals and birds were trapped, netted, arrowed, speared, and piked. Certain skins were specially valued, but, on the whole, land hunting came second to the sea chase. Plant foods were a poor third in the economy, although berries were popular; and around Puget Sound and on the Oregon coast the camas root was a staple. Acorns entered the diet in southwestern Oregon and northwestern California.

Of the many forest products of the central Northwest Coast region, the most variously useful were those from western red cedar. At birth the Indian had his first experience of something made from the wood: his cradle. For the rest of his life he used all manner of cedarwood containers—boxes, canoes, cooking vessels, houses. There was almost no end to the sizes, shapes, and functions of the famed Northwest Coast cedarwood boxes, their sides of a single plank, with corners kerfed and steam-bent, tops and sides exquisitely carved and painted with simple or elaborate designs. In every box, a plain cedar board thus became part of the signature of a people.

Cedarbark was no less prized a material. From Tlingit territory in southernmost Alaska to that of the Chinook on the Columbia, the bark of red cedar was bound up with the life of the Northwest Coast Indian even more intimately than the wood. Shredded fine as cotton, it swathed him in the cradle; and it was woven into robes, skirts, and other garments. Baskets to hold tools, pouches for harpoon heads, mats to sit on or spread a feast upon, ceremonial armbands and headgear, mattresses, even sails for canoes when the first crude copies of European canvas were made—these and many other things were fashioned of shredded cedarbark. The Indian's last contact with this essential stuff was likely to be within his burial wrapping.

Both bark and wood of red cedar were traded to groups living outside the region of the great tree's abundance. The north had a rival textile fiber in Alaska yellow cedar bark. Throughout the Northwest, other fibers were variously used: spruce root, alone or with cedarbark, for baskets; nettle for fishing cordage; goat wool along with cedar in the celebrated Chilkat blankets. Other woods had their uses, too: alder or yellow cedar, easily carved into masks and bowls without splitting; yew, toughly resilient for bows, harpoon foreshafts, and wedges for riving out cedar planks and posts. Maple and oak served these purposes in the south where, at the limits of the region, redwood replaced cedar for construction uses. But throughout the heartland of the Northwest Coast, western red cedar was of all natural resources the one most in evidence in the material culture of this well-endowed young civilization. Important economically, it also shaped a people's life style.

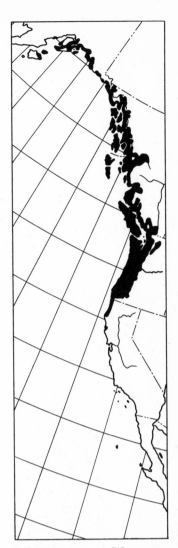

DISTRIBUTION: WESTERN RED CEDAR, WESTERN HEMLOCK, SITKA SPRUCE

Multifamily dwellings, lofty totem poles, and seagoing canoes were the big, bold strokes of the Northwest Coast signature in cedarwood. A forest as well as a sea people, the Indians of this culture doubtless used an instinctive forester's eye in selecting trees—this one for house timbers, that slender pole for carved figures proclaiming lineage and status, to stand richly colored and proud before a chief's lodge. For that most difficult technical achievement of these people—shaping a hull over fifty feet long and sturdy enough to sail hundreds of miles at sea (whose superb lines, some historians say, inspired the American clipper ship)—none would serve but the mightiest monarch of the grove.

The great cedar must be approached with appropriate spirit, felled as befitted its stature, worked with utmost patience and skill. They chose a tree near the shore for straightness, girth, and clear grain. They felled it in winter—with chisels of stone, horn, or shell, driven by heavy mauls; with massive chopping adzes; or by cutting a hole in the windward side of the base, making a fire in it, and letting the bole burn for two or three days, with a good draft, until the tree fell by itself. They left it to dry, then came

with adzes and roughed the outside shape. Some hollowed out canoes with fire, carefully controlled; others did the tedious job with adzes and chisels. After shaping the log, judging the thickness between their hands, the craftsmen filled the hull with water, added hot stones, covered it with cedarbark mats, and let it steam. As the wood softened, they gradually stretched it with thwarts until they had the proper hull width.

All in all, the sheerlines and curves of the sides, the proportions, finish, and general workmanship of the great Northwest Coast canoe made it a first-rate seagoing vessel, even when paddle-driven. Masts were stepped and sails added only after the Indians had seen European ships. There were many smaller models, for river and inshore use, for small crews and for lone sailors; and canoe patterns varied from tribe to tribe, region to region. In its time the Northwest Coast canoe was one of the finest vessels ever made by primitive man. The Haida war canoe and Nootka whaler, fifty- and sixty-footers carrying forty men with supplies and gear, were perhaps rivaled only by the great double-hulled ocean craft of the Polynesians.

The Indians' dwellings, commonly occupied by several related families, also varied in style, size, and construction from one area and tribe to another. Northern houses were between forty and sixty feet wide, almost square, and gable-roofed. In the south, longer and narrower homes with shed roofs were the rule (one building five hundred feet long and sixty feet wide has been recorded). Frames were massive, with upright posts often more than two feet square, and long, heavy horizontal beams, broad rafters, and wide, thick plank siding. The entrance might be a round hole cut through a huge central door post, carved and painted, and facing the sea. There would be a back doorway and a smoke hole in the middle of the roof. Interiors were cubicled

These old totem poles are quietly moldering and weathering to oblivion on Anthony Island, a speck of land in the southern tip of the Queen Charlotte archipelago, ancient home of the Haida Indians.

for the separate families, with the chief's apartment at the rear. In splitting planks and timber, the builders drove yew wedges in series along the desired lines: red cedar is notable for cleavage in even planes. Bark was saved and shredded for fiber—these people were good husbanders of their resources.

No single object has been more familiarly associated with Northwest Coast culture than the totem pole. Anywhere from ten to seventy feet tall, carved in animal figures and brightly painted, standing in rows before the village houses—certainly these cedarwood objects were the most conspicuous (if also the grossest) art form these Indians created. From some ancient time down to the present they have stood—gray-weathered, or reconstructed, or re-copied modern—often the first visible sign of human occupancy at shoreside forest clearings.

Voyagers approaching Vancouver Island's west coast and the Queen Charlottes saw them well before landing. As natives of treeless Easter Island raised up their megalith monuments hewn from the only material at hand, so the Northwest Coast people carved their memorials out of logs, sometimes three feet in diameter, and stood them erect as if to say: "In this land all things are of the tree."

THE INDIAN canoes are mostly gone now, and the old totem poles have moldered and fallen like ancient trees in the forest. Few houses still stand which were raised and joined in the old way, with wedge-split and adze-finished timbers and broad planking. Indians who remain on the Northwest Coast, no doubt with lessening reflection on the past, have mostly taken up the habits of the times. A potlatch dimly shadows past affluence and social glories and burdens, if it does so at all.

It is perhaps worth something to think of these people as they were, in their own long and high time on this coast, however they came and in how distant a past. They came, probably from less hospitable regions, and they made the ocean's edge and the forest their own—the abundant shore and the vast forest of spruce and hemlock and cedar. They mastered the deep sea with hewn logs. And they made a good living and a good life along this edge where the greatest forest and the greatest ocean meet. This is not a bad record for any people.

CHAPTER 18

A TIDE OF TIMBER

The Douglas-fir empire of Puget Sound —
the story of a mighty tree and the mighty industry it supports.

A Traveller wandering over these unfrequented Plains is regaled with a salubrious & vivifying air impregnated with the balsamic fragrance of the surrounding Pinery, while his mind is eagerly occupied every moment on new objects & his senses rivetted on the enchanting variety of the surrounding scenery where the softer beauties of Landscape are harmoniously blended in majestic grandeur with the wild & romantic to form an interesting and picturesque prospect on every side.

— Archibald Menzies, JOURNAL

WHEN CAPTAIN GEORGE VANCOUVER sailed the *Chatham* and *Discovery* into Puget Sound in 1792 to explore and survey that exceptional body of water for England, the expedition's naturalist, Archibald Menzies, became enraptured by what he saw ashore. A walk in the forest near where Everett, Washington, now sits among its stumps of old, second, and even third growth inspired the rhapsodic entry in his journal, quoted above.

The Royal Navy surgeon, serving as botanist on Vancouver's voyage, was avidly collecting new flora at every Pacific Coast landing where he had the opportunity. Thus the first specimens of the gigantic unknown "pine" reached Great Britain, along with some of the coast redwood and other trees of the Pacific slope. Aylmer Bourke Lambert, then England's chief authority on cone-bearing trees, described Menzies' new giant and named it *Pinus taxifolia* ("pine with leaves like a yew"). In those days, any tree with needles and cones was generally called a pine — and so it was, in the family sense.

Some natural landmarks of the world have had

to be discovered twice to win due notice, and Menzies' "pine" was one. In the spring of 1825, the English brig *William and Ann* brought to the Hudson's Bay Company's Fort Vancouver on the Columbia River a young plant hunter from the Horticultural Society of London, David Douglas. On the upriver end of the voyage that had taken him around Cape Horn, this eager and observant Scot was greatly impressed with the wilderness of "lofty hills well wooded with pines." In passing the Columbia's timbered banks, he took special note of "a species which may prove to be *P. taxifolia*" — showing he had done his homework in the current botanical literature.

Outfitted by the Company's friendly factor, Dr. John McLoughlin, Douglas lost no time getting out of the fort and into the woods. He knew his tree and set about measuring the biggest log he could find; it was 227 feet long and 48 feet in girth. He had to get seeds for his society — but how, he complained, when the cones on the standing giants were too high to bring down with buckshot and no tree could be felled with his hatchet? Somehow the determined collector got his "*P. taxifolia*" seeds in the end and rushed them off to London by an outgoing ship, together with his other specimens. The first examples of the great tree to be seen in Europe grew from David Douglas's seeds.

Fittingly, the king of North American timber trees now bears the names of both its discoverers. After a long and curious history of misnaming and renaming, several times over, this anomalous member of the Pine family appears at last to be firmly estab-

The Douglas-fir is most easily recognized by the slender,
three-pointed bracts that project from between the scales of the cones.

DISTRIBUTION:
DOUGLAS-FIR

lished as Douglas-fir, *Pseudotsuga menziesii* variety *menziesii* (distinguishing the Pacific Coast form from the Rocky Mountain variety, *glauca*). The generic name—still a boggler—says it is a "false hemlock" in a combination of Greek and Japanese!

DOUGLAS-FIR—the conifer that was described by botanists first as a pine and then as a fir, but is neither; that is known locally by the common names Oregon pine and Douglas-spruce; that is closely related to fir, spruce, and hemlock—is a tree of more contradictions than those of name and form. Although on the Olympic Peninsula it yields primacy in the rain forest area to Sitka spruce, western hemlock, and red cedar, it is there that some of the largest Douglas-firs are found. One giant has a diameter of fourteen and a half feet. Douglas-fir is, moreover, the most abundant and wide-ranging tree of the whole peninsula. Yet it is characteristically a tree of drier, more open land. It prefers sun to shade, well-drained ground to wet.

In the rain shadow of the Olympic Mountains, on the east side of the peninsula and throughout the Puget lowlands, summers are warmer and drier than along the outer coast. This is the heart of the coast Douglas-fir's range—the center of a belt extending northwestward along both sides of the Strait of Georgia and Queen Charlotte Sound, and south between the western Cascades and the coast to Northern California, where it divides to send a spur far down the western Sierra Nevada.

This wet winter-dry summer range of Douglas-fir is a region of fire—from both natural and human causes. And fire has been, since some ancient time of emerging adaptation to its ecological role, a prime factor in the spread of many plants; Douglas-fir is an excellent example of this.

Before modern man's extremes of carelessness and over-protection, fire was a boon to some plants and their natural communities; it still is, where natural controls are not thwarted. Fire opens the cones of certain pines, releasing their seeds; it fosters the vegetation of many chaparral and other shrubs by stump-sprouting; and it clears the ground. Natural fires in areas undisturbed by man are ground-fires. By keeping woodlands free of tinder-dry undergrowth, they guard trees against upflaring holocausts that consume all, from base to crown; and they open the way for seedlings that need more sun.

Douglas-fir has light, easily wind-borne seeds that sprout and grow best in the open. Given suitable soil, enough moisture and warmth, and clear ground to leeward, its forests live long and increase with amazing rapidity. Some "old-growth" Douglas-firs have lived five hundred to a thousand years. Second- and even third-growth forests now cover much of the tree's range, having invaded and reinvaded large acreages cut or burned over in our own times. But this ecologically "subclimax" tree will remain dominant over vast areas only so long as fire and other factors continue to work in its favor. Let the Douglas-fir's stands become dense, choked, and shaded, and some of its rivals for living space—the shade-tolerant western hemlock for one—will invade and supplant it.

With its tendency to take up open ground, Douglas-fir is a frequent mingler with other trees, especially where their stands thin out at the edges. Just as it appears conspicuously in the Olympic rain forest at the edge of wetness and shade, it is, in the southern part of its range, a common associate of coast redwood. Where fog-shrouded Sequoia groves thin out on the sunny side, or begin to climb hillslopes more open and better drained than their overcrowded creek-bottom flats, Douglas-fir is almost bound to appear. Its darker boles are scarcely of lesser stature, but they signal a change—welcome for some visitors—to a lighter forest cover on the whole. It is open enough to admit a graceful understory of tanoak, madroño, and other broadleaf trees and shrubs, and it is usually enlivened by more birds and animals than are to be seen or heard in the hushed nave of a redwood cathedral.

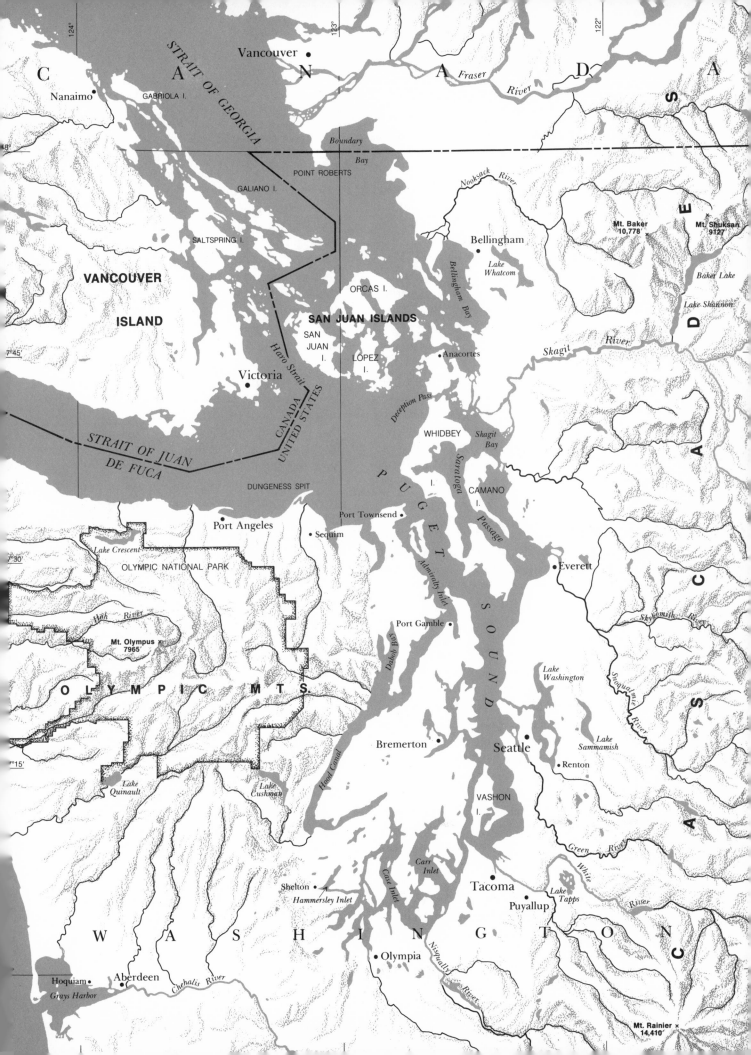

FOREST NORTH, DESERT SOUTH

THE ARRIVAL of the Pacific Mail steamship *Oregon* at San Francisco on December 1, 1849, was an event whose consequences would reach from that city to communities yet unborn in the north, from the Columbia to Puget Sound. Two young men from East Machias, Maine, landed in San Francisco that day: Andrew Jackson Pope and Frederic Talbot. With them was another gentleman from the same down-east lumber and shipping town, Captain Josiah P. Keller; a fourth, Lucius Sanborn, had arrived earlier.

Gold had not lured Pope and Talbot to the Golden Gate — gold in the ground, that is. A new city was rising: here was the main chance. Two days after arrival, the four easterners formed a company; five days later they bought an old longboat for five hundred dollars and were in the lighterage business. Within six weeks the Yankee quartet also possessed a yawl, two scows, and a seventeen-ton sloop for river freighting. By the end of January, 1850, they had earned the $9,100 cost of all vessels, sold one scow above cost when lighterage slowed, and divided nearly a thousand dollars in clear profit. Sanborn then sold out.

Meanwhile Pope and Talbot had set up their own lumber business. Today, the firm of Pope & Talbot, Inc., stands in the forefront of Pacific Coast lumbering and shipping; it got there by way of Puget Sound.

It is hard now to imagine the timber needs of nascent San Francisco, itself at the edge of the greatest coniferous forest realm on earth. In March, 1850, Captain William Chaloner Talbot, Fred's older brother, brought the 140-ton brig *Oriental* through the Golden Gate, out of East Machias via the Horn, hold and deck loaded with sixty thousand feet of lumber and, the records show, "two house frames, an assortment of joists and timber, and a few shingles" — profitable "coals to Newcastle" in those days. Settling down for a long stay, San Francisco needed a continuous and increasing flow of lumber. Some locally cut redwood and Douglas-fir was coming from a few small mills. But soon the Talbots and their partners saw big pilings for the city's new waterfront coming through the Gate, and sensed opportunity.

In November 1851, Pope, the Talbots, and Keller signed an agreement to build and operate a "Steam Saw Mill for manufacturing lumber in Oregon in the vicinity of Puget Sound." Thirteen months later, on December 20, 1852, with a fourth partner, Charles Foster, and capital of thirty thousand dollars, the long-lived Puget Mill Company was born.

The great Northwest Coast forest belt was still in its primeval glory. Throughout recent millennia it had furnished man the material for canoes, totem poles, plank lodges, and a few other artifacts; and it had been touched quite naturally by fire, as in all the geologic ages of its existence. But this forest was in splendid climax when sailing ships first entered the strait past the Olympic Peninsula, its great trees defying surf and mirrored in tidewater. Men shuddered at the darkness within their stands.

Such was the prospect before Captain W. C. Talbot and his handful of down-east lumbermen when in June, 1853, they coasted into Puget Sound and beheld "thousands of acres of land so densely wooded that they could supply dozens of sawmills with logs for generations." The plan was to choose a millsite on a good harbor yet close enough to the new settlements, Seattle, Olympia, and others, to draw labor.

Talbot's party took soundings, cruised timber in the vicinity, and landed cargo: a few thousand feet of Maine lumber for bunkhouse, cookhouse, and store, with tools, foodstuffs, and trade items. Leaving men to fell and square up the big timbers for the mill which was to be roofed before Captain Keller arrived with mill machinery from the East, Talbot sailed to Seattle for a load of lumber from Yesler's new steam sawmill, opened that March. Puget Mill Company lost no time getting into the profitable San Francisco lumber trade.

Off Port Townsend in the strait, Talbot spoke the inbound schooner *L. P. Foster,* 154 days out of Boston. Shouting directions to Captain Keller for finding the millsite, he squared away for the Golden Gate.

Skirting the timbered shores, the *Foster*'s people sighted the fresh-hewn uprights of the new mill. However dark the encircling forest, the crude framing and the glad shouts of the builders were welcome to Keller, his wife, daughter, and crew after five months at sea. And so Port Gamble was born.

On September 24, 1853, Puget Mill Company advertised in the *Columbian,* the territorial newspaper, that it was in business — lumber and general merchandise. Mill capacity was about two thousand board feet a day. Less than five months later, the little

Log rafts in Eld Inlet, Puget Sound, Washington.

muley had been supplanted by a new sash saw and a "live gang" of a dozen blades hung in one frame. These improvements boosted the cut to fifteen thousand feet per day of better, truer lumber, and bigger logs could be handled. Other mills which had started up at tidewater on the sound during this period were also cutting to capacity. Exploitation of the Northwest's fabulous timber resource had begun in earnest.

The romance of "green gold" and gang saws, of tough schooners and tougher skippers, of skid roads and bullwhackers, swampers, fallers, hooktenders and hand-skidders, of log booms and donkey engines, and of lumber port booms and busts—all this is to northwesterners what the golden argosy of the forty-niners is to Californians, or the saga of the sourdoughs and Klondike days is to Alaskans. And as with all such human stories, there is no end to its telling.

But here in the great Northwest—on Puget Sound and Grays Harbor, on the Columbia's many rivers and the plunging Olympic streams, up the straits of Juan de Fuca and Georgia, and now with rising crescendo on Alaska's island shores—where forest-green and sea-green tides meet, the story has a difference. It is not a story of some inert stuff man takes from the rock, something with no part in life, even human life. It is an epic of living things renewed in the earth and vital to man as all life is—precious vitality which he could use up but hopefully will not.

The tide of timber will serve man best if part is left to run free, to rise in its own time and place from the land, to meet the sky, and the sea where it will, on its own terms.

CHAPTER 19

FORESTS OF THE FOG

*The coast redwood and its sea-mist community; the silent floor
and the lively edge; a visit to a forest of the past.*

A COASTLAND of moderate, fertile slopes, deep-soiled valleys, numerous rivers, good rains, and much fog—this is the Northern California heart of the coast redwood belt. The redwood cannot live without loam and water for its roots, and it cannot live well without a summertime mantle of fog. River-mouth valleys are funnels to receive this ocean bounty; over the flats it may hang at treetop level, shredding softly down into the dark canopy, but it billows with the forest itself up hillslopes and over the lower mountain ridges.

The shade that fog provides is as vital to redwoods as the extra, dry-season ration of water condensing from mist to drops and percolating from leaf to limb to ground. During long summer days, when the sun beats down directly, the fog lends a warding parasol against transpiration and evaporation. But in deference to its own limiting factors of temperature and vaporizing, the fog thins out south of the Santa Cruz Mountains, its northerly high tide spent. And the redwoods do likewise in response to their own curbs, chief of which is the fog's frail edge.

Though written long ago, when research in Sequoia attributes and life history was still young, a brief observation (made in 1863 at Crescent City) by Professor William H. Brewer of the California Geological Survey, is pertinent:

THE FOREST is narrow, and mostly made up of gigantic trees—large groups of trees, each ten to fifteen feet in diameter, and over two hundred feet in height, the straight trunks rising a hundred feet without a limb. The bark is very thick and lies in great ridges, so that the trunks seem like gigantic fluted columns supporting the dense canopy of foliage overhead. They generally swell out at the bottom, so that a tree but ten feet in diameter at thirty feet high, will be fifteen or more at the ground. They grow so abundant that the sun cannot penetrate through the dense and deep mass of foliage above. A damp shady atmosphere pervades the forests, and luxuriant ferns and thick underwood often clothe the ground. Large trees fall, mosses and ferns grow over the prostrate trunks, trees spring up among them on the thick decaying bark. The wood is so durable that a century may elapse before the fallen giant decays and mingles with its mother earth. In the meantime, trees a century old have grown on it, their bases twelve to fifteen feet from the ground, sustained on great arches of roots that once encircled the prostrate log upon which they germinated. A man may ride on horseback under some of these great arches.

Appearing in the now classic *Up and Down California in 1860–1864* (New Haven: 1930), Brewer's description is clearly of old-growth redwood forest in climax upon the deep, rich alluvium of a river valley or creek bottom. Such places, within twenty miles or so from the coast in the fog belt between central California and the Oregon border, provide the ultimate fullness of life for this great tree.

A SPECIES with the genetic and ecological vitality of the coast redwood will make the most of its assets and push as far as its limiting factors allow. On the north, it reaches to Oregon's Chetco River, about

*Coast redwoods in Simpson Reed Grove, Jedediah Smith
Redwoods State Park, near Crescent City, California.*

five miles from the California border; on the south, to Salmon Creek on the Monterey coast. Amazingly, one small stand lives far to the east of the fog belt, just north of San Francisco Bay, on Inner Coast Range slopes draining to the Sacramento River—a holdover, perhaps, from cooler and wetter times.

This coast redwood range is four hundred and fifty miles long and roughly ten to thirty miles wide; it has many breaks along the way, and it seldom touches the sea. The region is marked by ridges alternating with river valleys, both trending northwesterly as they run to the coast. While redwoods grow from sea level to around 3,000 feet, they are most abundant between 100 and 2,500 feet, especially in lower reaches where streams become fat and sluggish with silt. For soil needs, this is the optimum, as Brewer found it.

A COMMON QUESTION is regarding the difference between the coast redwood *(Sequoia sempervirens)* and the "giant sequoia" or big tree *(Sequoiadendron giganteum)* of the Sierra Nevada. Although the term *redwood* is often applied to both trees in popular usage, there are distinct differences between the two and their growing and living habits. Until a few years ago, the big tree was called *Sequoia gigantea*, then botanists generally agreed it was distinct enough to be put in a genus all its own. But doubtless it will remain giant Sequoia for a long time.

The coast redwood attains the greatest height, the big tree the greatest diameter of all living tree species. Each has its special soil and climate needs, and neither would thrive in the territory of the other.

Redwoods engage light winds with grace—air sun-warm and dry, fog-moist, or ferrying gentle rain. Fresh, cool breezes are welcome. But a hard and steady blowing, as of our prevailing westerlies upon the forelands, is anathema: it sucks the juices out of plants, even from the leafage and vital tissues of trees. Redwoods are sensitive, also, to ocean salts sprayed inland by sea-borne storms—witness the hard-bitten, crusty old veterans facing everyday winds in Monterey canyon mouths, another extreme situation. They care little for cold: the bite of frost on both ends of a short summertime, or the burden of snow upon the weary spread of a long winter. Having found congenial latitudes, they shun both the exposed outer coastline and higher elevations.

DISTRIBUTION:
COAST REDWOOD,
SIERRA REDWOOD
(BIG TREE)

The middle ground is right. Redwood forests march over every type and exposure of moderate terrain in their territory until, in the southern part, they keep to the northern and western facings, huddling in the partial shade of canyon walls along the Monterey coast. Best of all are the broad flats of northern river valleys, which heavy rains and dependable flows perennially feed with the clay, silt, and sand of upland erosion. Rich loam builds up when these are mixed with the organic products of the forest's own decomposing. A season of heavy flooding may add two feet or more to the redwoods' larder.

To deal with a continually rising ground level and thrive on a glut of nutriment overlying a waterlogged subsoil, the redwood species has evolved a multistory root system. It has no taproot. After each major buildup of the soil around its base, the tree produces a new "story" of roots above the old. As the redwood's girth increases, each higher root growth spreads correspondingly wider. New rootlets have access to, or are able to reach, the oxygen of each fresh soil layer.

In Northern California a redwood was found to be over twelve hundred years old. Measurements of its root system indicated that seven major floods and many lesser ones had raised the ground level more than eleven feet during the life of this tree.

The coast redwood is no great seed producer in comparison with some other conifers, such as Douglas-fir, and its forest seedlings are relatively few. But it has marvelous regenerative power through stump and root-crown sprouting. This accounts for the familiar "rings" of redwood stands. Before an old tree dies and topples, it may be surrounded by its offspring—saplings, even tall young trees—rising from basal nodes of upper root system outliers. Each generation repeats a process: a redwood forest is virtually an infinite complex of rings clustered around rings to its farthest edge.

One of the best known properties of redwood is the resistance of both bark and wood to fire, insects, decay, and disease, long and widely heralded in accounts of redwood ecology and economic uses (which tend to sound like descriptions of a "wonder tree"). The magic is compounded of an abundance of tannin, an absence of pitch, and a great thickness of remarkably tough-fibered bark, which is inhospitable to flame and organisms alike.

THE GREAT AGE of redwoods, coast and Sierran both, is regarded as nature's supreme symbol of living continuity, from past to present and, hopefully, to some certain future for both earth and man.

A few miles north of San Francisco Bay, in deeply canyoned hills between the Sonoma and Napa valleys, one may enter a redwood forest of the past, a place called simply the Petrified Forest. Privately owned, but open to visitors, it is one of the best examples known of an ancient woodland.

Upon a gentle south-facing slope, great broken logs protrude from the rocky ground. Sunlight, falling through the open shade cast by a thin cover of living trees, strikes the bright green leaves of seedlings, which grow in tiny pockets of soil in bark fissures of the prostrate logs. Here and there a youthful oak or other tree springs from between sundered log sections. Had there been no sign proclaiming a "petrified forest," one might have contemplated the scene

for some time before he felt a dawning suspicion of these derelicts lying in partly dug trenches or half emerging from scarps of country rock; only a closer look would confirm that the logs were solid stone.

This is a volcanic area, merely dormant, as can be seen by its living geysers and hot springs (there is, in fact, not far away, a generating plant powered by live natural steam). Mount St. Helena, close by, is a rugged pile of volcanic fragments, although not an actual volcano. A volcano or great volcanic vent must have existed, however, not far north of the Petrified Forest. Some five million years ago, trees were thrown down, with tops pointing to the south, and buried beneath volcanic ash. An explosion is surmised, or a blast of wind rushing down the slopes of an ash-hurling volcano.

The greatest of the stricken trees were redwoods. With them fell spruces, firs, hemlocks, and those familiar redwood associates, Douglas-firs. Also recognized in the fossil debris of the once thriving forest are other trees and shrubs that live with redwoods today: red alder, wax myrtle, tanoak, chinquapin, California laurel, huckleberry, and rhododendron. Strangers existed here, too: the red bay, elm, and chestnut of our East, and an unfamiliar aquatic now found only in China, the water chestnut. Living redwoods stand close to the Petrified Forest today in canyon bottoms, while drier slopes support many Douglas-firs, madroños, and other trees of the redwood forest edge.

It was reported quite recently that in southern Manchuria imprints of foliage closely resembling the needles of our coast redwood were found in fossil-bearing beds of the Jurassic period, perhaps 150 million years old. More abundant evidence—petrified wood, leaf and fruit impressions, deposits of long-vanished lakes and basins—clearly shows ancestral redwoods existed 100 million years ago.

They took two main forms in response to climatic and perhaps other limiting factors of their environment: an evergreen, linked directly to the living coast redwood; and a deciduous form, adapted to a wet-summer growing season and a cold-winter time of dormancy, the conditions of the northlands. The latter redwood came to light among fossil relics of temperate forests that once lived as near the pole as northern Greenland. It was widespread in Alaska, and grew on the Bering land bridge, as shown by fossils from St. Lawrence Island. Associated with it were many species living today: maples, oaks, walnuts, and others. All were part of a complex known as the Arcto-Tertiary Flora, a plant association that early in the Cenozoic era flourished much farther north than its representatives do now. Other fossil redwood specimens have been found in lower latitudes around the world from Britain and southern Europe to eastern North America.

Shortly after World War II a startling and scientifically momentous redwood discovery was made. In 1944 a Chinese forester, T. Wang, found in central China a living tree like nothing he had ever seen, apparently new to science. The story has been widely told: how, at the war's end, the news burst upon western science that a live redwood of a type supposedly extinct for twenty million years had been discovered; how the American paleobotanist, Dr. Ralph W. Chaney of the University of California, went to China in 1948, examined the tall trees, and announced to the world a living fossil, *Metasequoia.* In his own words, "never has there been a more dramatic botanical discovery than the finding of the living Dawn Redwood by forester Wang." Research has since revealed it did exist at other times in other areas of the earth, but, as Dr. Chaney has written, it "disappeared from the living forests of North America before the close of the Miocene epoch, probably as a result of [climate] changes . . . from summer-wet to summer-dry," surviving to the present only in China's summer-wet interior.

That discovery led to the patient reexamination of the whole fossil record of redwoods around the world, in the context of time and climate. Before the true picture could be clearly understood, it had to be seen that certain fossil cones and leafless twigs represented a *deciduous* redwood—one that could have lived in the cold winter of Arcto-Tertiary times well to the north of the present coast redwood latitudes. In that Eocene period, each Northern Hemisphere climate belt extended far to the north of its present limits; our coast had a milder climate and gentler topography, along a warmer sea.

But as successive epochs passed, there were shifts in climate, crust, and ocean. It became cooler; mountains rising on the western rim brought dryness to the continental interior as they cut off ocean moisture. Forests and other Arcto-Tertiary plant communities gradually withdrew from polar and subpolar regions to a more temperate zone. In the Far West, tropical forms retreating south gave up a northern edgehold in Washington and settled back in Mexico and Central America, where relatives still carry on.

The great *Sequoia* migration, beginning perhaps fifty million years ago, can be charted through fossils of progressively younger rocks. Releasing old Rocky Mountain and other interior holdings, it moved southward for warmth and coastward for moisture. Coast redwood is, on the geological time scale, a relatively late arrival—its earliest known fossil is less than twenty million years old.

To DESCRIBE a magnificent stand of virgin coast redwood in its densest lowland growth as a veritable desert of lifelessness is to state a paradoxical but telling part-truth. On the ground of some such grove is stacked the greatest weight and bulk, acre for acre, of organic matter anywhere on earth. But this mass of matter is overwhelmingly constituted of *dead wood.* The heartwood of a Sequoia is dead, and so is the bark. Only the cambium layer next to the bark, and the leaves and branchlets, along with the active layers of the root system, are viable matter. It has often been remarked that such a grove of redwoods is a place of awesome quiet—not the quiet of death so much as the dearth of visible, touchable, audible life. If branches are a hundred feet and more above the ear, birdsong dies somewhere in the acoustical sponge of bark. The least of all mammals, a shrew, may be hidden in the duff underfoot. The scant understory of lesser plants is muted, no breeze stirring it, an occasional shaft of sunlight barely reaching a fern leaf. Such a place is for sober thoughts—a necessary place, for some of us.

But the edge of a redwood forest is the necessary part for the greatest number of its creatures. Meadow's edge, stream bank, rise of slope—there things come and go, mix, light up, look alive. There it becomes evident that the coast redwood community is one of many members—trees, shrubs, ferns, flowers, mosses, fungi, molds, bacteria, invertebrates, birds, and all the four-footed things from frog to elk. The edge of the forest is where life moves and sings.

"The Giant": a redwood log fifty-six feet long and eight feet in diameter, in the Petrified Forest, near Calistoga, California. Some five million years ago, a mixed evergreen forest of redwood and associated species was blown down by a volcanic blast and buried in ash and mud. Mineral-bearing water percolated through the cover, and the fallen trees gradually turned to stone, their forms preserved intact. The now world-famous Petrified Forest was discovered in 1870; Robert Louis Stevenson visited it in 1880 and wrote about it in The Silverado Squatters.

*In the Olympic Peninsula rain forest, where venerable Sitka spruces and other trees
are clothed in soft green, the clubmosses hang in curtains from every branch.
Light from the sun, itself unseen, filters palely down through the high canopy and
any sound is rare. The most accessible place to visit the rain forest is in the
Queets Corridor of Olympic National Park.*

A meadow opening in the Douglas-fir forest is likely to be invaded by various members of the broadleaf evergreen woodland, creating an example of mixed evergreen forest. This one is in the Point Reyes National Seashore, about twenty-five miles north of the Golden Gate.

The Far West is no rival for the Northeast in fall color, but the few touches of it are perhaps the more appreciated for their rarity, as here among the deciduous California black oak, in the Northern California Coast Range Preserve of the Nature Conservancy.

CHAPTER 20

WOODLANDS OF THE LONG DRY SUMMER

*Pines and oaks of the middle coast region today
and through the eyes of the first Spanish padres.*

THE MARK of a long, dry summer on the great middle part of the Pacific Coast, it was suggested in the earlier discussion of climate, is seen most clearly in the vegetation. The look and life-style of plants adapted to an annual sequence of several rainless months is exemplified in this coast-land by many of their communities: grasses and herbs, scrub and chaparral, and woodlands. Among the last, none are more characteristic of the extended region than the ones belonging to the oaks or the pines. In the world-circling genera of these trees are many species supremely suited to the Mediterranean-type climate this coastland enjoys. From central Oregon to northern Baja California, few indeed are the seaside, valley, or mountainous landscapes to which some pine or oak does not lend a particular interest and charm. Anciently woven into the fabric of nature, oaks and pines have long taken part in the human story.

A GROVE of valley oaks once arched tall and graceful over a clear, small creek north of the Golden Gate. In the winding colonnade of gray-barked, massive, and many-angled trunks, some California laurels stood nearest the water, their dense-leaved tops sharing the high canopy. Where the oak-grove floor verged on gentle slopes, sunlight caught the bright russet of smooth madroño bark. This was a community of trees, in which an oak played the dominant role. Grasses, herbs, and shrubs had their special niches in it, as well as a host of mosses, molds, lichens, ferns—all the major and minor elements of a plant community in this temperate coastland region.

This was an animal community, too. Many little trails led down from the dry, scrub- and grass-covered hills to the cool stream bank. After their drink, black-tailed deer lay in the oak shade for a siesta before the climb back to their evening browse. Gray squirrels raced in their aerialist way from branch to branch of the canopy—for miles, it would seem, without landing via some trunk. At night, ring-tailed cats took their turn playing on the crooked oak limbs, while raccoons dunked a variety of food at the stream's edge. Coyotes, and smaller predators such as weasels and striped skunks might prowl darkly through the little valley. At spawning time for steelhead, grizzly bears—now vanished—would come for good fishing.

Of the many birds that livened this oak community, none did so with more dash and color than the acorn woodpeckers, a colony of them. Black and white with yellow throat and scarlet crown, they would wing through treetops calling loudly, then settle on a high limb and whack with chisel-beaks to make countless holes of the precise bore for acorns. For vocal beauty in the woodland, the thrushes were unequaled, their songs lilting like flute solos at sunrise and dusk.

Man first entered this community, perhaps ten, twenty, thirty centuries ago, in a red-brown skin and little else. His shelter and food, as well as clothing, needs were elemental. Rabbit and venison, bear and salmon, quail, the shellfish and ducks from the creek's tidal estuary, some good herbs such as Indian lettuce, camas bulbs, buckeye or horse chestnut seeds, and the abundant harvest of the acorns—the larder was

*Bishop pines—like these of Northern California—or Monterey pines,
found south of the Golden Gate, make wonderful filters through which
to view the Pacific Ocean.*

193

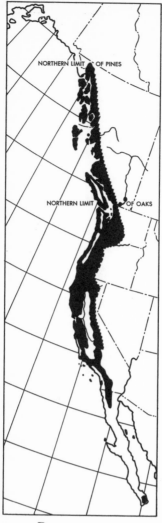

DISTRIBUTION:
OAKS AND PINES

full. And the climate was as ideal as man could find. A ridge between valley and ocean was skylined darkly with bishop pines, which made their own denser but drier woodland community as they climbed the lee slope up from the oaks, laurels, and madroños to face the sea wind and fog. The understory of the ridgetop was hardy scrub which merged at the seaward edge with a bunch-grass prairie running to the bluffs above the strand.

The Indians who for millennia shared this country with the oaks, pines, and wildlife were the Coast Miwok that greeted Drake on his New Albion landing in 1579. It was their country for another two and a half centuries, then they were gone. On some creeks that run inland to San Francisco Bay, a few oaks and laurels now arch over suburban streets and homes. Summer houses nestle among the pines on the ridge. The climate is still ideal.

Thursday, August 10 [1769]— . . . We set out at eight in the morning, following the valley [of the Santa Clara River in Ventura County, California] west-southwest, and also the arroyo, which runs with a good stream of water, and has banks well grown with cottonwoods, live oaks, and willows. . . . The mountains on either side are very high and bare, but abundantly covered with grass. On the summits are seen some live oaks and pines. . . .

The diarist is Fray Juan Crespí logging the journey of the Portolá Expedition; he is quoted by Fray Francisco Palóu in his *Historical Memoirs of New California.* Of entries covering 116 days of the epic coastland trek from San Diego to San Francisco Bay, this one is chosen from the forty-two that mention either oaks or pines, or both. The historic purpose of the wilderness *entrada* was to rediscover the Monterey Bay that Vizcaíno had found and named on his 1602 voyage along the coast. Mistrusting "certain" identification of that bay as earlier described from the navigator's, not the muleteer's, viewpoint, Portolá and Crespí pushed on from there to the unknown bay and its Golden Gate.

The Spaniards knew oaks well from their own Iberian landscapes, but Crespí may have used the word "pine" for various conifers, as was customary in those days. True pines grew along the routes, however, and it may be assumed that for the most part the padre called them as we know them. The long journey paced off a fair stretch of one of the world's chief homelands of oak and pine. Both kinds of tree play leading roles in our brief story of this central region of the Pacific coastlands for several reasons — historical, geographical, ecological.

Portolá was seeking a place which Vizcaíno, 167 years before, had described as a haven "well situated" for easting Manila Galleons and furnished with "a great extent of pine forest from which to obtain masts and yards, even though the vessel be of a thousand tons burden, very large live oaks and white oaks for shipbuilding, and this close to the seaside in great number." To the land-bound Portolá party, Monterey Bay did not measure up to the old navigator's picture. However, the next year Junípero Serra sailed to it from San Diego and wrote to Palóu: "This is indeed the famous harbor discovered by Vizcaíno." In another letter he reported: "The altar was set up under the same oak"—a great one, it is said, with huge and wide-spreading branches—"under which Vizcaíno's chaplains had celebrated Mass. . . . Everyone arrived singing, while the bells hung from the old tree were ringing at full peal." The historic tree, standing near the beach, was to the Spaniards an *encina,* or live oak; Vizcaíno's "white oaks" were *robles,* the word they applied to valley oaks.

The next year, retracing Portolá's march, Serra came to a place near the San Antonio River (in Monterey County), naming it *Cañada de los Robles* ("Valley of the Oaks"). Serra founded there Mission San Antonio de Padua — again with "bells hung from an old oak tree."

Returning to the Monterey Peninsula, the padre celebrated, on August 24, 1771, the first Mass at

The dry inner slopes and valleys of the Oregon and California Coast Ranges are open grass and oak country—and prevalently range country. Grassland that is almost level, with trees widely spaced, is savanna. Such land is this valley oak grassland near Ukiah in Northern California, but perhaps it is too steep to be called savanna properly. On many summer days the heat here is palpable; in spring the ground is bright green with the new grass.

195

The Torrey pine has stiff, gray-green needles, 8 to 13 inches long, in bundles of five; cones are large, 4 to 6 inches long, with scales thickened at the apex into heavy pyramids. In natural growth, the tree is irregular, extending about 20 to rarely 40 feet high; in cultivation, however, it has grown more than 100 feet high and straight.

There may be no more than 7,500 Torrey pines living on about 1,000 acres of their natural habitat on the Pacific Coast. These, along with the trees of the Santa Rosa Island stand, may seem like a large enough population of one species to ensure its survival. Yet that portion of the coastal environment, in San Diego County between La Jolla and Del Mar, where this relict from pre-Pleistocene times is making its last bid for a piece of the future, is one that has been constantly threatened with conversion to various human uses.

Mission San Carlos Borromeo Carmelo, built not far from Carmel Bay, in the dark embrace of the Monterey pine forest that had provided its timbers.

A LARGE BOOK could be filled with the story of oaks and pines, their roles in the lives of the Indians and in European settlement of the Alta California coastlands. Western North America, and especially the Pacific region between northern Baja California and southwestern Oregon, is scarcely equaled anywhere in the number of its species of these two kinds of tree. Of more than two dozen western oaks, a generous proportion reach the Pacific and a few are exclusive to the coastlands. Of a similar number of pine species in the West, some two-thirds are found in the coastal region, living within sight of the sea or in the Coast Ranges. One may be impressed by how many kinds there are of both trees, but interest centers on their history and how they live.

T HE PINES have been adapting to change for a very long time. Their class, the gymnosperms (plants with naked seeds), first appeared some 300 million years ago. In the Pacific borderlands the pines have spread gradually southward from a good deal farther north than any of them are found today.

Certain pines now singularly restricted to small and isolated coastal areas once enjoyed much larger ranges. Inland populations gradually lost ground to stronger forces of change than they could withstand: increasing cold, alteration of landform, competition from other plants. An example is the pine that colonized some of California's Channel Islands five or ten million years ago, when they were connected to the mainland. Late in the Pliocene epoch temperatures dropped, making life inland uncomfortable for pines and remaining mild enough only where the climate was softened by the sea. The bishop pine and its slightly divergent variety, the future Santa Cruz Island pine, survived on the coast. When the islands were later cut off by geological changes, the isolated trees formed a relict population and began to evolve still greater differences from the mainland relative. Curiously, besides the Santa Cruz group, a few small groves of the island pine are found on Baja's Isla Cedros. Almost as much reduced in natural range is the Monterey pine, with three very small colonies on

the California coast and one on faraway Guadalupe.

Pines are, nevertheless, extremely adaptable; they meet a wide range of environmental conditions, some quite harsh. Consider some extremes: the Monterey and bishop pines on coastal strands and fog-damp slopes facing the sea—tall, erect, full-foliaged, with big, long limbs growing high on the trunk and reaching away from the wind; and the bristlecone, living at high mountain timberline through the hot summers and frigid winters of the Great Basin region—wind-tortured, stunted, spare-leaved (yet with a possible life span of well over four thousand years). What we admire in each of these pines is the picturesque beauty it gives to its landscape. In their natural habitats they become wondrously misshapen, far from the concept of a "normal" pine tree, as they struggle against climatic and other adversities. For the Monterey pine, proof that its growth in its native stands is, in fact, abnormal can be seen in the plantations of this world-famed California tree flourishing in such places as New Zealand and Australia, away from the ocean, and yielding perfectly straight sawlogs a foot in diameter at twenty or thirty years' growth. Fine, tapering, healthy trees, not dried and pruned by the wind, not salt sprayed, not embattled in any struggle—and not specially charming.

It is ironic, that where pines delight us most as elements of landscape beauty—Japan's Matsushima or "Pine Islands" and her Inland Sea, many parts of the Mediterranean shore, Monterey Peninsula and elsewhere on the Pacific Coast, and in bristlecone country—the trees themselves are handicapped, in constant contention with natural adversity.

What, then, is their ideal environment? Pines will tolerate cold winters but not the frozen ground and cool, short summers of the Far North; sunshine and warmth, but not tropic heat. They need some dryness, but not the parching blast of strong winds. They endure salt soil and spray, but not sea water too close to their feet.

Since their seeds will not live in the brine, pines cannot migrate by sea from island to island or shore to shore; instead, the seeds must ride long distances on the wind, a major instrument of their dispersal. Pines readily invade land newly cleared, as by fire. After the retreat of glaciers from our northern

FOREST NORTH, DESERT SOUTH

coasts, the beach or lodgepole pine was one of the early pioneers in reclaiming the naked land. Pines will invade coastal dunes—witness the beach pines forming a ragged and beautiful crest along the high Oregon Dunes—but not true desert sands. The nearest to a desert pine is the piñon, at best a fringe benefit for the high deserts.

O AKS AND MEN live well together. They have done so for long centuries of alternating wet and dry seasons, nourishing and preserving each other, in several hundred miles of coastland and in the adjacent foothills and valleys. The oaks—valley, live, blue, black, and others of the *Quercus* genus—had settled first, by many millions of years. When men came, they found oak country hospitable, as acorn woodpeckers and other animals had before them.

The oaks had selected a land of gentle climate, between extremes. Winters were sometimes frosty, but not hard-freezing. The long summer was hot, but the oaks provided shade; it was dry, but where oaks lived, water was available. The land was big and open, with live oaks dotting the grassy hills, throwing cool canopies across steep canyons. Valley oaks spread in parklike savannas between riverlands and hill slopes. And on the rain-shadow side of the coast ranges, in the heart of the thousand-mile reach of the oak woodlands, the community of blue oak and digger pine rimmed the great interior valley.

Oaks like cold even less than pines do. One pine, the lodgepole, ranges coastally all the way from Northern California to Skagway, Alaska, and thence high into the Yukon. But the Garry, or Oregon white, oak alone represents its kind in the Northwest, and only as far north as southeastern Vancouver Island. And while a few pines such as the bristlecone and the whitebark will hold to high-mountain timberline as though it were the last place on earth, the oaks fade

The coast live oak is the most widespread and characteristic tree of the hills and valleys from the Golden Gate south into Baja. It branches close to the ground, extending outward an incredible distance, often touching the ground with an "elbow" and reaching up and outward again. This was one of the first trees from the Pacific Coast to become known in Europe, after it was collected in 1791 by the Malaspina Expedition, Spain's only scientific entrada into Alta California.

*On the northern ridges of Guadalupe — a volcanic
island probably never connected to the mainland —
some four hundred mature pine trees grow, a variety
of California's Monterey pine. The Guadalupe Island
pine, and a cypress, an oak, and a palm — all endemic to
the island — will doubtless become extinct when the existing
trees die, and other island vegetation will go with them.
Their seedlings, if any, are devoured by the swarming
descendants of introduced goats. The trees have aided the
survival of some of the small plants, despite the goats, by
condensing fog in their branches and letting the water
drip to the ground. As the trees die off, the island is
gradually becoming more desertlike.*

out in the middle elevations, or transition zone from lower slope to alpine height. Unlike the pines, however, some oaks have adapted to the conditions that make chaparral, and several species have become components of it. These are the various scrub oaks, the *bonsai* of the oak world.

OAKS HAVE MET PINES in this Pacific borderland for at least sixty million years. Coming to the present from different points in past time, the two genera are woven into a rich mosaic of vegetation, telling of a temperate, livable climate.

The great western pineries of ponderosa and lodgepole, in sometimes vast and pure-stand forests, belong to the interior. Where lodgepole spills over the rim in its beach pine variety, as on the coasts of Vancouver Island, and south to Mendocino County, California, it darkens the strand in wind-sculptured shapes of individual character. The bishop pine, in silhouettes recalling Japanese prints, takes up the coastal strip to windward of the redwoods. The Monterey pine fills this role, in part, on the ocean foot of the Santa Cruz Mountains and farther south. On the coast near San Diego, the relict Torrey pine is

for a brief space the only native tree in sight today.

Where pines grow in woodland numbers, they tend to be exclusive, allowing few lesser plants into their shade in comparison with the greater variety found in some of the oak associations. But if a pine stand is opened wide, as by fire, it may be quickly invaded by scrub or chaparral. It then becomes much richer in animal as well as plant life, more nearly fulfilling the idea of a community.

The mixed evergreen woodland blankets the outer Coast Ranges from southwestern Oregon to south-central California, where mountains are low enough to let the year-round ocean mildness penetrate deeply. Its great conifer elements — coast redwood and Douglas-fir — extend long fingers through a mesh of the slanting, curving, forking branches and sun-flecked foliage of tanoak, laurel, and madroño, black oak and maple, dogwood and red alder along streambanks. A giant chinquapin's stout limbs may interrupt the pattern now and then; the scene varies endlessly as vegetation, direction, slope, and elevation change for the wandering viewer. Shifting woodland patterns enchant the eye as long as daylight lasts — in summer or any season.

CHAPTER 21

ELFIN FORESTS OF THE SOUTH

*Chaparral — the seven million acres of hardy scrub
covering California hills and mountainsides.*

NOTHING SEEMS MORE hauntingly Californian than the sight and aroma of chaparral drenched in sunlight. Yet, for the Spanish *soldado* or *padre*, the oaks, pines, and chaparral so widespread over the face of coastal California must have aroused an aching nostalgia for the Iberian homeland. Here were raggedly rounded oak trees scattering blotches of shade on a parched savanna, the etched accent of pines on a distant ridge. And seldom absent from view along the mission trail from Baja far into Alta California was the mottled mosaic of scrub on rocky slopes. The tawny pelage of dry grass, muted gray-greens of trees and shrubs, a faint blue veil of volatile essences filling the heat-shimmer above billions of aromatic leaves — all were sensate reminders of Mediterranean coastlands a long, long voyage away.

They called the miles of stiff, woody brush *chaparral:* the place of *el chaparro,* their own familiar evergreen scrub oak. And that softly bristling word has become indelibly affixed to this far landscape.

What is chaparral? Technically it is a dominant, deep-rooted, shrubby vegetation, chiefly evergreen with leathery, often hard-surfaced leaves. The many-branched shrubs tend to look like miniature trees; clumps of them have been popularly called "elfin forests" — a poetic truth, for they have indeed become dwarfed as an adaptation to thin hillside soil and a Mediterranean climate. Other survival mechanisms of chaparral are the woodiness of trunks and stems, and the development of hard, thick, small leaves, both of which help these plants to conserve

the moisture of the short rainy winter-spring through a long, hot, generally rainless summer.

Where chaparral grows, the annual rainfall averages ten to twenty inches; less rain would spell desert, more might produce tree growth. This aridity often causes the plant to simply desiccate on the bush instead of properly rotting into the soil. Also, small particles are constantly moving downhill through the summer instead of building soil profiles, and the brief rains are apt to wash away everything loose — soil, dead leaves, and all. The lower layers of soil would go too, if it were not for the chaparral's extensive root system.

However, chaparral adapts to a wide spectrum of soils and exists on land that will support little else. The classic examples are on the Mediterranean shores of Europe and North Africa, and in California, from Baja California north via the Coast Ranges to the San Francisco Bay region, and then into southern Oregon along the inner ranges. In sparse patches a few species of "hard" chaparral persist north as far as British Columbia, east to the Sierra Nevada slope.

"Hard chaparral" (as distinct from the less woody and dense coastal sage scrub, sagebrush scrub of the Great Basin, and desert scrub) covers about 7,300,000 acres or 7 percent of California's land. The largest continuous acreages can be seen on one high-altitude flight from San Luis Obispo County to San Diego County and on into Baja California. Suppose the route to be along the axes of the Coast, Transverse, and Peninsular ranges. Darker patches and mottlings of coniferous forest and woodland appear on high

Chaparral often rises from the ashes of fire in forest, woodland, or chaparral areas. Sprouting from their own stumps or "crowns" is the secret of regeneration for many chaparral species. This happened in Santa Barbara County, California.

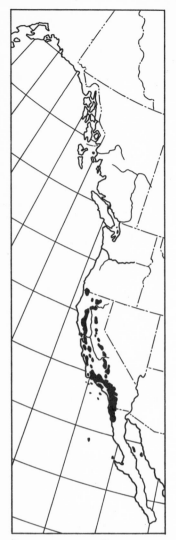

northern exposures, flats, canyonsides, dry slopes, and other upland areas. In lower canyons and intermountain valleys, oaks might be dumped or widely dotted over the grasslands. Slopes between, moderate to very steep, would seem to be carpeted with a gray-green to olive-colored pile, folded sharply over ridges and down into treeless canyons and gullies.

Nowhere but in Southern, and adjacent Baja, California are there such seemingly endless "mountains" of this particular plant cover. This is truly "chaparral country." Chaparral abounds from the Santa Lucias, southward past the Sierra Madre, San Rafael, and Santa Ynez mountains to Santa Barbara, and then across the Transverse Range of the Santa Monicas. The mountains fringing the San Fernando Valley still can claim chaparral cover between areas of human development, as can the rugged San Gabriel Range and San Bernardino Mountains, south of which the desert supports scrub plants, not chaparral. In those areas not relegated to desert scrub, chaparral shares the rugged terrain with oak, pine, big-cone spruce, and other growth of this arid region, far down into northern Baja California.

IF WE COULD go back some seventy-five million years, we would find this area part of a continent-wide lowland tropical forest. Among the broadleaf trees we would recognize the evergreen avocado, fig, and cinnamon of the spicy bark. It was warm then, the year around, with rainfall eighty inches or more. There was no desert in the Southwest. A sea of fog extended clear across to the East, and northward to Oregon. So it was until, about sixty million years ago,

a new long-range climate trend set in to change the picture. As it grew cooler and drier, conifers moved down from the temperate north—the redwoods, for instance, ultimately pushed even beyond the Santa Barbara coast. Meanwhile Southern California's future high mountains were rising.

Dryness continued to increase. In time it reversed the southward tide of the cool-moist-temperate coniferous forest, just as it had helped to doom the broadleaf tropical forest. Two different vegetation types, new to the Southwest region, were the forests' far-flung successors. The first was a grassland, spreading gradually over much of California and reaching its distant high tide on the Great Plains. The other was a small tree and shrub mixture, forerunner both of today's chaparral and of the leathery-leaved woodland so widely associated with it.

This mixture took ground inland from east of the Cascades all the way to northern Baja California. In the past 15 million years or so, there has been a sorting and regrouping of its components to form the modern communities. During this time the land became still more arid as summer rains ceased. Climate shifted to the Mediterranean pattern enjoyed today. As the Coast, Transverse, and Peninsular ranges rose in the southland, they attracted summer drought-tolerant conifers to their cooler and moister uplands, while the broad-leaved dry woodlands assembled in the next belt below. Grasses took over the drier coastal prairies and valleys. Most arid of all were the deserts, inland to the east, in the rain shadow of the mountains. There the most drought-tolerant vegetation developed: creosote bush and other types of desert scrub, cacti, and various herbaceous annuals.

Between these southland extremes of relatively cool and moist uplands and dry lowlands, there was the broad middle range of lower mountain slope and foothill crest. Chaparral claimed it.

Chaparral has come to represent the great norm of the coastal Southwest, holding the wide mid-band of the climate spectrum. At upper and lower limits it readily gives or takes ground as conditions fluctuate. Thus as the climate became cooler and rainier for long spells in successive Pleistocene ice ages, chaparral yielded to forest along its upper edges but gained on the grassland below. In the 12,000 years since the last great glaciation and its retreat, the climate has

Chamise: the most widespread of the
chaparral shrubs, extending from Baja
to about a hundred miles north of
San Francisco. The bushes in the
photo are six feet high.

Silktassel: a chaparral shrub with
tassels six inches in length. This and
related species are found on dry slopes
and ridges from Baja to southern Washington,
and bloom from February to April.

Manzanita: a Northern California species,
in bloom from January to March. The name
manzanita is applied to dozens of species and
varieties of the genus, represented in the
Pacific coastlands from Baja to the Arctic.

Western peony: a flower, two inches
across, which blooms from May to July.
Widespread over the West, it is one
of the few herbs to be found growing
beneath chaparral shrubs.

203

grown much drier. We are now in the driest period ever, by the evidence of geology and the fossil record of plant successions. Consequently the total area of chaparral is less now than it was in a recent past time. The trend is to still greater aridity. If it continues. chaparral is going to take over more yellow pine and upper woodland area, while giving way to grasses and coastal sage on the south and desert scrub inland. Because there is less land toward the top of the pyramid there will be a net loss for chaparral.

Two other factors have played decisive roles in the evolution and ecology of chaparral: soil and fire. It is an ecological truism that "things live where they do because they can." The condition of scant or poor soil, or both, exists in nature. Plants of some kind or other were certain to adapt to "poverty row" and make a living there, within the means afforded, by remaining small, while non-adapting types failed. On typical chaparral land, slope, rockiness, and occasional scouring downpours conspire to keep soil to the bone. Extreme summer drought and heat make a short-fuse certainty of fire by lightning or any other means of combustion. Chaparral country has been for thousands of years fire-climax vegetation country. Again, chaparral is one of the types that has adapted to periodic burning, some species regenerating through sprouting from charred stumps, others by seeds requiring heat to crack and germinate.

CHAPARRAL is a composite of many different species assembled from widely diverse plant families. Together they form a kind of fluid organism that masters every facet of its chosen environment by moving in and holding ground with the components best suited to the local situation. A look at some of the individual species will bear out this notion.

Chamise — A member of the rose family, this is the most abundant and widespread chaparral species, and best adapted to arid conditions. Though woody at the base, it branches up less stiffly than other chaparral types, and its pale gray-green leaves cluster short and needle-like around the stems. From February to July it adorns itself with large showy white flowers. Chamise predominates on the lower and drier lands, where stands of it form an uncommonly open chaparral, sometimes leaving half the ground surface of an area exposed—response to almost desert dryness. On the north end of its range, near the Oregon border, chamise is found only in small stands, mixed with other chaparral species. Through central California, it is commonly seen sharing mountainous acres equally with broad-leaved shrubs, and even dominating the area on dry, inland-facing slopes. In the south, from the rugged Ventura County ranges into Baja, chamise is the predominant native plant.

Scrub oak — In contrast to chamise, no chaparral species forms denser, more diabolically impenetrable thickets than the evergreen California scrub oak. It sends its short, rigid branches and brittle, prickly leaves in all directions, quite effectively barring human passage. A number of other shrub-forming oaks are variously distributed through the chaparral regions.

Manzanita — One of the most widespread and best-loved chaparral groups, belonging to the heather family, manzanita often forms compact mats covering the ground, or shrub gardens around large rocks. Some species grow to small-tree size, more than twenty feet high, making little forests in open flats. Their bark is smooth, dark red-brown, contrasting with the pale silver of dead branches and rich green of their leaves. Spring-flowering, the shrubs are often covered with waxy little white or pink blossoms, later with nutlets. Manzanitas are found on coastal dunes, in foothills, and high in the mountains.

Ceanothus — A member of the buckthorn family, the ceanothus is the most beautiful in bloom. Varying in different species from a foot-high ground mat to small trees twenty-five feet or more high, this shrub is resplendent in spring and early summer when its spikes of densely clustered tiny flowers may cover a whole hillside with blue—annual glory of California's chaparral. Others in this family are the coffeeberry and the buckthorn, known medicinally as cascara sagrada, a small tree of moister places in the North Coast Range and Sierra Nevada foothills.

Chaparral-pea — In May and June, this contributes to the color parade with typical wing-and-keel blossoms of rose-purple.

Chaparral-pea: of the pea family, this blooms in May and June from San Diego County to the Coast Ranges of Northern California.

Buckbrush: the showiest of the widespread chaparral shrubs in bloom, with white, pale blue, or deep blue flowers from February to May, from Baja to Oregon. Commonly called ceanothus, and a member of the buckthorn family.

Fremontia: also called flannel bush; sports bright yellow flowers from April to June in the inner Coast Ranges and Sierra foothills of California.

Clematis, or virgin's bower: a woody climber, part of the buttercup family, throwing blankets of cream-yellow blossoms over chaparral shrubs and even into trees, on canyonsides in the Coast Ranges from Northern California to Baja, and in the Sierra foothills.

Several plant communities form the vegetation mosaic so characteristic of open coastland slopes. In this scene of the Point Reyes National Seashore, one may see mixed evergreen woodland along the ridges and deep in canyons; chaparral adjacent to it, especially on the higher slopes and steeper canyonsides; grassland on the flatter midlevel areas; and coastal scrub covering most of the rest, including the foreground slope. This is an area well watered by winter rain and summer fog.

Lupines — Although associated more with coastal and sagebrush scrub, woodlands, dry forests, and grasslands, some of the lupines invade chaparral, their unmistakable pea-flowers often colored with magenta, violet and blue, or blue and white tones.

Returning to the rose family, among the most attractive chaparral shrubs are mountain mahogany; creambush or ocean spray, with tiny cream-white flowers clustered on many-branched panicles; and the white-flowering western choke cherry and holly-leaved cherry, or islay.

Chaparral flowers, when it does, with energy stored up from a short early-spring growth period. Its environment is harsh for plant growth in a normal year, especially in the southern region. In winter, rains moisten the ground, but the cold inhibits growth. In summer, temperatures are fine, but without rain the soil dries out and plants go into a dormant state. By adaptation, chaparral species can survive through exceptionally dry years, with growth and flowering almost nil. Just as individual chaparral plants respond in this way to extremes of drought, so the chaparral association has adjusted to the dry southern end of its range by reducing the number of species there and the density of the formation.

To LOOK for birds and animals in the apparently deserted chaparral is a challenge, but the quest can be rewarding. Who has not flushed a covey of quail on a grassy hillside, meadow edge, or dusty road, to see it whirr and melt into the bordering brush? Or traced a particular sequence of musical notes to a sickle-billed, long-tailed brown bird posing erect in a manzanita top?

The brown California thrasher, like the Costa hummingbird, the wren-tit and the Anna, is most at

The manzanitas are among the most easily recognized chaparral shrubs, with their smooth, skin-like reddish mahogany bark, and often with parts of limbs dead, barkless, and silvery gray — a handsome combination.

Coastal scrub, sometimes called "soft chaparral," is a common element of the vegetation mosaic between the coastal strand and the higher chaparral or woodland slopes. The coast sagebrush is frequently found in this association, from Monterey to Humboldt County, California.

home in chaparral or desert scrub. The green-tailed towhee has only one second choice—sagebrush. Bewick's wren is a chaparral and brush resident of wider range over the West, and so are the fox sparrow and others of the sparrow, finch, grosbeak, and bunting family. With an assortment of other hummingbirds, flycatchers, gnatcatchers, warblers, a vireo, brown and spotted towhees, scrub jay (when not in its preferred oak woodland situation), and mountain quail in the higher range, the "barren" chaparral can be bustling in nesting season and at the livelier times of day.

The forty or fifty surviving California condors sail out from their rock ledges and cliff caves to forage widely over hill and valley grasslands and also over great chaparral areas. Chaparral is not neglected by the turkey vulture, either, in its endless watch for carrion; nor by such predators as golden eagle and red-tailed hawk, although more open country—savanna, oak woodland, grassland—offers more to the soaring vision. Even the horned owl does some of its hunting in chaparral, though more by chance than by choice.

Many small mammals, especially rodents, find brushy places most to their liking for living, forage, and protection from skyborne or foot-pad assailants. Such small things as chipmunks, pocket mice, kangaroo mice and rats, brush mice, dusky-footed and desert wood rats, and brush rabbits find the "elfin forest" nicely scaled to their size, and its density gives good cover, at least from winged and larger four-footed predators. With their large numbers the rodents handily support sizable populations of gopher snakes and rattlesnakes, which are perfectly designed to penetrate the tightest little hideouts. Other snakes and a variety of lizards also frequent the chaparral.

The birds, mammals, and reptiles who spend most of their wild lives in and about the chaparral do so with no great visible effect upon the brushlands— all but one: the deer. Wherever there are deer, the shrubs display a familiar "browse line," made by deer cropping leaves and soft outer twigs of their favorite forage. The large mule deer and its smaller cousin the black-tailed deer are animals of the forest, but they roam to the brushland edge zones. There, in stands of manzanita, ceanothus, and other larger

chaparral species, the browse line is a common sight, five feet or so above the ground, as even as though cut with hedge shears and a calculating human eye. During the middle hours of a sunny day, when the overhanging unbrowsed branches shade everything below, this "topiary" line is startlingly prominent.

WHEN WHITE SETTLERS reached and took these coastlands, man and his domestic grazing stock became the animals most affected by chaparral and making the greatest impact upon it. For perhaps thousands of years the Indians sporadically burned the brushlands to drive game into the open. But they added little to the age-old effect of frequent lightning fires. Only in our time has fire been purposefully used in the management of these lands—as land. Cattle and sheep growers have burned the brush in the hope of increasing their acres of grasslands. This has worked sometimes, where the soil was good, and sufficient for grass. Sometimes the effort has "backfired," however, stimulating the increase of chaparral through its crown-sprouting regeneration and the heat-cracking of its seeds. The ecology of chaparral is a thing of natural balances that are easily upset.

Chaparral, and brushlands generally, present complex problems and controversial questions to all who live in the regions they dominate. At first problems chiefly involved the range; but now there are also questions of water supply, recreation, aesthetics, and mere everyday living, wherever—as in Southern California—large and growing numbers of people, not cattle, are taking over the chaparral country.

Answers to the questions and solutions to the problems can be found only in the course of objective, long-range ecological studies. It is now imperative, for example, that communities make intelligent decisions about the control of fire in chaparral, which is tinder-dry most of the year. They must learn all the facts about chaparral, grasses, and forest, to know the values of each for many potential uses—such as watershed protective cover—depending on slope, soil, climate, and other conditions.

Despite wholesale changes man is bound to make, wisely or unwisely, in this environment, chaparral and its special kind of landscape—for many of us a desirable, peculiarly beautiful landscape—will exist as long as we do, perhaps much longer.

*The elephant tree belongs to a large family
that includes poison ivy and the cashew nut.*

*San Ignacio is one of desert Baja's most important oases; it grew
around Mission San Ignacio de Kadakaaman and its lush gardens.
The little valley is filled with a sea of date palms.*

The cirio is probably best known to Baja visitors as the "boojum tree," a name out of Lewis Carroll's fanciful and humorous poem, "The Hunting of the Snark." To the aboriginal Cochimí of Baja it was "milapá". To botanists it is Idria columnaris, and a relative of the ocotillo. It ranges throughout central Baja from El Rosario south to Calmallí, except along the coasts and in the high eastern mountains.

A rock garden seemingly designed by a sculptor of animal forms, in the northern part of the Vizcaíno Desert, between El Mármol and Rancho Chapala. Cardón, cirio, and ocotillo all appear against the sky. The yellow flowering shrubs are of the aster family.

Another view in the same area is filled, to the left, with tall spiny yuccas (native to Baja only); next are cirio, ocotillo, and cardón. The upper picture shows clearly the wide spacing of desert plants, each shrub staking out its claim to whatever moisture there may be.

*How Baja ends: Cabo San Lucas. "When we rounded the
uttermost austral rocks of the peninsula," William Beebe
wrote in Zaca Venture, "we found them abounding in*

superlative attributes. The early Spaniards called them Los Frailes [the Friars] . . . . As we approached and encircled them they shifted and altered like moving, living creatures. A herd of monstrous, prehistoric reptilian dragons with scales of iridescent gray would have been only a parody on these great granites."

Baja begins, in the north, with great mountains: first, Sierra Juárez, then Sierra San Pedro Mártir, with the peninsula's highest summit, El Picacho del Diablo, 10,100 feet in elevation. Beyond the jumbled granite pile, which plunges steeply down to the east, one sees the coastal lowlands along the Sea of Cortés.

CHAPTER 22

DESERTS BY THE SEA

*The bare-bones life in Baja's coastal desolation
and a tropical finale in the lush Cape region.*

EL DESIERTO DE SEBASTIÁN VIZCAÍNO—the Vizcaíno Desert on most of our maps—has no precise geographic limits agreeable to everyone (not surprising since no two maps of Baja coincide in very many respects). The name generally refers to that lowland midsection where the peninsula reaches its greatest width in a westward-jutting hook. On the south it blends into the Magdalena Plains, a similar desert area where Baja again bulges west, toward Bahía Magdalena. Biologists recognize this region as part of a still greater and ecologically fascinating realm of aridity—the Sonoran Desert, a great horseshoe of hot, dry land around the Gulf of California.

Disregarding cities, "stop" or "*alto*" signs, and other evidence of human ecological development, with their frequently nationalistic overtones, a traveler could go from Southern California deep into Baja with little sense of change. Indeed, the five-hundred-mile sweep of coastland from Santa Barbara to El Rosario, two hundred miles south of the border, is uniform enough in climate, topography, soil, and other characteristics to be considered a single biotic entity. Zoologists call it a "faunal district," but it is marked by distinctive plant life as well. Sage scrub and tall agaves on terraces and low hills; a few sycamores in gravelly bottoms, with elderberry, willow, cottonwood, and oak appearing higher inland before the rise to airy pine forest under the summits—the pattern is consistent from the Santa Ynez to the San Pedro Mártir. In the southern part of this district, one senses the desert's approach as a scattering of prickly pear becomes a horde of cholla, with increasing numbers of the hook-spined, barrel-type cacti, *bisnaga* and others. When change comes, it comes quickly—across an arroyo, over a hill—life's response to changes in topography and climate.

Facing the coast, the Peninsular Ranges capture the modest flow of moist Pacific air in their latitudes, putting the low trough from the Salton Sink to the gulf in a rain shadow to the east. The westward slope is watered well enough to make it a "desert-chaparral transition region." The plants here are largely northern in their affinities. Where those ranges end, however, in the southward drop-off of Sierra San Pedro Mártir, a gap opens wide to the weather. Ocean winds sweep unchecked across the peninsula. Some of the moisture they bear reaches the Sierra Madre Occidental on the Sonoran Desert's southeast, but much is dissipated in the upsurge of hot air from the broad desert trough itself. In this region, ocean air is sucked into a continental climate system, and its beneficence to the coastal belt is largely lost. On the windward Pacific side, in fact, the effect of strong and virtually constant onshore winds is an extremely sparse and stunted vegetation. A paradox meets the eye along this coast, through about three hundred fifty miles from Bahía del Rosario south to Punta Pequeña: the curious sight of bushes, cactus plants, and even the rock outcrops from a bone-dry ground, all festooned with lichen and a ball moss. These rootless hangers-on thrive in the foggy humidity of the same sea winds that desiccate the plants which give them anchorage.

Sometimes a little winter rain falls, but any given

The graceful flower spikes of the succulent Dudleya, *here in bud, in the foothills
of Sierra San Pedro Mártir, are a modest introduction to the strange and
marvelous desert plants awaiting the traveler on Baja's southward road.*

217

inland spot in Baja's desert region may not see a drop for years on end. When it comes, it is not a general rain but a local deluge. From mid-July to mid-October especially, the meeting of moist ocean air with hot, turbulent updrafts over the highlands of the eastern peninsular rim generates towering thunderheads. Baja cloudbursts, like those in the American Southwest, may be sudden, destructive, and dangerous. A pinpoint area may be devastated by the initial impact; and a swath of instant calamity may follow a wall of floodwater down a winding arroyo, under a cloudless sky. The traveler camping or lingering in such an arroyo, and thinking less about rain than anything under the sun, can be caught and swept away with no more warning than an eerie rumble from around the bend. Wise explorers of central Baja cross arroyos quickly and limit their interior travel as far as possible to the seasons between late fall and early summer.

In the strike area, such a storm does great damage to land and life. Gentle rain soaks into the soil and nourishes roots, but even a short-lived torrent slashes and sweeps away soil, roots, plants, and all. The only benefit comes elsewhere, in the ultimate deposit of silt on some distant outwash plain to support an arid-land agriculture, or in the replenishment of subsurface water in those few broad-cut arroyos that are the true oases of this desert. If storms had never struck the Volcanes de las Tres Vírgines, Cerro Santiago, or other highlands of this drainage basin, the Jesuit padres could never have started the lush tropical gardens in the great arroyo at Misión San Ignacio de Kadakaaman. But thanks to springs in the bottom upstream and a water table to sustain wells, San Ignacio, today a town of a thousand souls, sits amid vineyards and groves of olives, figs, oranges, pomegranates, bananas, and the date palms for which this valley is famous. When on rare occasions a flood sweeps down the Río San Ignacio, it does little damage to a bottomland so generously interlaced with thousands of tree-size root systems.

Baja's heart is called desert, and it is indeed a sun-seared and largely rainless land. Yet, as the veteran naturalist of the California deserts, Dr. Edmund C. Jaeger, has written:

. . . under these severe conditions there has developed, particularly in this [Vizcaíno-Magdalena] desert, a much specialized and unexpectedly abundant flora which has given to the landscape a strange and often bizarre appearance. The visitor, finding himself suddenly in the midst of so many unfamiliar plant forms, . . . can almost imagine [he has] been transferred to another planet. This odd flora is one of the world's richest and most extraordinary assemblages of plants.

THAT "OTHER PLANET" feeling strikes the southbound traveler as he first leaves the coast road to cross Río del Rosario and take up the rugged eastward track to El Mármol. It is intensified by two tall vegetable apparitions: *cirio* and *cardón*. Trees the cirios surely are not, but what else in the plant world that is not a cardón can stand forty or sixty feet high and not be a tree?

What indeed but a "boojum tree." This anomaly is perfectly designed to prepare the traveler for entry into a strange new world of nature. (It is named out of Lewis Carroll by desert explorer Godfrey Sykes; the Mexicans call it "cirio" because it is like the "wax candle" of votive uses.) And the giant cardón reminds him, especially if he is acquainted with Arizona's giant saguaro, that what lies ahead is a desert of deserts. Rising up to sixty feet and weighing up to ten tons, cardón is the giant among giant cacti.

After passing those two gatekeepers of the peninsular heartland, one should be ready for every strangeness ahead. One such is the elephant tree, *torote* to the Mexicans, encountered at the inland point where one turns southward toward the Vizcaíno borderland. From a short and fat trunk, wildly contorted, swollen-looking limbs reach out and up, then ravel into ragged mops of quickly tapering little branches. The small compound leaves unfold to bright green maturity only after drenching showers. They soon fall, reducing water loss by transpiration, to be followed by showy flower panicles—peach-pink clouds of bloom that, in mass, set the desert aflame from miles away. But the sight is as rare as the rain.

From the northern part of the Vizcaíno all the way to the Cape, the peninsular tree yucca *datilla*, a close relative of California's famed Joshua tree, is an abundant landscape feature. Veritable forests of this grotesque yet beautiful plant are often interspersed with the contrasting spires of cirio and organ pipe cactus. Agave, ocotillo, and another of the organ pipe

Clam diggers work in shallow water on the ocean side of the San Quintín Peninsula. The clams are about four inches across and resemble Pismo clams.

group, the *pitahaya agria,* which provides Baja's choicest cactus fruit, bring variety to the assemblage thriving in the deep soils of the valley bottoms.

The *guayacán,* a relative of the creosote bush, that most characteristic shrub of our desert Southwest, is an evergreen shrub similarly widespread over the desert of Baja and western Sonora. Stout-branched but compactly rounded, it grows to twenty feet in height among other plants of the dry-wash edges. Guayacán is conspicuous for its large fruit capsules and a strong odor which some consider pleasant.

The rough wheel-tracks into Baja's desert heartland open to the adventurous a wonderful variety of terrain, habitat, and view. One's eyes shift from boldly sweeping distance to rich roadside detail and back again.

The five- to six-hundred mile Vizcaíno-Magdalena segment of Baja's granitic spine is ribbed and flanked with alluvial interior and sand-blown coastal valleys; outwash plains; ocean-facing lagoons, salt-pans, dunes, offshore islands; granite hills, volcanic mesas and plateaus, recent cinder cones and lava flows; rugged but not high mountain ridges; low playas, or dry lake beds; and a complex drainage pattern of barrancas, arroyos, large and small erosion channels, crosscutting the whole in every direction. Soils vary a great deal from place to place: fine volcanic clays in local pockets, gravelly material on outwash plains, alkaline clay of broad western lowlands; and there are beach sands blown inward from ocean shores. The larger topographic features and their local surface manifestations are groundwork for an intricate mosaic of life.

The kaleidoscope of impressions—astonishment, delight, bewilderment, perhaps satiety near the end of a long, hot, dusty day, leaves the traveler with more questions than answers. Why, for instance, are some plants incredibly abundant in certain areas yet totally absent from others? Where climate difference is not the obvious answer, one must look to soil, water, exposure, and so on through the ecological gamut. Baja is still, as Joseph Wood Krutch said in *The Forgotten Peninsula,* "a land where new discoveries can be made." Anyone with open eyes and a little curiosity can play the discovery game.

After crossing the line from Estado de Baja Cali-

The honey mesquite provides nectar for bees,
and beans which the Indians grind into meal.
A desert bush or small tree, it grows where
its long roots can reach underground water.

The night-blooming sour pitahaya is found with
its petals beginning to fade soon after sunrise.
Indians use the fruit for a jelly. This was
photographed near La Paz, Baja California.

A late spring to early summer resident of the
coastal foothills, the matilija (ma-til-i-hah)
poppy whitens large areas with its bloom, from
northern Baja California to Santa Barbara.

The yucca, blooming in late February in the peninsular
foothills between El Rosario and El Marmol, is
distinguished from the familiar yucca of Southern
California by its gray instead of gray-green leaves.

*One of Baja's unique trees is the blue palm, which the Spanish call
palma cenisa. Photographed in the north fork of Arroyo San Francisquito,
near the site of the Misión Santa María in the Vizcaíno Desert.*

fornia to Territorio del Sur, one can go westward into the vast Vizcaíno Desert plain, and on to that deep-thrust inlet, Laguna Ojo de Liebre (Scammons Lagoon) which is breeding ground for the "desert whale," the California gray. Or if he would like to experience the ultimate desert, a swing to Laguna Guerrero Negro will lead to coastal sand dunes and outstretched, lifeless salt flats.

Inland, reaching toward the south between the ocean and the tableland that rises to the peninsula's eastern sierra, a monotonous flatness expands to the horizon, broken only by widely spaced yuccas, with an occasional giant cardón. Between the weird plants the ground is bare, unless it has rained; then primroses, sand verbenas, and other flowering things spring up for their brief day.

When the road finally reaches the Magdalena Plains, south from La Purísima on one branch, from Comondú on another, it begins ninety miles of good sand track—the longest straightaway on the peninsula. Here is the same horizon-bound flatland as farther north, but nature does not repeat entirely. Now cardón is king, with yucca the infrequent interloper. Should one look, however, for the perfect symbol of the Magdalena region, as the boojum is of the Vizcaíno, he would find it in the "creeping devil." Krutch's description can hardly be improved:

Near Santo Domingo, only ten or fifteen miles from the ocean, we came upon a large patch of exceedingly curious cactus which grows only on this particular desert . . . *Machaerocereus eruca* the botanists call it or, when they descend to the vernacular, "creeping devil" and "caterpillar cactus"—either of which name is vividly descriptive. It is a creeping devil because the trunks covered with ferocious spines and larger than a man's arm lie prostrate on the ground and creep forward as they grow to make huge mats over which it would be almost impossible to walk. It is also a caterpillar cactus because it has the odd habit of rising here and there a few inches above the sand like a measuring worm, then arching down again. Where it touches the earth it sends out new roots and as the strange plant makes its strange progress the oldest extremity often dies off progressively as the other extremity advances. Apparently its combination of odd habits enables it to live in an area so nearly absolute desert that few other organisms can survive there and it is a strong contender for

second place (after the boojum, of course) in the hierarchy of vegetable queernesses in Baja.

THE CAPE REGION was an island once, and an island of tropical luxuriance it remains, compared to the land of boojum and creeping devil. Paved road signals the coming change even before Bahía de la Paz flashes into view around the final southward toehold of the Giantess. Here at Baja's narrowest point, its peninsular backbone appears to be broken, with no visible topographic connection or unseen geological relationship between the Sierra de la Giganta and the Cape's Sierra de la Victoria. For relatedness, one must look far to the north, for this sierra is a block of the same granitic batholith that forms San Pedro Mártir. What lies between is the outcome of another geological story.

The physiographic separateness of the Cape massif is coupled with, but not the single cause of, ecological change. Elevation and climate also play a part. The sierra, lying athwart the weather, is a mountain range complete with its rain shadow. The eastward bulge of the peninsular tip, ending at Cabo Pulmo and Los Frailes, is the final portion of the Gulf Coast Desert.

Baja's desert dies hard. It approaches its end in a mighty outpouring of its own kinds of life, the xeric vegetation crescendoing in miles of almost impenetrable thorn scrub, and thickets of nearly every spined and thorny thing the desert grows.

But trails, roads, and water courses do cut through, and there is a different country to be reached, a highland, woodland country. Other garden places—San Ignacio with its date palms, Magdalena Bay with its mangrove-jungled shores—are merely islands in the desert, oases on the way to somewhere else. The Cape is the climax. With a rainfall similar to Los Angeles's, it lays the desert to rest under plantations of bananas and mangoes, papayas and sugar cane, tomatoes and other fruits and vegetables.

La Victoria is victor, finally, over the desert below. It is meadow and forest—an echo, at least, of its geological kin, San Pedro Mártir, eight hundred miles to the north. Palms fill canyons on the way up the mountain. The highland meadows are large; there are three kinds of oak and a pine—a piñon larger than any on the northern desert borders. On La Victoria one knows the desert trip is ended.

Ruins of Misión San Francisco de Borja. The first adobe chapel was built by the Jesuits in 1795. The entrance to the stone building pictured was built by the Dominicans in 1801.

PART FOUR:

BARRIER
AND BREACH

*The eternal barrier of rock and mountain, and the
incontestible breaching power of wind-driven waves:
these are the antagonists in the timeless standoff along
the continent's edge, and neither can overcome.*

225

CHAPTER 23

THE UPRAISED RIM

*Mountains of the Pacific Coast—their characteristics,
geological history, and significance for man today.*

PACIFIC COAST MOUNTAINS more than hold their own in global comparisons of the edges of the continents. South America is the only other continent entirely rimmed along one side by superlative mountains. But for the most part, the Andes are fronted on the Pacific by a gently sloping coastal plain, until they break up in the islands and fiords of southern Chile. No other continent plunges so abruptly into the ocean as North America, along so great a length of coastland. The western edge, from the Aleutians to Central America, is a virtually unbroken chain of mountains.

The Alaska, Chugach-Kenai, St. Elias, Fairweather, and other ranges of Alaska's gulf coast; the Olympics of Washington; the Coast Ranges of Oregon and California, including the Klamath complex, King Range, Santa Lucias, the Transverse Ranges, and the San Jacinto massif—all these must appear on any roster of our Pacific coastal mountains. The Cascades and Sierra Nevada also have marginal relevance to this coastline. Ranges and peaks of the Alaskan gulf coast are the highest land borders anywhere on earth. But even the lesser ranges to the south are towering when confronted from the sea, a seemingly unbreachable wall guarding the continent.

The coast's mountains are extremely diverse in geological origins, structure, surface appearance, and the environments available for life. Crustal forces are responsible for the composition and gross forms of mountains. Climate, with changes rung through forty degrees of latitude, determines the kind of erosion—glacial, stream, wind—that detail their sur-face features. It is climate, too, that gives mountain faces their final character: it may crystal them with ice, clothe them softly with green, or strip them to bare earth-bone.

All factors, climate especially, combine to form the many habitats mountains offer to living things. It may be crags for Alaska's Dall sheep and mountain goats; moist lower slopes for Sitka spruce or redwood; snow-fed rivers and lakes for spawning salmon; dark, wet ground on the seaward side for northern rain forests; bold, sunny faces for southland chaparral. Every facet of these coastal mountains reflects a pattern of life, even if only lichen crusting a granite wall—or merely the promise of something to come with change.

Great changes in climate and the earth's crust gave the continent its upraised Pacific rim. Everything in the earth's repertoire of mountain building and leveling forces was brought to bear: vast deposition of sediments; crustal deformation such as folding and faulting, uplifting and downwarping; intrusion of molten magma beneath or between layers; volcanic eruption; glaciation and all forms of weathering in response to shifting climate patterns and land-sea relationships. We have already become familiar with most of these forces as they have shaped the major features of the long coastline which lies so largely at the feet of mountains. Our study of processes and their effects now reaches to the mountains themselves; some understanding of how they were formed will widen our appreciation of the coast's landscapes.

We are concerned here chiefly with mountains

*The barrier almost breached: ironically, Turnagain Arm of Cook Inlet, where Captain Cook
was defeated in his search for a northwest passage, knifes through the Kenai-Chugach Mountains.
A little deeper gouging by some glacier, and the Kenai Peninsula would have been an island.*

facing the shoreline, while we keep in mind that the outer and inner chains are closely related in the story of continent-building—sometimes joined either physically or by a common geological origin. The story takes us through far-reaching realms which overlap in both time and geographic area. The history of these mountains lies embedded in their own rocks, in the deposits of their valleys, and in the sediments covering the floor of the adjacent Pacific Ocean. Though most of it is lost to us or not yet read, we do know for certain that mountain and sea have changed places here in the past and will do so again.

Sometime in the Mesozoic era, 150 million years ago, the large continental borderland pattern of alternating troughs and mountain belts was evident, but offset from its present position.

Let us look at the extent of these Nevadan batholiths on the map, and consider their import for the Pacific Coast. At the tip of Baja, the Nevadan rocks form the cape region massif and the backbone of the peninsula's northern half, climaxing with the Sierra San Pedro Mártir. They continue in the Peninsular Ranges of Southern California. From the Sierra Nevada they skip northwestward to emerge again in the Klamaths. But it is in British Columbia's Coast Range that the Nevadan system comes truly into its own. The batholithic complex in its thousand-mile northern arc is one of the greatest of its kind on earth. Another point of interest is how the Nevadan system switches from the outer to the inner of our parallel ranges and back again, ending finally on the inner prong of the far north.

What of the gaps unfilled by Nevadan granitics— the Coast Ranges of California, Oregon-Washington, and Alaska? As vast intrusions of molten magma forced the overlying beds higher along eastern California, these washed away to reveal the sun-reflecting granitic rock of the future Sierra Nevada, and washed down on the western side to become part of the material of the future Coast Ranges. It is interesting to ponder that some of the rock of California's mountains along the sea was once rock of mountains standing between the Sierra and the Rockies. The rise of these ranges that began before the end of the Mesozoic era is, in fact, still going on. The Mesozoic sea ebbed away, and its shrunken trough became the great Central Valley of rich alluvial soils that is Califor-

nia's world-renowned agricultural heartland today.

It would take a whole book to recount in detail the building of those small but many-faceted mountains —the Transverse Ranges, Santa Lucias, Northern Coast Ranges, and their numerous extensions and satellites, including the Channel Islands. Theirs has not been a single or uniform rise. Uplift, downwarping, and reinvasion of the sea have followed each other in some areas, as we have seen in San Francisco Bay; major faults—notably the San Andreas— have also played a part in the shifting about of building blocks. Volcanoes have flared up and died down; under various crustal pressures rocks have changed form many times over. These mountains are very much alive!

The Klamath Mountains form a rugged and massive link between the coastal ranges and the inner belt of the Sierra Nevada–Cascades. To the north, the topography of the Oregon-Washington Pacific borderline—coast range, valley trough, higher but parallel inner range—is similar enough to that south of the Klamaths to suggest a comparable history, but such is not the case. We read in the rocks of later origins and a greater role of volcanism. One similarity does appear: coastal and inland events are definitely connected.

Noting from the map that Nevadan mountain-building takes a wide swing eastward from the Klamaths to Idaho and back to the British Columbia Coast Range, we see an intriguing possibility. One geologist has speculated: "Could the western edge of the Nevadan arc have formed the continental border until late in Mesozoic time . . . ? If so, the recess was made continental later by filling with sediments and volcanics, and the coast was straightened by growth of a new set of volcanic structures along the Cascade Range."

What we find in the upraised Coast Range and a hundred miles inland, from north of the Klamaths to the Olympic Peninsula, is a deep interbedding of Cenozoic marine sediments and lava flows. The basalt was mostly erupted onto the sea floor, as its "pillow" structure shows; it is the material of the crust beneath the ocean. In some places the outpouring rose above the sea and was weathered. Non-volcanic layers are composed of erosion detritus, their structure showing that they were laid down in deep water.

A portion of the San Andreas Fault near San Francisco Bay, as seen through the medium of radar image, stripped of vegetation, with only hard geological and man-made structures showing. The most prominent, continuous, and almost straight line from left to right is the main fault rift, which runs northwest-southeast. The black portions of the rift, center, and to the left below the big **X** of San Francisco International Airport, are a chain of lakes which serve the city as storage reservoirs. The short white line to the right is Stanford University's linear accelerator, about two miles long. The fault crosses the coastline diagonally and goes under the ocean off the Golden Gate, reappears in a trench from Bolinas Lagoon to Tomales Bay and, generally following the coastline, crosses the Mendocino Fracture Zone and heads into the sea. On its southeastward course, out of this picture to the right, the rift is clearly traceable all the way to the Gulf of California.

A modern perspective on a historic landfall. The King Range, with Cape Mendocino just out of the picture to the left, and grassy Point Delgada in the center were the landfall target of easting Manila Galleons. After crossing from the Philippines, the ships turned here and coasted — always in danger of being blown onshore — to Cabo San Lucas and on to Acapulco.

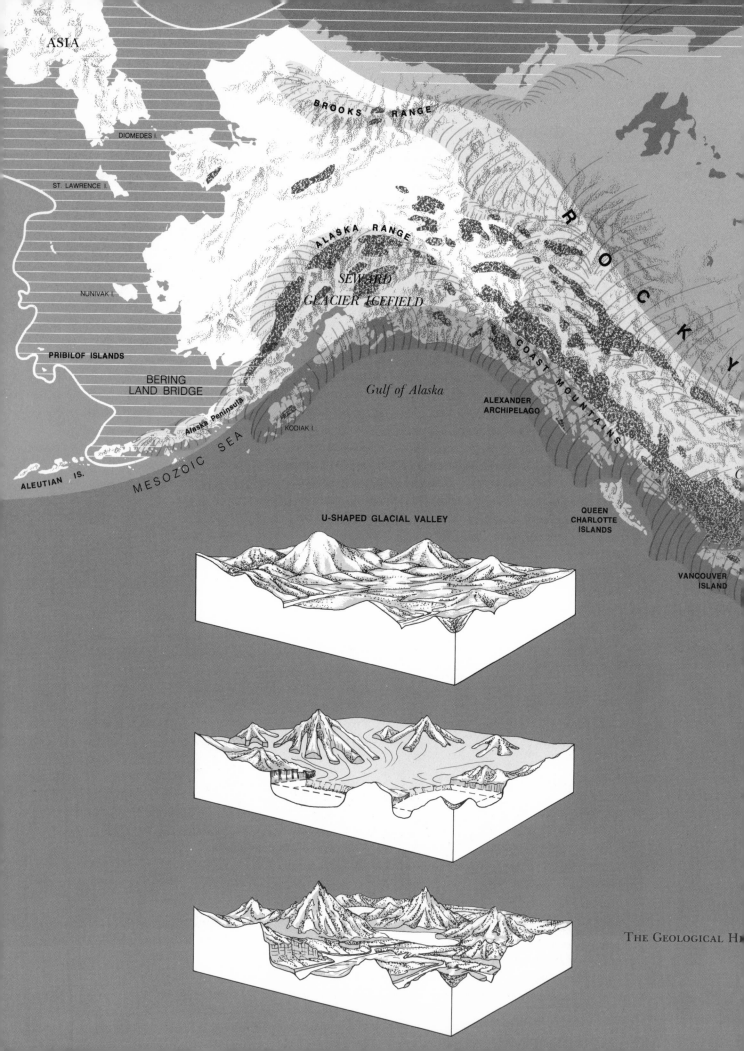

ASIA

DIOMEDES I.

ST. LAWRENCE I.

NUNIVAK I.

PRIBILOF ISLANDS

BERING
LAND BRIDGE

ALEUTIAN IS.

Aleska Peninsula

KODIAK I.

MESOZOIC SEA

BROOKS RANGE

ALASKA RANGE

SEWARD
GLACIER ICEFIELD

Gulf of Alaska

ROCKY

COAST MOUNTAINS

ALEXANDER
ARCHIPELAGO

QUEEN
CHARLOTTE
ISLANDS

VANCOUVER
ISLAND

U-SHAPED GLACIAL VALLEY

THE GEOLOGICAL HI

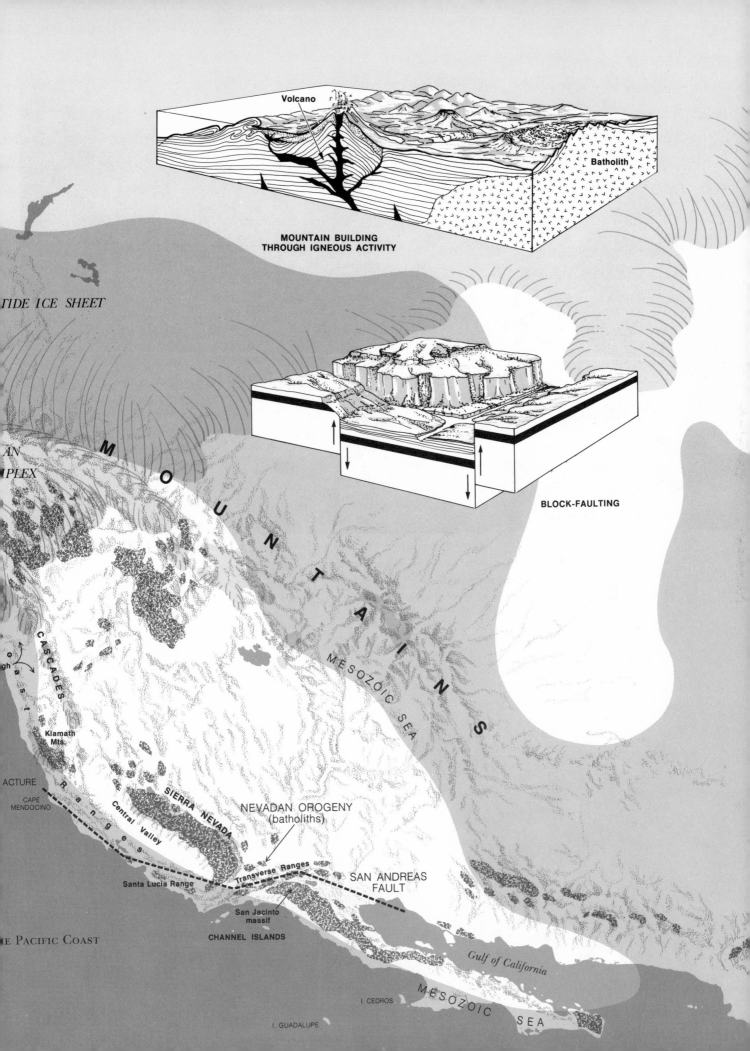

Volcano

Batholith

**MOUNTAIN BUILDING
THROUGH IGNEOUS ACTIVITY**

BLOCK-FAULTING

TIDE ICE SHEET

M O U N T A I N S

CASCADES

Klamath
Mts.

M E S O Z O I C   S E A

ACTURE

CAPE
MENDOCINO

R a n g e s

SIERRA NEVADA

Central Valley

NEVADAN OROGENY
(batholiths)

Santa Lucia Range

Transverse Ranges

SAN ANDREAS
FAULT

San Jacinto
massif

PACIFIC COAST

CHANNEL ISLANDS

Gulf of California

M E S O Z O I C   S E A

I. CEDROS

I. GUADALUPE

Mountains as climate barriers: a view west toward the King Range (Humboldt County, California) and parallel ridges of the Coast Range to the east. The range nearest the ocean captures the heaviest precipitation and is most densely covered with forest and chaparral. The inner ranges begin to show a rain shadow effect, and the increase of open grasslands signals even greater dryness.

The alternating rock layers total 10,000 to 15,000 feet in thickness, except in the Olympics where they are several times thicker.

Eventually, these layers were building up faster than they were sinking—in part because the volcanoes of the Cascades were beginning to tower and thus erode to the east—and the shoreline was moving westward and straightening out, to eliminate the deep ocean embayment from the continent. A gentle upwarping parallel to the new coastline raised the plateau that with much stream-cutting became the Oregon Coast Range. The Willamette–Puget Sound trough was sinking to east of it, and the still greater upwarping of the Cascades' platform was taking place along the east side of the trough.

A remarkable feature of the range is the many rivers that have deeply dissected its mass, like crooked streets meandering among stone-tiered blocks of some ancient city. A few that cross it altogether are antecedent to the range; their courses were set upon the earlier plain where they started sawing channels before it rose as a plateau. Such are the Umpqua and the Chehalis. One, the Columbia, which alone compares with the Strait of Juan de Fuca as a major breach of the continental barrier, levels the Coast Range in crossing it. The lesser streams give character to the Oregon-Washington coastal highland, as one discovers when driving between the coast and interior valley all the way along the low level, winding course of the Umpqua, Siuslaw, Alsea, or Nehalem. Some of their gorges plunge past the low-tide line and reach out to the sea across the narrow continental shelf; they are drowned by tidewater for several miles inland, too—this coastland has been sinking recently, since the general Coast Range upwarping.

The summit of the Coast Range plateau trends unevenly lower from the Klamath Mountains and Rogue River region in the south, to zero elevation at the Chehalis River in the north, then rises again to new heights in the Olympic Mountains. Mount Olympus —at a shade under eight thousand feet—is not only almost twice as high as any peak between the Rogue and the Chehalis; it is the highest Coast Range summit from the Olympics to the Transverse Ranges of Southern California.

The Olympics are among the youthful mountains of the coast. Only about fifty million years ago the peninsula was just emerging from the sea. The mountains attained their height and their dramatic glacier-carved forms during the Pleistocene ice ages. Olympic peaks are jewel-box sculptures arranged on white velvet. Though miniature as compared to the overarching Alaska Range or the congregation of giants around St. Elias, the Olympics are nevertheless a stunning prelude to that Gulf of Alaska borderland where ice is both the major geological material of the surface and the chief agent of its shaping.

THE STORY of the continent's western edge has been one of sea, shore, and mountains—they are inseparable here. Of the three the mountains give this edge of land its strongest character in our time. The ocean was primordial; the shore came into being with the continent, and will remain as long as sea and land exist. But the mountains, the stanchions of this great upraised rim we know, have come and gone and come again. Barrier against the sea, seldom breached in the past while they stood; yielding to forces within them, which raised them up again—the mountains were here to meet man, to thwart him, invite him. Undoubtedly, they will outlast him.

The sea and the mountains together *are* the coast to us, and we would not change it. But for the mountains—the sea notwithstanding—this coast could be a desert: witness the coastal plains of Peru and Chile, in corresponding latitudes. The ocean winds would blow across the shore and leave their moisture elsewhere, on inland slopes. The mountains give us rain and snow, and with them forests and glaciers— resources, scenery, tempered climates. Man has the means to level hills, but happily the mountains are above him. The natural desert of this coast is where the mountains break, in Baja. Man makes small deserts of coastal plains and basins, as in Los Angeles, by spoiling air and water, destroying woodlands and chaparral—and goes up to the mountains to escape them. And man can deface the mountains to a degree; but they will remain a longer time than man, and renew their ancient faces.

The eastern escarpment of Sierra Juárez, Baja California, looking north. Like the Sierra Nevada, this range traces its origin to the Nevadan Revolution. Sierra San Pedro Mártir, just to the south of Juárez, is the major part of the same granitic batholith and subsequent uplift. Note that the steep scarp is to the east, and the long, gently sloping plateau to the west—as it is with the Sierra Nevada.

233

CHAPTER 24

THE LAST OF THE ICE CAP

*Living glaciers of John Muir's Glacier Bay
and their Ice Age ancestors that carved the Northwest shore.*

THERE WAS a great ice-filled bay to the north; it was enclosed by mountains, and no white man had ever seen it. Only the Indians knew this place, and they called it Sitadaka. Such was the word given John Muir at Fort Wrangell. It was late fall, the season running out, but he was determined to go there. With his missionary friend Hall Young, the old Stikine chief Toyatte, and a crew of paddlers, he followed island channels up into Icy Strait and Cross Sound, turning north from there into the unknown waterway. And so, in 1879, Muir and Hall became the first white explorers to enter Glacier Bay, to penetrate the inner recesses of this great ice wilderness behind the coastal Fairweather Range, and to report them to the outside world.

During the few days before a threatening wintry freeze-in, they discovered several of the major inlets and glaciers, including the big northeastern arm and its active glacier which were later named for Muir.

Late the next summer the "Great Ice Chief," as the Indians had titled him, spent a week with Hall on Muir Glacier, measuring its flow. Every twenty-four hours, they found, it advanced fifty to sixty feet.

Ten years passed before Muir's next visit to "his" glacier—on a tourist steamer! This time he spent ten days alone on the glacier. He found it still flowing, its midstream moving toward the bay at a fair rate, but more slowly than a decade earlier. As is usual with glaciers, friction with the valley walls slowed the ice considerably along the sides. A line of measuring stakes across the ice bowed downstream in the center.

What he soon discovered, however, was of major import: Muir Glacier was in fact retreating. Its front was melting back faster than downward flow from parent snowfields could replenish its total mass. He found his 1880 campsite a mile farther from the glacier's snout. And in 1899, on his last visit to Alaska, he measured yet another mile of withdrawal

> THE Cordilleran Glacier Complex of the Pleistocene was a network of glaciers, 2,350 miles long, with its center in British Columbia. Ice sheet, valley glaciers, and piedmont glaciers fused together in a continuous mass. The complex was fed largely from the northern Cascades and from the high Coast Range to their northwest, with the Rockies contributing a small share. Glaciers flowing eastward from the two western ranges and westward from the Rockies coalesced in the lowland trough between, to form the Cordilleran Ice Sheet, which may have been fully 7,500 feet thick at its domed center. This was more or less trapped in its intermountain basin, the Interior Plateau of British Columbia, which now holds some of the province's largest lakes. Seeking outlets, this huge ice mass found them in a few river valleys cutting through the Coast Range, which the outlet glaciers deeply and widely eroded on their westward way to the sea.

of the Muir Glacier. Significantly, most of Alaska's glaciers were, by then, known to be in retreat.

Muir's 1890 observations marked the beginning of a continuous glacial fluctuation study in which Glacier Bay has been one of the world's principal laboratories for observing glaciers as indicators of long-term climate change. Not all glaciers are remnants of a vast single ice sheet of the last Great Ice

*The front, or snout, of Mendenhall Glacier, a few miles north of Juneau.
Its retreat from its small coastal plain on the Lynn Canal gave Alaska's
capital the only possible site for a vital landplane airport.*

BARRIER AND BREACH

Age. Glaciers in the High Sierra, for instance, were never continuous with those in Alaska or with the Wisconsin ice sheet. Alaska's glaciers—in the Pleistocene they were part of the Cordilleran Glacier Complex of that time—still exist where they are because of regional climate patterns and snow-trapping mountain ranges. They were never physically connected with, say, the glaciers of the Alps. But all glaciers respond to global temperature as if they were members of a worldwide system.

The first half of the twentieth century was, over most of the earth, a period of glacial shrinkage brought on by a general rise in temperatures (and consequently the sea level rose two or three inches everywhere). Despite the advance of a few, glaciers have lost more ground in our time than they have won. The fact has been plainly evident in Glacier Bay.

In 1925 this area became a national monument. One of our most magnificent parklands, it is truly a monument to John Muir. Still flowing down at the uncommon speed of twenty to thirty feet a day, the Muir Glacier is one of the most active and interesting glaciers of the park or, in fact, of the entire Alaskan coast. It is almost two miles wide, and its face rises 265 feet sheer above the tide.

With a keen eye for telling detail, Muir saw evidence of more than one advance and retreat of these glaciers. He was intrigued by ancient stumps in Muir Inlet and along other shores of Glacier Bay. They stand where Sitka spruces once grew on a moraine left by earlier glaciers' retreat; in time they were overwhelmed by sand and gravel washed down by the great floods preceding another glacial advance, and eventually were crushed beneath the glacier itself. A later retreat then bared the relict stumps. They were evidence of a climatic pendulum swinging through the centuries in its own ineluctable rhythm.

GLACIERS ARE BORN and continue to grow only in areas of perennial snow where, moreover, a greater quantity falls than is yearly lost by melting, evaporation, or blowing away—where it is freezing much of the time, but the land is not constantly attacked by strong winds. There must be a build-up of snowpack in the glacier's starting area, or firn-basin, greater than the capacity of the place to hold it. The accumulating weight of snow crystals presses the mass

down to squeeze out air and meld particles into ice, slowly—so slowly it may take many decades for glacial ice to form, then to flow down from the basin.

At the other end, its front or snout, a glacier is constantly "dying," where it meets the greater warmth of lower land or the sea. The sun's warmth each day melts away some of the surface, like a sharp knife peeling an onion layer by layer; rain will etch the ice; and finally the sea's edge receives the glacier's broken front. A cycle is completed: water from the sea, to the icefields, and back to the sea.

No matter how fast it may be receding, a glacier is still a "live" one as long as it gains increment at the source and keeps flowing. A "dead" glacier is not being replenished and so does not move. A good, healthy glacier going down to the sea or to a lake-shore meets its "living end" grandly every day in the thundering fall of bergs.

Glaciers do not come into being simply because somewhere there is a great massing of snow turned to ice. Although the high plateau of Antarctica is buried beneath an ice sheet of enormous thickness, it is on mountainous rims of land masses that the factors of latitude, altitude, temperature, and snowfall combine to create the greatest glaciers. The Gulf of Alaska coastland is a supreme example, The great glaciers of the Northwest Coast are not merely holdovers from the Ice Age. The essential conditions for their creation have persisted since the beginning of the Pleistocene epoch—over a million years. These are a cold, long-winter maritime climate and a mountain-bound coastland receiving heavy seasonal snowfall. Theirs is a partnership of forces.

The Pacific Coast's weather is from the ocean, borne upon prevailing winds. Just as surely as the shore stops the sea waves, the coastal mountains trap the precipitation. If they did not exist, most of the sea-borne moisture would be wafted inland to dissipate (or, in an ice age, to build a continental ice sheet). But the mountains are here, a maze of peaks and basins, folds and pockets, ideal for catching snow and holding it, like the rooftops of a village. The greater the mountain mass, the more snow it will catch; and the higher and steeper its slopes, the greater the momentum of the snow impacted to ice and moving downslope as glaciers. These Alaskan and British Columbian coastal mountains are massive

Like a turbulent sea of ice at the mouth of a frozen river, the Matanuska Glacier ends its winding course down from the peaks of the Chugach Range above the Gulf of Alaska.

Naked mountains and flowing ice: the Raven Glacier cuts its wide trough through Alaska's Chugach Range, near Turnagain Arm. Rook Mountain (6,685 feet) is the clouded summit peak.

and exceedingly high; they have spawned many and mighty glaciers.

For more than a century, since the fact of periodic worldwide glaciation in the higher latitudes was recognized, men have asked what caused the major climate changes that bring on an "ice age." Half a hundred theories have been proposed: shifts in solar radiation; aberration of the planet's orbit; reduction of solar energy reaching the earth's surface because of unusual amounts of volcanic ash and smoke in the atmosphere. But no certain explanation is yet at hand. For whatever reasons, the stage was set with a rising land and the Great Ice Age was upon the earth, and upon our northern Pacific Coast. It was the lengthiest and farthest reaching period of chill climate yet found in the geological record.

Colder and colder the climate became, the chill creeping southward from the Arctic, northward from the Antarctic. For tens of thousands of years it continued cold, with minor fluctuations now and then. At the same time, ocean water was piled up into the atmosphere, dumped on the high land by the wind in one frozen form or another, or in chill rain, and compacted into ice in mountain basins and lower valleys. The ice piled up deeper, to upwards of ten thousand feet in some regions. The buildup was greater and faster in some areas, from which it pressed outward in vast, slow but relentless sheets.

One need not journey to Antarctica to visualize this land sheeted over entirely as in the Great Ice Age. In 1891 the glacialist Israel C. Russell stood on a divide three-fourths of the way up Mount St. Elias and looked northward to a region no one had glimpsed before. He had anticipated a forested lowland, with lakes, rivers, and "some signs of human habitation," but

What met my astonished gaze was a vast snow-covered region, limitless in expanse, through which hundreds, perhaps thousands, of bare, angular mountain peaks projected. There was not a stream, not a lake, and not a vestige of vegetation of any kind in sight. A more desolate or utterly lifeless land one never beheld. Vast, smooth snow surfaces without crevasses stretched away to limitless distances, broken only by jagged and angular mountain peaks.

This was the Pleistocene landscape — how it was, over

the greater part of Cordilleran North America in the glaciered latitudes, from the Rocky Mountains to the Pacific Coast Ranges.

Overwhelming the lofty British Columbian Coast Range, the Northern Cascades, and Vancouver Island, the Cordilleran glaciers filled the deep northern end of the long Puget Trough (now the Strait of Georgia) The ice slid down the steep southwest face of the island, blocked the river outlet the Strait of Juan de Fuca then was, covered the triangular lowland behind Cape Flattery, and ended at the northern slope of the Olympic highland. That group of middling high peaks had meanwhile grown its own collective ice cap, which hung down to its shoulders but never merged with the larger mass flanking it from north to southeast. On the continental side of the Puget lowland, with its many confluent rivers, the Cascades sent high valley glaciers down the gorges to merge as fewer piedmont glaciers fanning out across the gentle lower slopes.

Southward the great broad tongue of the main ice sheet moved into the Puget basin, brushing past the Olympic massif on its west and the fronts of the Cascadian piedmont glaciers to the east. This is known as the Vashon Glacier. At least the second hugh ice sheet to invade the Puget Trough, it was also the last. Pushing up the river valleys of the Puget lowland, it stopped at the low divide between them and the Chehalis drainage to the south and southwest. Its terminal moraine and lateral signs are still to be seen. After the enormous Vashon Glacier had finally melted back to the north, and the deepened river gate of the Strait of Juan de Fuca was once more unlocked, the sea flooded in and Puget Sound came into being.

The pattern is repeated on a somewhat broader scale with Vancouver Island and the Coast Range of the nearby mainland. Moderately elevated, the island has lost altogether the glacial ice that once capped it. Winds, not robbed of all their moisture by the seaward slope of the 280-mile-long island, ride over its 5,000- to 7,000-foot backbone, across Queen Charlotte and Georgia straits, and strike the 10,000-foot wall of British Columbia's Coast Range. Many fairsized glaciers still file the sawteeth of the Coast Range at this southeastern end.

The Cordilleran Ice Sheet built up on the Interior Plateau behind the range until its overflowing mass found outlets through several river valleys leading westward across the mountains to the coast. Chief among these ice-scoured gorges is that of the Skeena; down it the Canadian National Railway and the only highway crossing the mid-province now go to Prince Rupert. Whether rising in the interior and cutting through the range or starting high on the Pacific Slope, all the many river valleys from Puget Sound northwestward to the Gulf of Alaska became pathways to the sea for glaciers. Their V profiles were ice-chiseled into the characteristic glacial U. Millions of tons of rock, gravel, sand, and silt were stripped from upland slopes and canyon walls and bottoms. Glacier snouts pushed the material downriver, while bottoms and sides of the solid ice streams dragged it along, grinding and gouging, smoothing the very surfaces that supplied the abrasives.

With more or less continuous uplift pushing the crust against them (as a machinist pushes metal against a rotary grinder-head), the glaciers deepened gorges and widened valleys across the entire slope from the northern Cascades to the soaring St. Elias Range and on around the curve of Alaska's gulf. In some places, such as Kodiak Island and Prince William Sound, existing river valleys were scoured by glaciers to depths then below sea level. Broad submarine troughs in the sound's entrance and off Yakutat Bay are regarded as the work of glaciers. To a large extent, however, the coastal features of today —the intricate maze of channels, islands, fiords, and inlets of all sorts—mark the ocean's repossession of a glacier-altered coastland from which it had very gradually withdrawn as more and more of its water was sequestered to land as glacial ice, and to which it just as slowly returned as glacier melting restored its accustomed level.

Earlier glacial periods have also left their sign in the Northwest's geological record—as many as six of them, each, like the latest one, divided into glacial and interglacial ages. These periods cycled in intervals of 200 to 250 million years, but there is reason to regard the most recent series as the greatest ice age of them all.

The beautiful and sometimes awesome landscapes of the Northwest Coast region are altogether glacial.

Although glaciers performed no basic construction of the land and no great amount of total demolition, they lastingly reshaped and resurfaced every part of it that felt their living grip. Even the tops of many peaks were plucked to knife-edge and needle-point by ice expanding in cracks and pulling down rock at glacier headwall and cirque rim. As the glacier melted away in death, their work went on in a secondary phase: continuing erosion and downward transport of material by runoff streams of meltwater, and continuing build-up of alluvial outwash plains and deltas. As if to prove that nothing on this earth is lasting, on the other hand, many such streams set vigorously to work tearing down moraines and flushing the glacial drift deposits of centuries out of deep gorges and valleys. Glaciers and interglacial rivers of the Pleistocene brought enormous quantities of their erosion products down to the coast. The material is one thousand feet thick near Vancouver, and much of the offshore sea bottom is covered with it.

No tale of glaciers upon the Pacific shore should neglect certain famous names of present-day glacial "Who's Who": the handsome Mendenhall, whose recent retreat enabled Juneau to build an airport on its outwash plain; the Llewellyn, flowing into the long trough of British Columbia's Atlin Lake on the upper Yukon; Columbia, a favorite of excursionists in Prince William Sound near Valdez; Mount McKinley's Muldrow and others known to climbers; the lofty inland ice cap of the Wrangell Mountains back of the Chugach and St. Elias ranges; and between those massifs the gigantic Bagley and Seward Glacier ice fields. And there are many more.

In truth, perhaps, the glacier story Muir began for us can never be all told. No one can foresee its ending, or whether in fact it might be approaching a new beginning. In any event, the study of the whys and effects of glacial variation goes on. And the Southeastern Alaska coast—easily reached, relatively mild in climate, with the longest record of glaciological and climate and weather observations of all large North American glacial regions—has been expertly called the world's best place for such studies. At least we may be able to chart a trend toward the next great ice age! Meanwhile the beauty and wonder of grand and approachable glaciers are here to be enjoyed for a long time.

CHAPTER 25

RIVERS GREAT AND SMALL

*The role of rivers in the discovery, exploration
and settlement of the coast, and their present-day importance.*

IN THAT SPRINGTIME of our history on this continent, when the great western wilderness was largely uncharted, the most vigorously sought highroads to new discovery, rewarding enterprise, and tenacious settlement were water roads: ocean tracks with favoring winds, navigable rivers to relieve the foot and the wheel. In equal demand were suitable shore bases: fit harbors and roadsteads, facilities for shipbuilding and repair; depots for handling and bartering goods; points of access to the interior. The mouths and confluences of big rivers gave the best sites for such bases. The Dutch built New Amsterdam at the entrance of the Hudson's estuarine highway to rich farm and timber lands. Explorers and settlers of the vast mid-continent found the Mississippi and its tributaries an almost limitless arterial system. Factors and *voyageurs* plied the northern fur trade over lakes and streams left by the last retreating ice sheet.

The Far West, on the other hand, was not comparably favored. What did the *conquistadores* find? The Colorado, churning in tortuous gorges, becoming only briefly navigable before its silty discharge into a desert sea. For the men from arid Iberia, *entradas* were a dusty business; all of New Spain from the Rio Grande to the Golden Gate was as devoid of usable waterways as their homeland. For human transport needs beyond the primitive, the Southwest was a riverless land.

Men of other backgrounds and compulsions, oriented to more northerly latitudes—Cook, Vancouver,

Mackenzie—were lured by the myth of a fabled "River of the West" that would connect with the eastward drainage by a short, hopefully easy portage, thus providing a transcontinental waterway. In 1793 Alexander Mackenzie, in a canoe with Indian paddlers, followed the small Bella Coola River to tidewater at Point Menzies on the British Columbia coast. He did not realize his goal of finding an inland water route by which his North West Company might tap the profitable trans-Pacific fur trade with China, but he became, at twenty-nine, the first white man to make a northern crossing of the continent.

His own explorations in the Northwest and, later, news of Gray's discovery of the mighty Columbia River prompted Mackenzie to return to England to urge British expansion into this promising frontier. In the end he also contributed to exploitation of the area by the United States: among the interested readers of his 1801 *Voyages . . . Through the Continent of North America* were Thomas Jefferson and the president's young secretary, Meriwether Lewis.

The search for a great "River of the West" was not in vain. In 1776 Heceta had reported evidence of a large river mouth in the north. Two years later Cook in search of a Northwest Passage fetched the "New Albion" coast, at 45°N latitude, but the rough conditions that prompted him to name Cape Foulweather hid both the Columbia and Strait of Juan de Fuca.

History missed its next chance to turn in British favor when Vancouver passed that way in 1792; he later wrote:

*View toward the mouth of the Russian River, the first
large stream flowing to the Pacific north of the Golden Gate.*

BARRIER AND BREACH

The sea had changed from its natural, to river colored water; the probable consequences of some streams falling into the bay, or into the ocean north of it, through the low land. Not considering the opening worthy of more attention, I continued our pursuit to the N.W. being desirous to embrace the advantages of the now prevailing breeze and pleasant weather.

Coasting northward two days more, Vancouver spoke a strange ship standing in toward the Strait of Juan de Fuca. It was the *Columbia,* commanded by Captain Robert Gray, some two years out of Boston (between 1787 and 1790, Gray's 85-footer had completed the first American circling of the globe). Gray told Vancouver of the great river just passed, where the *Columbia* had earlier lain off the entrance nine days, unable to cross the bar.

After the meeting with Vancouver, Gray bore away to the south again, discovered Grays Harbor, sailed past Willapa Bay, and again faced the forbidding bar of the great stream. Gray sent a pinnace to scout the channel, then the *Columbia* shortened sail and followed through the wracking breakers. The date was May 11, 1792. The little ship deserved to name the river she had conquered.

Vancouver's turn came. When he left Nootka Sound in mid-October for California, he was determined, on the way, to force the Columbia and survey it for England. After sending Lieutenant Broughton ahead in the *Chatham,* a sixty-foot brig of broad beam and light draft, Vancouver attempted the seething shoals with his larger vessel. But unlike the *Columbia,* the *Discovery* was not to make it. When soundings showed three feet of water beneath her bottom, Vancouver hauled her out, wisely leaving the river to Broughton.

With dawn the *Chatham* made some fifteen miles into the estuary (to the *Columbia's* twenty), at which point Broughton saw he had best use his boats to extend the survey upriver. The lower Columbia was broad and shallow with a maze of channels—no Northwest Passage, Broughton concluded. He named Point Vancouver, where one hundred miles inland he turned back, and Mount Hood, which gave a climactic view of this country as they took possession for England. Broughton and his crew were the first white men to set foot there.

On the trunk of a "big pine" on the north shore of the Columbia, just behind Cape Disappointment, a signature is carved:

WILLIAM CLARK DECEMBER 3RD 1805.
BY LAND FROM THE U. STATES IN 1804 & 1805

The party had made its first miserable camp at that spot in days on end of rain. Moving thence to the south side, a mile up the little Lewis and Clark tributary, they built a stockade naming it Fort Clatsop after the local Indians, and wintered there from December 7, 1805, to March 23, 1806.

American claims to the Northwest were advanced by two decisive events in American history: the Louisiana Purchase and the Lewis and Clark Expedition. The Columbia was Lewis and Clark's highway down the Pacific slope, its mouth their farthest and designated goal. Though burying under a mound of geographical fact the almost dead idea of a usable waterway linking both coasts, the expedition took nothing from the stature of the mightiest river flowing into the Pacific.

WITH ITS chief tributary, the Snake, the Columbia drains a basin at least the size of Texas. The combined system draws water from British Columbia, Washington, Oregon, Idaho, Montana, Wyoming, Utah, and Nevada. Collected in the main trunk of the lower Columbia, the flow is double the Missouri's, carries to the sea ten times the Colorado's water and adds up to more than the total volume of all streams, large and small, reaching the Pacific between the Mexican and Canadian borders. Vital as this flow is for irrigation east of the Cascades, it is the combination of tremendous volume with fast fall that distinguishes the Columbia today. It has been called the greatest power stream in the civilized world, a source of cheap energy far mightier than the Mississippi or any other stream in the world outside of Africa. But a hundred and fifty years ago nobody judged a river on its hydroelectric output, or even perhaps on scenic beauty. It was a *way*—or an obstacle.

Ross Cox, a young Irishman clerking in Astoria for the Pacific Fur Company made an upriver trip that was subsequently described in his book *The Columbia River* (1831):

The Columbia is a noble river, uninterrupted by rapids for 170 miles; 100 of which are navigable for vessels of three hundred tons. It is seldom less than a mile wide; but in some places its breadth varies from two to five miles. The shores are generally bold and thickly wooded. Pine in all its varieties predominates, and is mixed with white oak, ash, beech, poplar, alder, crab, and cotton-wood, with an undergrowth of briers, &c., through which our hunters made many ineffectual attempts to pass. The navigation is often obstructed by sandbanks, which are scattered over different parts of the river below the rapids, and are dry at low water. In the neighborhood of these sandbanks the shores are generally low, and present some fine flat bottoms of rich meadow ground, bordered by a profusion of blackberry and other wild fruit shrubs; in the deep and narrow paths of the channel, the shores are bolder. The river, up to the rapids, is covered with several islands, from one to three miles in length; some of which are fine meadows, and others well wooded. Great caution is required to avoid sunken . . . snags.

Five days out of Astoria the fur traders reached the first rapids, whose upper part

is a perpendicular fall of nearly sixteen feet; after which it continues down nearly one interrupted rapid for three miles and a half. The river here is compressed by the bold shore on each side to about two hundred yards or less in breadth. The channel is crowded with large rocks, over which the water rushes with incredible velocity, and with a dreadful noise. Above the portage the river widens to about half a mile, and is studded for some distance with several rocky and partially wooded islands . . . On the evening of the 8th [of July] we reached the foot of the narrows, or, as the Canadians call them, *les dalles*.

Midway between the rapids and the since-famous Dalles, "a bold promontory of high black rock" jutted far into the river. There were whirlpools here, and "great numbers of seals" on some islands, a most interesting fact if its truth may be accepted. When they came to the narrows,

the shores on each side were less covered with wood, and immediately close to them it had entirely disappeared. The land on the north side was bold and rocky, . . . rather low, mixed with rocks, a sandy soil, and totally devoid of

vegetation, except loose straggling bushes some distance inland. The Columbia, at the narrows, for upwards of three miles is compressed into a narrow channel, not exceeding sixty or seventy yards wide; the whole of which is a succession of boiling whirlpools.

Straining through a fifty-yard funnel, "the immense waters of the Columbia are one mass of foam, and force their headlong course with a frightful impetuosity." In the next portage leading to the falls,

the river is strewed with immense masses of hard black rock, mostly honeycombed, and worn into a variety of fantastic shapes by the perpetual friction of the water in its fearful course downwards. The appearance of the country here is high, rocky, barren, and without timber of any kind. We found this a sensible inconvenience; for we were obliged to purchase some drift wood from the Indians for the purpose of cooking.

At Celilo Falls the fur traders bought some salmon, thus partaking of an ancient economy of the Columbia. In their next view the country took on "a new aspect, . . . free from any rising grounds or timber, and on each side nothing is to be seen but immense plains stretching a great distance to the north and south. The soil is dry and sandy, and covered with a loose parched grass, growing in tufts." They saw their first rattlesnakes on these near-desert plains.

Geologically and ecologically, Ross Cox presented a truthful portrait of the Columbia River.

LIKE ALL great rivers and many small ones, the rivers of the Pacific slope rise in mountains. Every stream of this drainage, moreover, runs its entire course within or in sight of mountains. Born in ranges of the interior, the largest of our rivers have cut through coastal barriers to reach the ocean.

Thus, the only major system south of the Columbia, the Sacramento–San Joaquin, rises through a web of tributaries draining the entire western slope of the Sierra Nevada, the southern Cascades, and in a minor way, the Inner Coast Ranges. The two main trunks flowing from opposite ends of the Central Valley trough meet midway at the delta to form one short, broad river that first breaks through the Inner Coast Range at Carquinez Strait, then cuts through

*At its mouth, the Quillayute River of Washington's Pacific Coast finds itself
no longer an insignificant forest stream, but the main artery of the Quillayute Indian
Reservation, whose metropolis is La Push, where the placid stream escapes the fish nets to find the sea.*

the coastal mountains at the Golden Gate to meet the Pacific Ocean.

Going north 250 air miles up the coast from San Francisco Bay, we pass the sea mouth of many a Coast Range river that rises and runs its crooked course without knowing the level of a plain. The Klamath, a vigorous, deep-gorged river, rises east of the Cascades in Oregon and snakes through the Siskiyou and Klamath mountains to find the Pacific south of Crescent City, California.

The Rogue River, rising in Oregon's Crater Lake region, is familiar to many who enjoy white water and steep mountain terrain. A hundred years ago this was gold-strike country. More than twenty million dollars in gold came out of Oregon in 1857 alone, a large part of it washed out of Rogue River gravels. Taking the mail boat upriver the thirty-two miles from Gold Beach to Agness, when walking the old Indian trail up the canyon, one sees unhealed red-earth gashes where the miners' hydraulic nozzles started the erosion of the Rogue's banks. The huge monitors have been gone for decades, but their destruction lives.

The river too is long-lived, and has outlasted far greater, if much slower, processes of change. Indeed, it is a great deal older than all the mountain

chains that continue to nourish it with their seasonal snow mantle.

Two other fair-sized rivers cut through the coast range, the Umpqua and the Chehalis. The latter spells the northern end of the Oregon Coast Range and marks the beginning of the Olympic Peninsula. From Olympia, Washington, at the southernmost reach of Puget Sound, due west across the neck of the peninsula to Grays Harbor, the distance is sixty miles, and the Chehalis cuts across most of it. With nature's forces of change quietly and continuously working toward a future we can only guess, there is the intriguing possibility that the Olympic Peninsula will in a future geological age become an island.

From Puget Sound northward, the history of rivers is intimately bound up with that of glaciers: their courses were either created or permanently altered by ice. We will return to these wild northern rivers in the following chapter.

THE SOUTHWEST, a waterless land in terms of river transport, has become water-short for other human needs as well, simply through population growth. Plants and animals first, then Indians, made do with the existent water supply: if there was not enough to take care of the increase, their numbers leveled off. Adjusting to what the land offers, fitting into the ecology of nature, has not been the white man's way—at least not in our culture—but the old balances continue to function in the desert peninsula south of Los Angeles and San Diego.

On Baja's cape region, lying hot beneath the Tropic of Cancer, rain falls mostly in September, averaging about eight inches a year. But it gives no permanent rivers. A modest runoff down the flanks of the Sierra de la Victoria makes a few mountain streams and through time has silted the lowlands, building up on ancient flood plains some wondrously rich agricultural land. South of La Paz even the desert is more abundant—plants grow bigger, denser, and mountains are forested here and there. But like all the peninsula it is a land without true rivers.

High in the north, on the Pacific slope of Sierra San Pedro Mártir, Baja's ten-thousand-foot backbone, some fine trout streams are born of snow. But from about latitude 24°N—the region of the Vizcaíno Desert—only ghosts of rivers stalk across the earth, silent and deeply entrenched within their arroyos. A stranger here might wonder how this sere landscape was ever slashed to the bone by running water. It looks moon-dry. Then he might recall tales of flash floods in desert washes. It is wise to believe them, and watch the sky.

Some Southern California rivers today are wide, gravel-bottomed, partly concrete-lined "ditches," familiar to all who cross the gray metropolitan plain on the Santa Ana Freeway. No single view can be reconciled with Crespi's description of a riverside camping place which the Portolá Expedition enjoyed two centuries ago in "a valley full of large alders and live oaks." The native trees gave way to oranges, which yielded to industrial parks and satellite subdivisions.

The Portolá party left the San Fernando Valley, which was drained by a branch of the Los Angeles River now all but obliterated by a main freeway route, and crossed the pass between the Santa Susana and San Gabriel mountains. They came next to the Santa Clara River, near Castaic Junction. Crespi liked what he saw, on an August day of 1769: "the watering place consists of an arroyo with a great deal of water which runs in a moderately wide valley, well grown with willows and cottonwoods."

How strange it sounds, the padre's word of "a great deal of water," months along in California's dry season, in an area we know today as semiarid at best. Had there been exceptional snows that winter? Modern maps show only intermittent streams in all the rock-walled tributary canyons, and the Santa Clara as a broad sandy wash to the coastal plain between Oxnard and Ventura.

From Ventura the Spaniards walked the hundred miles of narrow coastal terrace beneath the Santa Ynez range, past the site of future Santa Barbara, and around Point Arguello to the mouth of the Santa Ynez River. On the way, frequent gullies and ravines "had running water and some live oaks." Today the Santa Ynez waters Santa Barbara via the Cachuma reclamation project and the seven-mile Tecolote Tunnel. Its remaining trickle meanders westward to the sea over tidy dairylands around the Danish community of Solvang, past ranches and irrigated farm country, to end under a mainline railroad bridge flanked by huge military facilities.

Continuing north, the Portolá party made its way up the coast until the Santa Lucia Mountains rose steep from the rocky shore. No choice here but to strike inland. And so they came, after much hardship, to the inviting valley of the Salinas River.

Ninety-two years later William H. Brewer, field chief for the new California Geological Survey, found this trough-like lower valley of California's 170-mile, third-longest river "much less verdant" than expected. His journal describes the river as it was in Indian and *ranchero* time, before irrigation brought vast acreages of lettuce, strawberries, beans, onions, sugar beets, and artichokes (near the foggy Monterey bayshore)—and before the Californians exterminated their state animal, the grizzly bear, which apparently abounded on this savanna in the 1860s:

The Salinas Valley for a hundred or more miles from the sea [actually rather less], up to the San Antonio hills, is a great plain ten to thirty miles wide. Great stretches are almost perfectly level, or have a very slight slope from the mountains to the river which winds through it. The ground was dry and parched and the very scanty grass was entirely dry. One saw no signs of vegetation at the first glance—that is, no green thing on the plain—so a belt of timber by the stream . . . stood out as a band of the liveliest green in this waste. The mouth of this valley opens into Monterey Bay, like a funnel, and the northwest wind from the Pacific draws up through this heated flue with terrible force. Wherever we have found a valley opening to the northwest, we have found these winds, fierce in the afternoon . . .

Brewer caught every salient fact of the Salinas River and valley of the time but one: however dry its bed looked much of the year, the Salinas flowed copiously—underground. Its willows and pale cottonwoods have told the story; they must keep their feet wet. Most of the Salinas's water, in fact, percolates through the deep sand and gravel of its broad lowland channel, leaving a quiet and sometimes slight flow, or none, upon the bed. It is America's biggest underground river. And today its valley is one of California's greenest gardens.

IN STRIKING contrast to that sluggish and recondite stream percolating beneath its cottonwood roots, the lively small rivers of the northern California Coast Range, the Douglas-fir and redwood belt, run properly above ground to the sea, through deep canyons, minuscule valleys, and shady groves of conifers. Until our day, they furnished an Indian economy of abundant salmon. A hundred years ago they were sending timber down to steam sawmills near their mouths, whence schooners carried lumber for the building and rebuilding of San Francisco Bay's fast-rising communities.

Giant coast redwoods still fall beside their gutted banks and down their watershed slopes to feed the mills in the once lively little valleys; freeways span them; scant runs of steelhead make their way upriver to spawn. A few Indians farm, in a marginal way, between stream-side and forest, and work for the loggers and road bosses. Unattractive riverbank communities house millworkers, cater to tourists, hunters, and fishermen. Cutover slopes bleed yellow muck in the heavy winter rains, swelling jaundiced floods that gut redwood parklands in the bottoms and stain the sea.

But much remains of wildness, and so of beauty, in these northern watersheds. There are still some unslashed hills to let raindrops fall softly through black oak, madroño, rhododendron, laurel, tanoak, and Douglas-fir, sword fern and deer fern and lady fern, to merge in clear little creeks. There are mossy rocks and clean-washed gravels and low, carpeted banks where redwoods stand tall between mirroring rivers and misty meadows.

A WILD RIVER has the continuity and wholeness of a living organism. It is in fact a linkage of countless communities of organisms. These—the amoeba in the water drop, the redwood on the bank—are bound to each other and to the whole of their environment, from specific habitats to the larger context of the total watershed or drainage system. A river is a living continuum. Whatever happens upriver is bound to have repercussions downriver. The quantity of water in a region governs the populations, and in part the kinds, of its animals and plants.

In nature's terms, Southern California and all the Southwest is an arid land with its own characteristic, well adapted flora and fauna. But for human needs, we find it a deprived land; and as we fill it nevertheless with our excessive numbers, we complain of a growing water shortage. So we look northward, hoping by some technology of long-haul transport to make up the deficit. What of the ecological consequences to northern riverlands?

An entire drainage basin of any size, still wholly natural or largely undisturbed by man, is a rare thing. Where one exists, it is now priceless—not only for wild nature's sake or for pure water, precious as these are, but also as a standard of comparison, an unspoiled sample for long-term scientific study.

Steps have been taken to save one such wild watershed from destruction. Elder Creek, flowing into the south fork of the Eel River in Mendocino County, California, is a complete river system in miniature, earmarked by the U.S. Geological Survey as perhaps the last of its kind in the California Coast Ranges. Purchased with funds raised by a national conservation society, the area has been dedicated by the National Park Service as a Natural History Landmark.

Few Elder Creeks are left along great stretches of the Pacific Coast. Those that remain are vital for what they can teach us about ecology—the relationships of living things—and about nature's ways of conserving water, in quantity, and safeguarding it, in quality. These are things we must know as inevitably we approach total use of all our water resources.

Fishing boats ride quietly on the Noyo River, Mendocino County, California, while morning mist rises from the edge of the redwood forest upstream.

Glaciers have scooped countless small basins which filled with meltwater or rain to become lakes or the smaller tarns. When surrounded by trees, and reflecting mountains, they are numbered among the beauty spots of a region, such as here in the mountains above Juneau. Many of them ultimately become filled with silt and detritus and form equally lovely meadows covered with grasses and wildflowers.

The glacial geologist Richard Foster Flint has likened a glacier to the crust of the earth; its rigid outer shell
is a zone of fracture in which crevasses open up, while its mobile inner mass is a flow zone.
In glaciers, crevasses greatly increase the amount of surface exposed to the heat of the sun.
From the clothing of the hikers, it can be judged this is a warm day in Alaska, and Mendenhall Glacier
is suffering ablation, or removal of some of its mass.

*Paradise Mountain, as it is known to climbers, stands on the
Kenai Peninsula in view of the road from Anchorage to Seward.
It supports its own minuscule glacier, and is wreathed in spruce
forest with an outer fringe of black cottonwood, whose yellowing
leaves will soon fall.*

When standing close to the towering snout of a glacier (such as Mendenhall Glacier, pictured here), one might reflect on the probable age of the ice at the bottom of the mighty mass. It may have taken as many as three hundred years for a certain fall of snow to become ice through a process of recrystallization and compression. When this has taken place, ice is rock—metamorphic rock, moreover, because it has changed form as a result of compression under its own weight. Undoubtedly there are places on earth where the ice capping the earth is more than a million years old—in continuous existence since the Pleistocene epoch.

254

*Of rivers draining into the Gulf of Alaska, the Matanuska is one of the best known outside of Alaska
because of the federally supported farm colony, planted there in 1935 as a depression remedy. A few miles
to the west, the larger Susitna empties into Cook Inlet; the other great river of the gulf is the Copper.
This view up the Matanuska is eastward to King Mountain of the Chugach Range.*

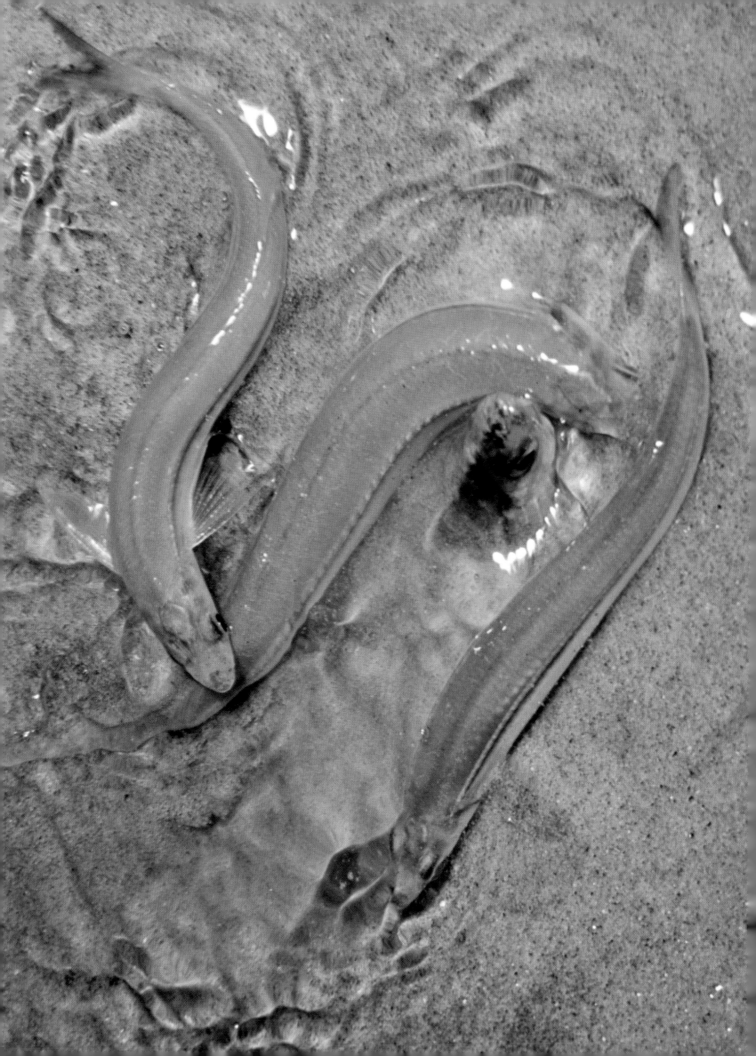

CHAPTER 26

FISHING IN COASTAL WATERS

*Some distinctive Pacific fishes — their spawning patterns,
economic importance, and struggle to survive.*

HOME WATERS of Pacific Coast fishes range from Alaskan mountain streams to subtropical Gulf of California shoals. Within that spectrum can be found every sort of piscine habitat except tropical reefs and the great ocean deeps. Many open-sea and mid-depth fishes also venture close to our shore. The shore itself — its shallows, reefs, rocks, kelp beds, tidepools, surf, open reaches, coves, bays, and river mouths — provides a rich variation in fish habitat which is manifolded by the wide range of ocean temperature over forty degrees of latitude.

From the Gulf of Alaska to Bahía de Sebastián Vizcaíno, these coastal waters hold some of the world's most intensively exploited commercial fisheries and are a sport fisherman's paradise. The wealth of this area has been known for thousands of years, as earlier people all along this shore formed the final link in a food chain beginning with the plankton of the sea.

On the Northwest Coast were the salmon-fishers: Coast Salish Indians with their anciently devised gill-nets; Kwakiutl building elaborate midstream traps of stakes and stones in inlets of Queen Charlotte Sound; Nootka poising twin-pronged spears along the Vancouver Island coast. On the central California shore, Coast Miwok and Pomo women filled baskets with mussels and clams; south and east of Point Conception, the Chumash plied the channel in sewn plank canoes, using fishhooks made of shell. Baja's more primitive inhabitants scoured beaches and rocky shores for whatever the tideline offered — gathering and fishing in their simple fashion. The modern surf fisherman, with his ready-made tackle, is enjoying an ancient pursuit on this Pacific shore.

Usually alone, this salt-water angler has been called "the aristocrat of ocean fishermen." Choosing an early high tide, he is on the beach before dawn, while the tide is still out, to dig his bait of sand crabs, or take sand worms and mussels from nearby rock exposures, and to select the deeper holes where fish will come under the breaking surf of an incoming tide. South of Point Conception, a skillful cast with his 12- or 14-foot rod may return with such prizes as yellowfin croaker or the delectable California corbina, most difficult of all surf fishes to hook.

The shores of all the Pacific states yield a variety of other game fish, going by such names as cabezon, yellowtail, tomcod, greenling (which change color to suit the environment), mackerel, and the many kinds of rockfish. A great deal of Pacific shore fishing is done from surf-beaten rocks, which provide dangerous footing at best. All too frequently fishermen are plucked off by an unexpectedly high comber. The wise angler knows the next wave may be higher.

Another kind of fishing — a hard-to-believe spectacle that is unique to California — may be observed from San Luis Obispo County to Coronado when the grunion are running.

MIDNIGHT is less than an hour away. More than a thousand men, women, and children, on this particular March 17, have formed a long line at the tide's edge. The night is dark but for the city lights to the east. An occasional flashlight beam shoots into

*Grunion spawning on a Southern California beach: the female has buried herself
in the wet sand to deposit her eggs; the males are ready to release their milt which
will reach the eggs as the female thrashes to free herself and escape to the surf.*

Fishing for "whitebait" or surf smelt (found from Long Beach to Alaska) in an ancient way: with A-nets, which the Indians invented and used long before white men arrived. The fisherman stands facing the breakers and may scoop as much as twenty-five pounds of the small fish at a time.

the phosphorescent surf, then quickly goes out. At 11:38 someone shouts, "Here they come! Let's go!"

First a few, then hundreds, and soon thousands of slim, silvery six- to seven-inch fish come boiling out of the frothy edge of a wave, to land wriggling on the wet sand. The people grab with bare hands, stuffing fish into buckets. The grunion run is on.

That same scene could be observed on most major beaches along three hundred miles of California coast. Each year since the early 1930s, during the high tides following each full and new moon from the end of February until July or even August, increasing numbers of bare-hand fishermen have flocked to the beaches, as in a tribal rite—the now famous California sport of grunion fishing.

Until he has looked into the life history of this unique little silverside (its common name), one seeing a grunion run for the first time might think he had stumbled upon a reverse-lemming catastrophe of nature—a horde of fish swarming suicidally onto dry land. In reality the purpose of the mass landing is not destruction but propagation. The California grunion goes ashore to spawn, and writes in southern California sands a most wonderful fish story. The marvelously timed, tide-geared onshore run of the California grunion is the best known event of its kind in the whole world of fishes.

The grunion schools for a normal three-year life span in areas just offshore. Who knows how many eons of evolution taught it that eggs deposited in teeming offshore waters merely became food for other species, that land offered breeding security?

To spawn on land, the grunion faced a three-fold problem. Adult gill-breathers must land themselves, deposit, fertilize, and bury quantities of eggs, and return alive to the sea. The eggs must remain covered by moist sand until mature. At the right time they must hatch, and the larvae make their first trip to their ocean home. The grunion has had to master a complex tidal mechanism to survive.

Timing is the vital factor. In order to fulfill their obligation to posterity, the grunion must make their beach rendezvous, first, in certain months of the year; second, on one of a group of three or four nights falling immediately after the high tide of either full or new moon; and third, within a one- to three-hour period of the night selected.

Swimming as high as they can go with the edge of the wave, the females arch their bodies and frantically dig in with their tails as they reach the shore, stirring water with sand to make an ooze into which they expel their eggs. The one to eight males accompanying each female curve their bodies around her and eject milt so that it flows down her sides to reach and fertilize the eggs. All this takes half a minute or even less. The males then flounder back into the next, or sometimes even the same, wave, leaving the gasping, spent females to extricate themselves from the sand and escape to the sea after perhaps several minutes out of water. A large female lays up to three thousand eggs at one time and as many as four times in a season.

After about ten days, the next series of high tides will begin to reach and dislodge the ripened eggs. Agitation by sea water causes the release of a hatching enzyme within the egg which softens its cover, allowing the grunion larva to escape and be washed out to sea within two or three minutes. If some eggs are not dislodged by the first series of tides, they will keep another two weeks until the next series of highs.

Nature has thus provided rather well for the grunion's future. Its range along the shoreline is but a few fathoms in depth and not many more yards in width, but the length of it makes up for these limita-

At Celilo Falls on the Columbia, an Indian lands a magnificent salmon while his companion waits for his net to fill. Fishing officials once tried to place a seasonal limit on fishing at the falls, but the Indian Tribal Council maintained the "perpetual" rights given in a treaty with the federal government.

tions. The grunion may be called abundant from Morro Bay to Punta Abreojos, Baja California.

For thousands of southern Californians and their often incredulous visitors from Missouri, grunion exist for no better reason than to furnish an excuse for an occasional tasty fish fry. This potential threat to the species was recognized early, hence the closed season during April and May, the requirement of a fishing license, and the prohibition of all tackle except bare hands.

Unfortunately, this kind of concern came too late to save one of the most important commercial fishes on this coast—the Pacific sardine.

Pride of California's fishing ports—San Diego, San Pedro, Monterey, San Francisco—were the big purse seiners. On moonless nights from August to December they would zigzag back and forth over the offshore grounds, their lookouts scanning the inky swells for the faint phosphorescent glow where a school of sardines had stirred up a cloud of shimmering plankton. A seiner coming upon a luminous patch of sea quietly lowered a skiff with two men, to carry out an end of the long seine and, in utter silence, surround the school. With the net encircling perhaps a million fish, a line was pulled in through rings at the bottom to close the "purse," and the squirming catch was hauled up the vessel's side.

In the booming days of the California sardine fishery, each seiner of a fleet might come home from a night's work with two to four million fish. With the catch at dockside, in came the machinery and warehouse hands; out to trucking sheds and boxcars went cases of tinned sardines for lunch tables and picnic baskets, barrels of oil for paints and varnishes, sacks of high-protein fish meal for cows and chickens. In full swing it was a sixty-million-dollar industry employing upwards of twenty-five thousand people afloat and ashore. From the early '30s to the mid-'40s, the Pacific sardine fishery accounted for 25 percent of the total fish catch of the United States.

All seemed well until the 1945–46 season, when the catch produced more long faces than profits. At first, it was considered just a "bad year," but hoped-for improvement never came. For over twenty years one of the most extensive and exhaustive oceanographic, biological, and ecological investigations has

been carried out to solve the "mystery of the disappearing sardine." The story has had no happy ending, but some of the questions that investigators asked have import now and in the decades ahead, when mankind will be looking more and more urgently to the sea for its margin against hunger.

Were the vast sardine schools simply "fished out" after years of netting? Did they migrate to other grounds? Have there been changes in the environment—shifts in temperature, food supply, currents, predators, pressure from other species? Did some unknown factor affect the sardine's reproductive capacity? Whatever the cause, the disappearance of the Pacific sardine has proven that, as one biologist has put it, "the sea is not a cornucopia spawning an endless supply of fish." The same may be said of our rivers. Clear, freerunning streams are exquisitely balanced devices of nature. Every thoughtful angler knows or senses this. A river, with all the animals and plants in and around it, is a delicate living system. Flowing water and leaping trout are one. Together they are viable—and hence violable.

Up from the sea they come, some in the spring, most in the fall; up the Fraser, the Columbia, the Klamath, the Eel, the Sacramento, the San Joaquin. A few at first, then many, until solid, seething phalanxes of salmon fill the rapids bank to bank. Not lingering, not feeding or resting, they swim against the current with one instinct-driven purpose: to return to the distant waters of their hatching, there to spawn and die. Five distinct species of salmon, each in its established range offshore, return thus to the fresh waters of their genesis. They are the large coho or silver, at home from Alaska to Point Conception; the pink, numerous from the Strait of Juan de Fuca to Alaska; the chum, extending its abundance south to the Columbia; the sockeye or red salmon, especially plentiful in Puget Sound; and the king of them all—the chinook, ranging from British Columbia to San Francisco Bay.

Of whatever stripe, hue, or size, they come up from the deep ocean with a built-in compulsion, an instinct that guides each fish back to the same stream from which it made its first journey to the sea, three, four, five, even eight, years before.

Having lived to make the seaward run, and sur-

Fishing boats and sportsmen's launches in the harbor at La Push on the outer coast of Washington. Formerly there was an extensive fishery of the Pacific sardine off the Washington coast, where the name "pilchard" was commonly used for this now scarce fish.

vived the perils of the deep, they now take another succession of hazards—brush weirs of coastal Indians, spears and dipnets of upriver tribes, claws and teeth of black bear and grizzly. And then the falls! Indians came from up and down the Columbia basin to Celilo's roaring scarp, where the salmon waited, gathering strength for that prodigious upspring. Many a wearied fish failed its first leap and fell back into the plunging whiteness. Indians and falls together took a heavy toll.

Pushing on upstream, each fish must fork again, and again until at last in some mountain streamlet or lake its tired, gaunt body is at home. And there, with almost its last gasp of life, it deposits or fertilizes the two to six thousand eggs—its share of a new spawning.

Patient scientific experiments are helping us to understand this odyssey. When eggs are transferred to other streams, the salmon hatched from them return, not to where the eggs were laid, but to where they were hatched. Other experiments have shown that the fish can distinguish by smell samples of water minutely different in chemistry. Salmon have been observed before their upriver run, rising and milling around in the top, fresh-water layer in front of river

mouths. It is conjectured they are picking up the "scent" they will follow.

Science still does not know the precise nature of the salmon's memory mechanism. Whatever it may be, it evolved millions of years ago and has worked unfailingly ever since.

The homing drive has enabled the salmon to keep its populations well distributed, not over-concentrated in certain favorable areas. It remained for modern man to challenge and in large part destroy the salmon's ancient leasehold of inland waterways.

If we wish to enjoy salmon fishing and eating, and preserve these wildlife species for their own sake, it is obvious what we must do: spare the breeding stock, and preserve the habitat.

The beginning of the potential end for this valuable resource was the commercial fishery that started in 1850 in the waters from San Pablo Bay to the Sacramento–San Joaquin delta. The business spread northward in long leaps—to the Columbia River, to Puget Sound and British Columbia and then, by 1878, to Alaska, where salmon packing became a giant among Pacific Coast industries. As late as 1936 the territorial catch alone, by 2,900 fishing boats, was

BARRIER AND BREACH

over a hundred million salmon. And at a peak before the inevitable decline owing to overfishing, the Alaska pack was worth 100 million dollars a year.

The "cornucopia" idea of the sea's bounty dies hard when heavy investments and twenty thousand jobs are at stake. Like the California sardine industry, Alaska salmon packing grew far past the point where common sense suggested that the fish population could withstand only so much taking, year in and year out. Restriction was difficult, for exhaustive research was necessary to determine the permissible limits of exploitation. In 1924 the Congress acted; at least 50 percent of the salmon must be allowed to pass upstream to their spawning grounds. Yet this breeding quota might now be quite inadequate, for the salmon is clearly vulnerable to man on another front. Its fresh-water breeding grounds, to a large extent remote from the sea, have in many areas suffered from logging, dam building, and other exploitations. In some cases they have become veritable battlegrounds for conflicting human interests. Can we have development of watershed slopes for timber, rivers for power—and salmon too? It has been proven we can, if we consider salmon important enough that planning any development project *begins* with provision for their continuing access to their accustomed spawning grounds, even at some cost in human convenience and profits.

C ONCEIVABLY, in a not far-off time when abandoned dams block river after river while lowland atomic plants fill all power needs, man will be seeking every means to augment the fish resources of the sea and inland waters for their enormous high-protein food potential. Along the Northwest Pacific Coast the chief of these resources is salmon. Evolution is too slow to change the ways of salmon in time to suit our needs. It must reach clear, gravelly streams or mountain lakes to spawn. Man is the only threat to the salmon's future.

Now, most urgently, we must look to every fishery resource we have left, weighing its future in terms of our own. It is terribly clear that we are heedlessly—needlessly—destroying by pollution and other means some of the links in the food chains of which fish are the link next to the last—ourselves.

Seeing any Norteamericano in a boat in the Sea of Cortés, one might safely infer he was a biologist of some sort—or a fisherman. Some believe that the world's best saltwater fishing is found in this gulf, and from north of the border the fishermen come by growing thousands. This is Bahía San Luis Gonzaga, south of San Felipe.

CHAPTER 27

BRIDGES ACROSS TIME

*The Bering land bridge—ancient highroad of life
between the continents of Asia and North America.*

IT WAS A BROAD PLAIN perhaps a thousand miles wide, reaching from Siberia's broad, high Chuekchi Peninsula to the mountains of western Alaska. The Arctic Ocean washed it on one side and the Bering Sea on the other. The Japan Current warmed its southern shores; and tall grasses, like those still found on the Alaskan Peninsula, supported many kinds of mammals. Because of its strategic location, this rich plain had a significance that would last long after its grasses had disappeared beneath the icy sea.

A bridge of dry land joining the continents meant an unbroken continuity of North America and Asia. With the Pacific rim alternately rising and sinking, and with sea level now low, now high, as successive ice sheets built up and melted down, such a bridge has come and gone many times in the last hundred million years. It is more than probable that during the Ice Ages a Bering land bridge existed simultaneously with the Isthmus of Panama (which has also come and gone). The Pacific shoreline would then have curved, unbreached by the sea, from the Strait of Magellan to the Malay Peninsula—three-fifths of the Pacific rim.

In this world of perpetual geologic and climatic change, it is no more than an accident of timing that Asia and North America are today sundered by fifty-six miles of open water while the two Americas are joined. In some future epoch the one juncture will no doubt be closed again, the other opened. For perhaps most of the last sixty or seventy million years, the region of Central America was an archipelago, with islands sometimes near enough to allow "island-hopping" exchanges of life between the continents, sometimes not.

The story of geological change in the two Americas and the fragmentary picture of their ancient life as seen in the fossil record both indicate long separation of those continents from each other. Asia and North America, on the other hand, appear to have been more intimate neighbors. And it is this connection, far more than the Panamanian one, that has affected the life forms of our own Pacific Coast.

Structurally, the alternate downwarping that let Arctic and Pacific waters mingle and unwarping that raised an earth dam between them showed that the earth's crust is continuous from one continent to the other and subject to a single set of tectonic forces. Obviously no great vertical movement of the crust was needed to lift the land at one time or lower it at another. Quite possibly such shifts were fairly frequent during those sixty million years, making a bridge for a few millennia, a strait for the next few. Thus it is reasonable to suppose there were many successive waves of life migrating between the continents, with waves of vegetation inching ahead of the animal transients and laying down feed for them.

Among the first mammals to use such a bridge were probably the marsupials, now represented in North America by the opossum alone. Our Virginia opossum is a late Mesozoic mammal, a "living fossil." Ancestors to it and its many relatives in distant Australia spread across Eurasia and North America, and are thus evidence for a bridge between them.

*The intimate relationship of predator and prey through all eons of
animal life is exemplified by the reassembled skeletons of a saber-tooth
cat and a mylodont ground sloth from the La Brea tar pits.*

There is also evidence of at least three periods of animal migration over this bridge in the past 60 million years, each one of them lasting several million years. By the Pleistocene epoch, mammalian life had advanced to dominate suitable areas of the earth.

During each of its rises from the sea, the Bering land bridge not only provided dry ground for the spreading of many forms of terrestrial life, but stood long enough to insure another essential—time.

However the bridge came into being at a particular time, whether by lift of land or lowering of water, it must have appeared above sea level first as broad tidal flats, broken only by ridges and hills which had but recently been islands. When all had risen above the highest tides, conversion to dry land was well under way. Algae and wet-footed salt marsh grasses had begun to creep outward from old shores onto the rich, newly-exposed alluvial muds, holding the salty clays and sands against tidal erosion.

Winds and the low arctic sun began to dry the ground that was now beneath the sky, not sea. Rains leached more and more of the salt away from the surface, and river deltas continued to spread fresh alluvium upon it, fanning outward from basins and valleys between endlessly eroding hills. From those older lowlands, salt-intolerant grasses and other true land plants marched out upon the delta fans and onto the new ground. The march was slow, year by year and decade by decade, but relentless.

Animals drifted and spread out upon the bridge along with the advancing vegetation. The primary plant consumers—grazers, browsers, bark and root and seed and fruit eaters, mammals, birds, insects— led the wave. Then came secondary consumers—all the predators and scavengers of the animal horde. And there were the several omnivores, chiefly bears and their smaller relatives. Animals and plants were interdependent members of a complex of biotic communities upon the bridge.

We speak of such a land bridge crossing as "migration." So it is in effect; many forms of life may thereby extend their range from one continent to another, transiently or permanently. But the term should not imply intent, like that of, say, migratory water-fowl on the Pacific Flyway; such population shifts are seasonal, rapid, instinctually purposeful, and certain of destination and return. The crossing of a Bering land bridge, on the other hand, was a gradual, even haphazard spread of populations outward from long-held continental homelands into newly available territory. Virgin land had, as always, the pulling power of a vacuum. And for some there was also the push of changing conditions on the old home front. Chief among these, during the million-year Ice Ages, were the climate changes. Plants and animals have always been likely to head toward more inviting horizons, but only man actually reasons that "things might be better on the other side."

What picture can we draw of those critical times of vast and profound upheaval that changed the scene, uprooted the life of one continent to plant it in another, and set the stage for the living drama of our own coastland in its most recent period? Who were the actors?

EARTH AND ATMOSPHERE were turbulent in the Ice Ages. Mountains rose high upon the northern Pacific rims of Asia and America. Slopes and peaks caught the wet of boreal storms wheeling eastward and poleward across the central Siberian plateau, up from the Sea of Okhotsk and Bering Sea, around the Arctic Ocean rim and in vast sweeps across the North Pacific. Driving snows were trapped in clefts of the ranges, packing and forming ice sheets. The burden of ice grew heavy on eastern Siberia's mountains and on the slopes of the Alaska Range, the Coast Ranges bordering the gulf, and the great Cordillera of North America.

The groaning ice moved down to the ocean and upon it, toward the steppes and lowlands of arctic Siberia; it encroached upon the broad, low trough of central Alaska. Inching glaciers threatened the northern lowlands and their grasses, sedges, shrubs, and mosses. Animals living upon them grew restless. All were adapted, through countless generations, to a chill habitat, so probably a gradual climatic shift to colder would not alone have driven the herds toward strange lands. But with food dwindling, hunger would have compelled them to seek forage in any hopeful direction. If storms moved eastward then as now, the grazing animals might be pictured hunching along, the wind at their backs. Their drifting numbers in time found the wide, warmer plain of a grassy young land, and made it their own.

Reindeer, long accustomed to sojourning where food was in seasonal supply, found willow leaves and shoots plentiful in summer, pawed the snow for mosses and lichens in winter. Stripping the same stunted willows in summer and foraging for dead grass bunches beneath the snow, hardy musk oxen swelled the bovine bands. Bison, moose and antelope joined the eastward trek; mountain sheep were temporarily "grounded" on lowland flats until they could claim the craggy heights of a new continent. Towering over all were the shaggy heads of mammoths, as those hugest of land mammals lumbered toward a brief American future.

The shift was overwhelmingly eastward. Only a few species negotiated the opposite passage. Both camel and horse, which had evolved in North America, migrated to Asia during the Ice Ages and became extinct in their original homeland until reintroduced by man in recent historic times. The small west-bound company may have also included the wolf and various rodents. The rodents' "journey" to Asia might best be pictured, not as a goalward march of mice and such, but as a grassroots infiltration, an inching and generation-by-generation spread by which North American forms in time became established on the neighbor continent.

If we could probe the Bering Sea's most recent sedimentary shallows, we might find fossil remains of some of the migrants that perished in transit upon the bridge itself. Not far to the west, however, close to the surface in the central Alaskan corridor, abundant evidence of the once teeming animal trail has been found. There the permafrost—ground perennially frozen to depths of fifty and possibly a hundred. feet—has yielded not only well preserved bones but sinew, hide, hair, and eatable flesh of mammoth, sabre-toothed cat, and others that gained the bridgehead and won the continent.

WHERE have the mammoths gone? What brought to extinction those huge beasts that so lately dominated a vast range? A large assemblage has gone over the hill with them during the few thousand years since the close of the Great Ice Age, notably the larger animals. Shifts of climate, failure of food, ecological disruptions—doubtless many hazards took toll of their populations. In some cases, perhaps, the most dangerous predator was man. Spear points of Pleistocene hunters have been found among the remains of mammoths, giant bison, ground sloths—each providing a great deal of meat in one kill.

The saga of man's first coming to America must remain forever untold, but for a few broken sentences, faintly readable to the archeologist. From these bits we can be certain of little but surmise much. On one point there is general agreement: the first human beings on our continent were Stone Age hunters following game over the Bering land bridge.

How long has man lived in America? No question is more intriguing or less certain of any conclusive answer. Scholars have long been cool to suggestions of more than a dozen millennia or so. Nonetheless, diggers into the past have found on one of California's Channel Islands some evidence which indicates that mammoths and quite probably man, too, came at least two or three times that long ago.

On Santa Rosa Island there is a seacliff exposure of Pleistocene sediments. In 1948 a scientific team from Santa Barbara found and began excavating a site in this formation which was marked by brick-red earth containing bits of charcoal and burned bone. They appeared to lie in what had been a pit. There were, besides, large bones that were not burned. Some of these bones proved to be part of the skeleton of a dwarf mammoth, which radiocarbon dating has placed at 29,650 years old, plus or minus 2,500 years. Phil C. Orr, of the Santa Barbara Museum of Natural History, reviewed his find: "We believe the conditions under which these bones were found strongly indicate the presence of man on the Island at this time, and that the burned ribs and vertebrae and brick-red earth could only have been caused by a hot fire burning for a period of time, probably as a 'barbecue,' in which the smaller bones, consisting of 'steaks' and 'spare-ribs,' would be roasted, while the larger bones would be stripped of their meat and put in the fire."

Whether man—western "barbecue culture" and all—has lived on the Pacific Coast for thirty thousand years may long remain controversial. Radiocarbon dating leaves little room for doubt concerning the antiquity of the presumed "cook-out" victim. And the incident of the mammoth on Santa Rosa Island adds a paragraph to the story of land bridges.

BARRIER AND BREACH

Fossils of a dwarf mammoth—the adult height ranged from under six to perhaps eight feet—have been found on San Miguel, Santa Rosa, and Santa Cruz Islands. Geological evidence shows these three northern Channel Islands to have been a single mass in the past and strongly suggests that the whole was a peninsular extension of the Santa Monica Range. Paleontologists support that belief. Elephants do not swim—not across several miles of ocean, as in a Bering Strait or Santa Barbara Channel. The little "exiled" island mammoth is thought to be the descendant of no less than the emperor mammoth, whose bones are found in the tar pits of Rancho La Brea, just south of the Santa Monicas. The great elephant had extended its range, perhaps a hundred thousand years ago, to the long westward peninsula. There it was when the inevitable forces of change destroyed the land bridge and isolated the island mass. A combination of evolutionary factors led rapidly to the dwarfing of the relict mammoth, which may have lived on one or more of the islands until as recently as fifteen thousand years ago. With increasing drought in the period following the Ice Ages, the once huge animal may have had to adapt to a drastically reduced food supply. (Paradoxically, the island fossil beds have also yielded up a giant mouse!)

The last small mammoth may well have fallen not to starvation but to human predators, to end its imperial line forever in a barbecue pit. The last of the emperors themselves, the mainland giants, may have closed their splendid dynasty in the tar pits of La Brea, amid a suffocating retinue of lesser creatures.

Dark forms wheel in the sky. Soaring in long slants from rock ledges of the Santa Monica Range close by to the north, the great birds, heavy-bodied, long and broad of wing, gather in a loose, circling concourse high above a blackened area on the valley floor. Singly the planing forms spiral down to the rim of a small but noisome lake of tar. The aim of each bird's ponderously controlled descent is the broad, upturned flank of a dead animal whose bulk is slowly sinking into the viscid blackness of the pool. So large is the hairy island of flesh, the mired mammal is perhaps a mastodon or mammoth, for some future man to identify by its bones.

As rapidly as the landing Teratorns gain a foot-hold, with rather weak claws, they sink great hooked beaks into the loosening hide. Hungrily they tear at the still sweet flesh. Vulturine, not of the hawk or eagle tribe, these birds were not built to attack and kill for their meat. Winging aloft, they spot with keen eyes any newly dead or dying animal on the ground far below. They are not lured to high-smelling carrion—food for scavenging insects, and the final consumers, bacteria.

Teratornis ("wondrous bird") remains the largest known flying bird of past or present. A number of the great birds were entrapped in the seeping La Brea tar, where they first became known to science when their bones mingled with those of the unfor-

California condors patrol the "Hurricane Deck," the primitive mountain area behind the Santa Ynez Range and the Santa Barbara coast. Across the Santa Barbara Channel, Anacapa, Santa Cruz, Santa Rosa, and San Miguel islands lie low on the horizon. (From a landscape painting by Ray Strong, with birds painted by Harry C. Adamson, for the Oakland Museum.)

tunate animals on whom they fed. They, too, may have been the last of their dynasty.

An echo of Teratornis, itself impressively large and of identical feeding habits, still soars silently above Pacific coastlands. How long will that darksome symbol of the Pleistocene, the California condor, remain aloft? Man, through the quality of his concern, will help decide its fate. There may be some who are saying: condors—they are bound to go anyway; what difference does it make, whether sooner or later? And that is a hard question to answer. Intrinsic difference? Probably little. Aesthetic? There are relatively few persons who see beauty in a great, lonely, not conventionally beautiful bird, soaring above

wild hills looking for a dead animal. But we know that to shrug it off with indifference is to deny some basic attributes of humanity, one of which is the capacity to be concerned about other than human life. Another, perhaps, is respect for something very old.

Bridges across time are fragile and must all fall down one day. They do not require careless or willful destruction. However, if we hasten the falling of one such bridge as the condor—and in these times of danger to all life we do so merely by making no effort to preserve it—we somehow know we are losing something of ourselves. The loss may be only a little more of our own sense of time and of wonder, but without these we are less than human.

269

CHAPTER 28

MAN ON THE WESTERN EDGE

*The dilemma man faces—how to use and enjoy
the magnificent coast and still preserve it for tomorrow.*

IN WONDER did man first behold this coastland, this new continent unfolding. In truth, the moment of wonder has come twice, perhaps more, in the history of this land. But who can speak for that other man, that Asian, or descendant of an Asian who first knew the curving, the cliff-rise, the surf-beat, the mist, the gull-cry of this shore? Who can know the degree of his sense of discovery and wonder? Who can imagine his response, his dawning of knowledge, with no record remaining of where or whence he came, no notion whether from sea or from land that first human being in all time filled eyes and brain with the reality of this coast?

One can speak with truthfulness only from within the bounds of his own view, his own culture, and experience. Mind and reflection, then, must leap an unknown long way from the present into the visible, knowable realm of historic context and continuity, to find ties between past and future.

Within that context, we can free imaginations for a kind of return journey—a mind-flight back to the beginning of discovery and the dawning of wonder. And although passengers of a particular culture we can identify none the less with every man who has discovered a new or wondered at an unknown thing. The trip will not end, however. When it has circled to bring the starting point of the present again into view it will continue, hopefully, as a spiraling onward through insight to some convictions about the worth of many things. Wonder might head the list—it preludes understanding. Acceptance of the fact of change can make one both philosophical and hopeful. Knowl-

edge and enjoyment of nature go hand in hand, and foster the sense of belonging to the earth and all time, or to this place and this moment, which may satisfy most human needs. Or some may watch a breaker rise to its plunge, and know that earth, sea, time, the instant, and man, are one.

STAND WITH BALBOA on a bare high hill in Panama and glimpse for the first time through Western eyes the most immense ocean on the surface of the globe. Wonder lies, at this shining moment, in understanding the impact of this awesome sight on Europeans of his time, who knew so little about the world. For Balboa suddenly the world is vastly bigger than it was a moment ago.

Sail the chartless Vermilion Sea with Cortés, Ulloa, and Alarcón. Venture with Bolaños past Los Frailes, around the stormy Cape, and northward up Baja's unknown ocean coast. Join Cabrillo and Ferrelo on the first long coasting voyage; cross the northern Pacific with Legaspi and Urdaneta, raise the bold headlands, and know the immensity of the ocean confronting this coast.

Discover some bay with Drake and leave the world a puzzle to solve. Coast southward with Cermeño after shipwreck at latitude 38°, and return with Vizcaíno to sight Mendocino's high cape and reach to 43°N; the parallels are the coast's measuring tape.

Walk north with Portolá and the padres, over pine-topped hills, through oak-groved valleys, along the rocky strands, and begin to read the coastland's book of nature.

*Symbolic of man on the edge of land: a lone fisherman, facing the setting sun off the
Golden Gate, for a brief hour in his own timeless world of rock, surf, and—hopefully—fish.*

Sail the icy waters with Bering and Chirikof, past the Aleutians into the glaciered gulf, to discover *Alyashka*, the Great Land. Go with Malaspina, Cook, and Vancouver to a Northwest of snowy mountains and coastland forests. Wonder at mighty trees with Menzies and Douglas, at Glacier Bay with Muir. Cross the Columbia's bar with Gray; float from the Dalles to the ocean with Lewis and Clark. A continent's edge is met from both land and sea.

On no other coast could the total experience be reenacted. In no other span of centuries could the human drama have equaled it; for the discoverer's journey has lost, along with certain dangers, the trauma of utter remoteness. Ours is an age in which vehicles of exploration do not leave port or launching pad without every conceivable assurance of mechanical mastery over all conditions of the trip. Communication is instant, constant, and complete, both auditory and visual. Yet man continues to perfect his means. Future generations will view Apollo moonships in museums as clever but crude prototypes of space exploration vehicles—"how did they ever get *there* in *that*?" Consider the sailing ship of four hundred years ago, not as vehicle alone but as a life support system—the means of communication that were available, for example, and the state of medical and nutritional knowledge. Yet people crowded into the impossible little tubs and pushed off into a total void of knowledge and communication, knowing that the experience of returning from such previous ventures was statistically not much in their favor.

The feats of discovery and exploration of this coast were accomplished just as soon as mankind was technically and culturally ready for such tasks. Then, with overwhelming speed and thoroughness, the succeeding age seized upon and converted to its own uses the accomplishments of the pioneers. In this are both wonder and warning.

In the past hundred years, the Age of Sail was quietly furled and stowed into memory, and the Age of Atom, Jet, and Space exploded into being.

A century ago, some of this coast's original discoverers were still alive and working; Muir was yet to bring Glacier Bay to the world's view. The offshore ocean was largely unfathomed. Cities were rising, trees were falling, steamships were plying, rails were

being laid. But this greatest of coasts still belonged mainly to the nourishing, shaping sea, to the freshening winds, to the restless, rising crust, and to all the living things that flourished in these wild habitats. Man was still small here, even a half century ago.

Viewing the picture now, is there some shock value in contemplating the degree of change that man has wrought? Portolá or Serra, returning today, would not recognize El Camino Real; De Anza would not grasp the outcome of that first transplant colony. Royal Navy Captains Cook and Vancouver would rub salty eyes at the bristling military might of San Diego Bay, Vandenberg Air Force Base, and Mare Island and Bremerton navy yards.

What has happened is too closely bound up with what *is* happening and what *will* happen to be merely studied and filed as history. The fate of the "pineries" and all the Pacific Coast's other resources and attractions is bound up with attitudes and actions which are still with us in the present and which will, in turn, shape the future.

The pace, now so fast, was slow starting. Men from western Europe first saw this coast as the far edge of a strange continent, a land mass which stood in the way of reaching the East and its treasures by a westward water route—land first considered to *be* the Indies. For a long time the Pacific Coast was explored more as an accessory to traffic with the Orient than as land worth knowing for its own sake.

At length, men began going to the coast simply because it was there. It offered new wealth for the Old World establishment—land to take for earthly kingdoms, with peoples to conquer for a heavenly one. It was a long time before this coast became an intrinsic part of the New World establishment of power and wealth, and still longer before it became not only a thing to exploit but a place to *be*, to develop as a new domain for Western civilization.

The people of the brief, explosive, and still recent period of settlement and growth gave little thought to values other than those inherent in their own material well-being. The idea that anything in nature could possibly be used up and therefore should be used moderately just did not exist. The western edge of the continent seemed as illimitable as it was wild and rugged; only a few parts were hospitable to shipping, farming, and town-building. Yet from all who came to make a new life, not just to take the gold out of the earth or other men's pockets, the cry went up for more and yet more people. They came —they still come—and we experience what Neil Morgan has called the "westward tilt, . . . the largest migration in the history of the world."

Inevitably the Far West's largest cities grew up around the major Pacific seaports (except for Los Angeles, which in the midst of its early boom had to reach across the open plain and build itself a harbor at San Pedro). The nuclei were well planted on the coast and ready when World War II and its aftermath triggered the present and most precipitous phase of the national population tilt.

Doubtless the impact on the long shore itself— first within arm's reach of the cities, then along farther and still farther stretches—would not yet be nearly so great but for two factors. One, the automobile, had begun an exploratory seaside crawl early in the century, but was limited by roads as well as by potential owners with leisure time. This weapon of assault upon the coastline came into its own in league with the other factor, the explosion of the nuclei and their even faster-growing surburban satellites into hordes of people endowed with spare time, spare cash, and the urge to spend both away from home. For some, there is the second home in the mountains or along the coast. For more and more of the rest of us, there is the leisure-time home on wheels. And obliging governments have provided the roads to ever remoter target areas for both classes.

We who dearly love this coast are now rapidly smothering it with our numbers. If we do not live here already, we pour in great streams from the interior on every warm weekend, and we drive to it from distant states. It is our privilege to do so, given the time, the money, and the wheels. Yet clearly a way must be found to lighten our impact, as we are now having to pull our punches upon the reeling Yosemite and other national parks. We face a dilemma, one viewed with alarm, sadness, or frustration in a growing spate of words in all media. Yet we, the public, are slow to muster our will and our power to resolve it. Power resides in the legislative process, whose ultimate control is the ballot. The chief obstacles to achieving desirable goals are general public apathy and particular private interest.

Oregon and California divide between them a major portion of a distinctively scenic sector of the Pacific Coast, where high, dark headlands, reefs, rocks, and sea stacks alternate with dunes or lovely crescent-beach coves where the forest meets the strand. From the Golden Gate to the Columbia, except for a stretch of the California coast on both sides of Cape Mendocino, one may view this superb shoreline from his car window. By some prophetic stroke of public wisdom, the State of Oregon as early as 1913 reserved its shoreline for all the people; access is now unrestricted to all but twenty-three miles of the outer coast. In contrast, 65 percent of the entire California coastline is privately owned. Of the rest, much is taken out of public use by military reservations.

The argument is most strongly and rightly made for a maximum of free public access (and a minimum of denial or restriction of it, whether in the name of military security or private ownership) to all the most beautiful, inspiring, and unique portions of our natural heritage—mountain peaks, deserts, wild rivers, seacoast. Yet herein is part of the manifold dilemma. By sheer numbers we tend to destroy these things we cherish. There is detrimental private ownership, which is allowed to result in the desecration of a Morro Bay by huge smokestacks, or of a fine Washington coastal spit by an ill-suited subdivision. Then there is a fortuitously beneficial kind, through which an appreciable percentage of California's coastland has been long preserved in huge ranches. Public ownership and access take an unhappy course when they lead to cheek-by-jowl crowding of people and the cars that bring them, trampled dune plants, and windrows of beer cans. Then arises the dilemma of quantity versus quality of experience. There are persons who find no pleasure in a beach that has all the charm of a garbage dump at the edge of a parking lot; their right to a different experience is not to be denied.

Mankind is here to stay, or so we constantly reassure ourselves—with the environment deteriorating around us. Now we know the causes as well as the consequences of such degradation; therefore we need not delay in reversing its course. Surely we can hurry into environmental improvement as readily as into war. It may cost as much, but will be a far greater bargain.

If man always lived along the sea as simply and tastefully as in the gentle community of Mendocino, California, and never tried to swarm at any seacoast point in unrestrained numbers or in disregard and deliberate violation of natural laws, he would create no problems for himself and the coming generations vis-à-vis the outer edge of land. And as the land surrenders a terrace face to the ever-cutting waves, it is better for man to yield a modest cottage than a mansion, a cowshed than a factory or skyscraper. It is better to think as a short-term leaseholder than as a perpetual owner. The edge of a continent is a temporary thing.

The first step is a reordering of priorities; the next is to educate people in the whats and whys of natural balances. An enlightened public will raise its own sights and back its choices with financial muscle. We have seen the process working in a small region with the San Francisco Bay Conservation and Development Commission. Finally, we must plan and carry through, on a broadly regional basis, the hard tasks of renovation.

The 1967 legislative creation of a California Advisory Commission on Marine and Coastal Resources, charged with reviewing the "known and estimated future needs for natural resources from the marine and coastal environment" and preparing a report "which sets forth the public interest in the coastline of California," was recognition, at least, of both the necessity and the possibility of tackling the obvious economic and political aspects of the problem.

Cry California, the journal of California Tomorrow, has emphasized the importance of legislation calling for "creation of a comprehensive Ocean Area Plan to delineate the present and future needs of the coast." A proposed California Coastline Commission, with teeth, will be a long step forward. Perhaps a multistate commission, and ultimately a three-nation body, for the governance of human ecology on the Pacific Coast, are not improbable dreams.

All discussion of the problems of the coast (problems common to our Atlantic, Gulf, and Pacific coasts alike), and proposals for action to solve them are useless if they are not addressed to the present and a very immediate future as well as the long term, and to the broad regional concern as well as the narrow local interest. The basic problem is, simply, to ensure for the largest number of people the greatest possible enjoyment, fairly shared, of the intrinsic bene-

people can use it annually without its residual wildness being trampled and spoiled?

No such questions can be resolved without sanctions in both senses of the word: approbation and intervention, consent to the restriction of rights, and denial of their violation.

Few would disagree that every child should have some chance not only to see a redwood tree but to feel its bark, to play on the beach to his heart's content, to swim or fish in an unpolluted stream, to peer into a tidepool and see all the fascinating things nature put there. Nor would they deny adults such pleasures. Yet as fifty people per day at some attraction turns into five hundred, the very traffic kills the forest garden, debauches the stream, makes the tide zone a desert. No one wins with too many players on the field at once. How can we give everybody a chance to play and win some worthwhile experience?

Perhaps there are no easy solutions, and probably none that will satisfy all of us. But there is little argument that if the rules are not changed the stakes are in danger of being lost.

FOR US WHO LIVE on this coast, visit it, or read books about it, there can be no such amazement at what has happened here as would strike a returned representative of some previous age. There can be, however, a healthy and repeated shock reaction to the "march of progress," warning us to be alert lest much that is devised and produced for us in the name of growth and progress becomes responsible for the loss of still more of the sources of wonder and beauty that have endured on this coast through all ages before the present one.

That last sentence is loaded—biased in the extreme. It is loaded in favor of wild dunes and mountains, pelicans skimming the surf, wind-shaped pines, salmon, tidepools, storms, and the clearing skies.

And it is biased on the side of everyone who enjoys such things, who would keep them where they are meant to be and as they have come through time to an incomparable meeting of land and sea; who would strive to keep ocean, river, and air pollution-free, tides running clean, beaches wild, vistas open, surf-sound unchallenged, forests growing tall to the sun; who would cherish these things and hold them in trust for a long future.

fits of a finite resource, now and for a hopeful future.

The dilemma is evident. "Greatest possible enjoyment" implies, for any individual, unrestricted access to whatever benefits there are, as he sees them. Obviously, the benefit of untrammeled wildness, for one to enjoy, is incompatible with the benefit of ownership, development, or pure exploitation, for another. As coastal residents and visitors both increase, the law of diminishing returns takes effect for everyone. For the democratic ideal to remain operative, there must be allocation and apportionment. This requires planning, unselfishly as well as realistically undertaken, at the highest public level. There must be the most searching consideration, by private interests, and the public through its representatives, together, of every alternative. Should development be permitted here, and what kind? Should that portion become a park, and how many

Overleaf: When all is said and done, and man has had his span of time, waves, and shores, sea and land will still be meeting in patterns too old for Earth to remember when they began.

SOURCES AND SUGGESTED READING

Land, Sea, and Sky

The Earth Beneath the Sea. Francis P. Shepard. Rev. ed. (New York: Atheneum, 1969.) Illus. An exceptionally readable textbook; the Pacific Coast well represented.

Earthquake Country. Robert Iacopi. (Menlo Park, Calif.: Lane Book Co., 1964.) Illus. The life and times of the San Andreas and other prominent faults.

The Evolution of North America. Philip B. King. (Princeton, N. J.: Princeton University Press, 1959.) Illus. A geologist explores the continent through its ancient past.

Evolution of the California Landscape. Norman E. A. Hinds. Bulletin 158: Division of Mines. (San Francisco: California Department of Natural Resources, 1952.) Illus. Written for taxpayers as well as professionals.

Geology Illustrated. John S. Shelton. (San Francisco: W. H. Freeman & Co., 1966.) Illus. The fine photographs include many from the air and of West Coast subjects.

Glacial and Pleistocene Geology. Richard Foster Flint. (New York: John Wiley & Sons, 1957.) Illus. A textbook, but not too technical for general understanding.

Landscapes of Alaska: Their Geologic Evolution. Howel Williams, ed., with contributors. (Berkeley & Los Angeles: University of California Press, 1958.) Illus., maps. In layman's language by experts, with relevance to the present scene and life of the region.

Marine Geology of the Pacific. H. W. Menard. (New York: McGraw-Hill Book Co., 1964.) Illus. Textbook for the serious student.

The Ocean of Air. David I. Blumenstock. (New Brunswick, N. J.: Rutgers University Press, 1959.) One of the most readable books about the atmospheric part of our environment, and how we respond to it and depend on it.

Physiography of the United States. Charles B. Hunt. (San Francisco: W. H. Freeman & Co., 1967.) Illus. Clear, simple text with much natural and human ecology.

The Scenic Treasure House of Oregon. Warren D. Smith. (Portland: Binfords & Mort, 1941.) Illus. The geology behind the scenery.

The Sea. Robert C. Miller. (New York: Random House, 1966.) Illus. For the layman, by an eminent marine biologist, oceanographer, and philosopher.

Waves and Beaches: The Dynamics of the Ocean Surface. Willard Bascom. (Garden City, N. Y.: Doubleday & Co., 1964.) Illus. Makes science an exciting adventure.

The World of Nature

The American West: A Natural History. Ann and Myron Sutton. (New York: Random House, 1969.) Illus. The gamut from desert to glacier, handled both in breadth and detail.

Autumn Across America. Edwin Way Teale. (New York: Dodd, Mead & Co., 1956.) Illus. The West Coast part of this journey went from Vancouver, B.C., to the Big Sur River.

Bent's Life Histories of North American Birds. Henry Hill Collins, Jr., ed. Vol. 1: *Water Birds;* vol. 2: *Land Birds.* (New York: Harper & Brothers, 1960.) A classic of observation.

Earth Song: A Prologue to History. Charles L. Camp. Rev. ed. (Palo Alto, Calif.: American West Publishing Co., 1970.) Illus. How the western land and life evolved together.

The Edge of the Sea. Rachel Carson. (Boston: Houghton Mifflin, 1955.) Illus. Of other coasts, but universal nevertheless.

Face of North America: The Natural History of a Continent. Peter Farb. (New York: Harper & Row, 1963.) Illus. Masterful overall account, with much ecology; the West given its due.

Island Life: A Natural History of the Islands of the World. Sherwin Carlquist. (Garden City, N. Y.: Natural History Press, 1965.) Illus. Inclusive of the California Islands.

Late-Pleistocene Environments of North Pacific North America: An Elaboration of Late-Glacial and Postglacial Climatic, Physiographic, and Biotic Changes. Calvin J. Heusser. Special Publication no. 35. (New York: American Geographical Society, 1960.) Illus. Source for the *refugium* concept and the role of pollen studies.

The Living Past. John C. Merriam. (New York: Charles Scribner's Sons, 1930.) Illus. Chapters on La Brea tar pits, redwoods of the past, a philosophy of evolution.

The Natural Geography of Plants. Henry A. Gleason and Arthur Cronquist. (New York: Columbia University Press, 1964.) Illus. A great deal about range and migration of plants, and an account of the vegetation of North America north of Mexico. Not difficult ecology.

Plant Ecology of the Channel Islands of California. Meryl Byron Dunkle. (Los Angeles: University of Southern California Press, 1950.) Illus. Technical but not difficult for the deeply interested layman, to whom so little on these islands has been addressed.

Proceedings of the Symposium on the Biology of the California Islands. Ralph N. Philbrick, ed. (Santa Barbara: Santa Barbara Botanic Garden, 1967.) Illus. Remarks: same as for above.

The Redwoods of Coast and Sierra. James Clifford Shirley. (Berkeley & Los Angeles: University of California Press, 1947.) Illus. Slim but informative.

The Road of a Naturalist. Donald Culross Peattie. (London: Robert Hale Ltd., 1946.) Illus. The last chapter is an entrancing West Coast journey, by one of the best of all nature writers.

The Sea Around Us. Rachel Carson. Rev. ed. (New York: Oxford University Press, 1961.) Illus. The incomparable book on the nature of the sea.

Union Bay: The Life of a City Marsh. Harry W. Higman and Earl J. Larrison. (Seattle: University of Washington Press, 1951.) Illus. Absorbing for its own sake; compelling as a lesson in the ecological importance of preservation.

Wandering Through Winter. Edwin Way Teale. (New York: Dodd, Mead & Co., 1965.) Illus. Reading Teale is an experience only surpassed by meeting him on his continental journeys. Southern California coast, with gray whales.

The Ways of Fishes. Leonard P. Schultz. (New York: D. Van Nostrand Co., 1948.) Illus. Source of the grunion spawning account, and much about salmon.

Wild America. Roger Tory Peterson and James Fisher. (Boston: Houghton Mifflin, 1955.) Illus. "A 30,000-mile journey around the continent," with West Coast points including Los Coronados,

Point Lobos, Destruction Island, Anchorage, Pribilof Islands. The two bird men are good raconteurs.

Exploration

Balboa of Darien: Discoverer of the Pacific. Kathleen Romoli. (Garden City, N. Y.: Doubleday & Co., 1953.) Combines true scholarship and vivid style.

Book of Bays. William Beebe. (New York: Harcourt, Brace & Co., 1942.) Illus. The great naturalist tells of a scientific expedition from Baja to Columbia, including offshore islands.

Coastal Exploration of Washington. Robert Ballard Whitebrook. Foreword by Henry R. Wagner. (Palo Alto, Calif.: Pacific Books, 1959.) An account of Vancouver's survey of Puget Sound, with course charts. Annotated.

The Columbia River. Ross Cox. (Norman, Okla.: University of Oklahoma Press, 1957.) Illus. First published in 1831; a compelling narrative.

The Costansó Narrative of the Portolá Expedition: First Chronicle of the Spanish Conquest of Alta California. Ray Brandes. Translated, with introduction and bibliography. (Newhall, Calif.: Hogarth Press, 1970.) An objective and impersonal account by Portolá's engineer, who deserves wider recognition.

The Explorations of Captain James Cook in the Pacific as Told by Selections of His Own Journals, 1768–1779. A. Grenfell Price, ed. (New York: Heritage Press, n.d.) Contains the story of Turnagain Arm, among many others.

The Flight of the Least Petrel. Griffing Bancroft. (New York: G. P. Putnam's Sons, 1932.) Illus. Remarkable personal narrative of an ornithologist's voyage completely around Baja California; detailed nature exploration and observation.

Font's Complete Diary of the Second Anza Expedition. Herbert Eugene Bolton, ed. Anza's California Expeditions, vol. 4. (Berkeley & Los Angeles: University of California Press, 1931.) The journey that brought San Francisco its first settlers.

The Forgotten Peninsula: A Naturalist in Baja California. Joseph Wood Krutch. (New York: William Sloane Assoc., 1961.) Illus. A great writer-turned-naturalist explores and philosophizes.

A Journal of Explorations: Northward along the coast from Monterey in the year 1775. Fr. Miguel de la Campa. Edited by John Galvin. (San Francisco: John Howell Books, 1964.) Narrative of the most northerly Spanish voyage, from San Blas to southeastern Alaska, with Heceta, Pérez, and Bodega y Quadra; observations of Indians and wildlife.

The Journals of Lewis and Clark. Bernard DeVoto, ed. (Boston: Houghton Mifflin, 1953.) Maps. Classic modern edition.

The Last Wilderness. Murray Morgan. (New York: Viking Press, 1955.) Illus. The Olympic Peninsula, discovery to national park.

Sea of Cortez: A Leisurely Journal of Travel and Research. John Steinbeck and Edward F. Ricketts. (New York: Viking Press, 1941.) Illus. A science and adventure classic, philosophical, often humorous. Original edition includes "Annotated Phyletic Catalogue." Issued later: the *Log* of the voyage only.

Surveyor of the Sea: The Life and Voyages of Captain George Vancouver. Bern Anderson. (Seattle: University of Washington Press, 1960.) Maps. A U. S. Navy rear admiral gives a Royal Navy officer his due for exceptional performance in Pacific Coast exploration and pioneer surveying.

Travels in Alaska. John Muir. (Boston: Houghton Mifflin, 1915.) Illus. The whole story of Glacier Bay and Muir's other Alaskan discoveries.

Up and Down California in 1860–1864: The Journal of William H. Brewer. Francis P. Farquhar, ed. (New Haven: Yale University Press, 1930; Los Angeles & Berkeley: University of California Press, 1966.) Illus. Classic account of life in early California.

Zaca Venture. William Beebe. (New York: Harcourt, Brace & Co., 1938.) Illus. This Beebe voyage was mainly in Baja waters, with Clarion Island thrown in.

The Human Drama

Black Robes in Lower California. Peter Masten Dunne, S.J. (Berkeley & Los Angeles: University of California Press, 1952.) Scholarly but highly readable, on the founding of Baja's Jesuit missions.

California. John Walton Caughey. 2nd ed. (New York: Prentice-Hall, 1953.) Illus. History from the land upward.

The California Coast: A Bilingual Edition of Documents from the Sutro Collection. Donald C. Cutter, ed. Translated and edited in 1891 by George Butler Griffin; reedited with emended translations, annotation, and preface. (Norman: University of Oklahoma Press, 1969.) Illus. Includes letters of Vizcaíno, Serra, and their respective contemporaries, and part of Crespí's journal.

The California Indians: A Source Book. R. F. Heizer and M. A. Whipple, eds. (Berkeley & Los Angeles: University of California Press, 1951.) Illus. See contribution by E. W. Gifford which begins: "Balanophagy, or acorn eating, was probably the most characteristic feature of the domestic economy of the California Indians."

California's Missions: Their Romance and Beauty. Hildegarde Hawthorne. (New York: D. Appleton-Century Co., 1942.) Illus. One of the most complete and readable accounts, with E. H. Suydam's delightful drawings.

California: Two Centuries of Man, Land, and Growth in the Golden State. W. H. Hutchinson. (Palo Alto, Calif.: American West Publishing Co., 1969.) Illus. Past and present in timely perspective.

Empire of the Columbia: A History of the Pacific Northwest. Dorothy O. Johansen and Charles M. Gates. (New York: Harper & Row, 1967.) Illus. Definitive is the word.

Empire on the Pacific: A Study in American Continental Expansion. Norman A. Graebner. (New York: Ronald Press Co., 1955.) Background to "manifest destiny" and the events of its fulfillment, focusing on the critical period 1844–46.

From Wilderness to Empire: A History of California. Robert Glass Cleland. Edited by Glenn S. Dumke. (New York: Alfred A. Knopf, 1959.) Illus. Of many "Californias," this is one of the best.

George Davidson: Pioneer West Coast Scientist. Oscar Lewis. (Berkeley & Los Angeles: University of California Press, 1954.) Absorbing biography of the U. S. Coast Survey geodesist and astronomer, who charted virtually every mile of the coastline from Mexico to northern Alaska.

Historical Memoirs of New California by Fray Francisco Palóu, O.F.M. Herbert Eugene Bolton. (Berkeley: University of California Press, 1926; New York: Russell & Russell, 1965.) In 4 vols., contains the Crespí diary.

Indians of the Northwest Coast. Philip Drucker. Anthropological Handbook, no. 10. (New York: McGraw-Hill Book Co., 1955.) Illus. An anthropologist writes for the layman.

Journey of the Flame. Antonio de Fierro Blanco. (New York: Brandt & Brandt, 1933.) An early nineteenth-century journey through the Californias that could have happened.

Land of Giants: The Drive to the Pacific Northwest, 1750–1950. David Lavender. (Garden City, N. Y.: Doubleday & Co., 1958.) Maps. How everybody got to the Northwest, and why.

The Last of the Conquistadors: Junipero Serra (1713–1784). Omer Englebert. (New York: Harcourt, Brace & Co., 1956.) The sweep, color, and action of a historical novel.

The Manila Galleon. William Lytle Schurz. (New York: E. P. Dutton & Co., 1959.) First published in 1939; *the* source on this romantic enterprise.

Observations in Lower California. Johann Jakob Baegert, S. J. Translated from the original German, with introduction and notes by M. M. Brandenburg and Carl L. Baumann. (Berkeley & Los Angeles: University of California Press, 1952.) Telling and truthful account of a strange land and people in the eighteenth century; still worth reading because much of it is still true.

The Pacific States: California, Oregon, Washington. Neil Morgan and the editors of Time-Life Books. (New York: Time-Life Books, 1967.) Illus. They call it "the restless edge."

The Royal Highway (El Camino Real). Edwin Corle. (Indianapolis: Bobbs-Merrill Co., 1949.) Illus. The path of the padres in California, down to the twentieth century.

Russian Influence on Early America. Clarence A. Manning. (New York: Library Publishers, 1953.) From Vitus Bering to the sale of Alaska, with a possibly gratuitous conclusion.

San Francisco Bay: Discovery and Colonization, 1769–1776. Theodore E. Treutlein. (San Francisco: California Historical Society, 1968.) Illus. Scholarly and fully documented.

The San Francisco Bay Area: A Metropolis in Perspective. Mel Scott. (Berkeley & Los Angeles: University of California Press, 1959.) Illus. History with emphasis on city and regional planning.

Skid Road: An Informal Portrait of Seattle. Murray Morgan. Rev. ed. (New York: Viking Press, 1960.) Captivating biography of the city on the sound.

The Story of Alaska. C. L. Andrews. (Caldwell, Idaho: Caxton Printers, 1947.) Illus. History to early World War II period; well documented.

Time, Tide and Timber: A Century of Pope & Talbot. Edwin T. Coman, Jr. and Helen M. Gibbs. (Stanford, Calif.: Stanford University Press, 1949.) Illus. Solid history, not just a "company book"; the Puget Mill story in full.

Vizcaíno and Spanish Expansion in the Pacific Ocean 1580–1630. W. Michael Mathes. (San Francisco: California Historical Society, 1968.) Illus. A scholarly, thoroughly documented evaluation.

Westward Tilt: The American West Today. Neil Morgan. (New York: Random House, 1963.) Maps. An often cited book.

Conservation

Alaska: A Challenge in Conservation. Richard A. Cooley. (Madison, Wis.: University of Wisconsin Press, 1966.) Illus. There are still too few expert analyses of Alaska's particular conservation problems and threats; this goes far in filling the gap.

Between the Devil and the Deep Blue Bay: The Struggle to Save San Francisco Bay. Harold Gilliam. (San Francisco: Chronicle Books, 1969.) Illus. An examination of events and efforts.

The Destruction of California. Raymond F. Dasmann. (New York: Collier Books, 1966.) Illus. On the terrible price of "progress."

Island in Time: The Point Reyes Peninsula. Harold Gilliam. Photographs by Philip Hyde; foreword by Stewart L. Udall. (San Francisco: Sierra Club, 1962.) The book that launched the Point Reyes National Seashore.

Man and the California Condor: The Embattled History and Uncertain Future of North America's Largest Free-living Bird. Ian McMillan. (New York: E. P. Dutton & Co., 1968.) Objective reporting with a strong message.

Wildlife in Alaska: An Ecological Reconnaissance. A. Starker Leopold and F. Fraser Darling. (New York: Ronald Press Co., 1953.) Illus. The wildlife resources of a great region and the use-impact upon them.

Views of Places

Fishing the Pacific: Offshore and On. S. Kip Farrington, Jr. (New York: Coward-McCann, 1953.) Illus. The sport fisherman's arm-

chair book. Chapters on Mexico, Catalina, Washington, and British Columbia.

Inside Passage to Alaska. Morten Lund. (Philadelphia: J. B. Lippincott, 1965.) Illus. Descriptive account of a sportsman's cruise.

The Pacific Coast Ranges. Roderick Peattie, ed. (New York: Vanguard Press, 1946.) Illus. Mixture of description, anecdote, personal reminiscence.

San Francisco Bay. Harold Gilliam. (Garden City, N. Y.: Doubleday & Co., 1957.) Nature, history, lore; nothing more readable on the bay.

The Sea of Cortez. Ray Cannon and the Sunset editors. (Menlo Park, Calif.: Lane Magazine & Book Co., 1966.) Illus. A fisherman's book: tidbits of nature and history to garnish a fish fry.

Guides and References

Between Pacific Tides. Edward F. Ricketts and Jack Calvin. 4th ed. (Stanford, Calif.: Stanford University Press, 1968.) Illus. The essential book.

The Birds of California: A Complete, Scientific and Popular Account of the 580 Species and Subspecies of Birds Found in the State. William Leon Dawson. 3 vols. (San Diego: South Moulton Co., 1923.) Illus. Stupendous opposite of a handbook: 2121 pages. Source of the Farallon eggers' story and others.

California Natural History Guides. Arthur C. Smith, ed. (Berkeley & Los Angeles: University of California Press, 1959–71.) Illus. In this comprehensive paperback series, upwards of 30 books by well-known authors have appeared.

A Field Guide to Western Birds. Roger Tory Peterson. 2nd ed. (Boston: Houghton Mifflin, 1961.) Illus. A new printing of this edition in 1969; still the best of the handy guides.

Forest Trees of the Pacific Slope. George B. Sudworth. U. S. Department of Agriculture, Forest Service. (Washington, D.C.: Government Printing Office, 1908; New York: Dover Publications, 1965.) Illus. Still the western tree man's Bible.

Geologic Guidebook of the San Francisco Bay Counties: History, Landscape, Geology, Fossils, Minerals, Industry, and Routes to Travel. Olaf P. Jenkins, ed. Bulletin 154: Division of Mines. (San Francisco: California Department of Natural Resources, 1951.) Illus. A gold mine of information.

How to Fish the Pacific Coast: A Manual for Salt Water Fishermen. Raymond Cannon. (Menlo Park, Calif.: Lane Publishing Co., 1964.) Illus. Not only the how-to, but the fish themselves in great detail, for reference and identification.

The Living Land: An Account of the Natural Resources of British Columbia. Roderick Haig-Brown. (New York: William Morrow & Co., 1961.) Illus. Authoritatively but popularly presented by a noted author.

Lower California Guidebook: A Descriptive Traveler's Guide. Peter Gerhard and Howard E. Gulick. 3rd ed. (Glendale, Calif.: Arthur H. Clark Co., 1962.) Illus., maps. The most comprehensive and detailed Baja guide; all roads, places, mileages, much local history.

A Natural History of Western Trees. Donald Culross Peattie. (Boston: Houghton Mifflin, 1953.) Illus. More than a guide: to be read for pure pleasure.

Plants of the Oregon Coastal Dunes. Alfred M. Wiedemann, La Rea J. Dennis, and Frank H. Smith. (Corvallis, Oreg.: O. S. U. Book Stores, 1969.) Illus. A regional guide which describes the formation and ecology of these great dunes.

Rancho La Brea: A Record of Pleistocene Life in California. Chester Stock. 6th ed. (Los Angeles: L.A. County Museum, 1963.) Illus. A detailed and documented account.

Shore Wildflowers of California, Oregon, and Washington. Philip A. Munz. (Berkeley & Los Angeles: University of California Press, 1964.) Illus. Has many full-color photographs of living plants.

GLOSSARY

Aleutian Low: an area of low atmospheric pressure prevailing seasonally in the northeastern Pacific region.

alluvium: a deposit of sand, mud, etc., formed by flowing water.

arborvitae: any of several pine trees of the genus *Thuja,* of North America and eastern Asia.

archipelago: a group or cluster of islands.

arroyo: a small steep-sided watercourse or gulch with a nearly flat floor; usually dry except after heavy rains.

arthropod: any segmented invertebrate of the phylum Arthropoda, having jointed legs and including the insects, arachnids, crustaceans, and myriapods.

atoll: a ring-shaped coral reef or a string of closely spaced small coral islands, enclosing or nearly enclosing a shallow lagoon.

autumnal equinox: the time in the fall (about September 22) when the sun crosses the plane of the earth's equator, making night and day of equal length all over the earth.

bar: a long ridge of sand, gravel, or other material near the surface of the water at the mouth of a river or harbor entrance.

barranca: a steep-walled ravine or gorge.

basalt: the dark, dense igneous rock of lava flow or minor intrusion, composed mainly of labradorite and pyroxene and often displaying a columnar structure.

batholith: a large body of igneous rock, bounded by irregular, cross-cutting surfaces or fault planes, and believed to have crystallized at a considerable depth below the earth's surface.

bedrock: unbroken solid rock, overlaid in most places by soil or rock fragments.

berg: a large floating mass of ice, detached from a glacier and carried out to sea.

berm: the nearly flat portion of a beach, formed of material deposited by the action of the waves.

bog: wet, spongy ground, with soil composed mainly of decayed vegetable matter.

browse line: line marking the upper reach of a browsing animal (deer, etc.) in cropping foliage and twigs from shrubs and trees—very noticeable in brushlands with sizable deer populations.

bryozoan: any marine or fresh-water animal of the phylum Bryozoa, which forms branched, encrusted, or gelatinous colonies of many small polyps, each having a circular or horseshoe-shaped ridge bearing tentacles.

cambium: a layer of delicate tissue between the inner bark and the wood, which produces all secondary growth in plants and is responsible for the annual rings of trees.

chubasco: local name for violent, usually sudden windstorms that strike the west coast of Mexico, especially the area where the Gulf of California opens to the Pacific.

cinder cone: a conical hill formed by the accumulation of volcanic debris around a vent.

conglomerate: anything composed of dissimilar materials or elements.

conifer: any of chiefly evergreen trees or shrubs (of the gymnospermous order or group Coniferales or Coniferae), including the pine, fir, spruce, and other cone-bearing trees and shrubs; also includes yews and their allies which bear drupelike seeds, or stone fruits.

continental borderland: a land region bordering a coast and influenced by the ocean climate.

continental shelf: a comparatively shallow submarine plain forming a border to a continent, often several hundred miles in width.

Cordilleran Ice Sheet: the glacial covering of the western mountain regions of North America during the Great Ice Age.

current: the part of a fluid body (as air or water) moving continuously in a certain direction.

deadwood: the heartwood, or layers beneath the growth layer under the bark, of a tree.

deciduous: shedding the leaves annually, as trees, shrubs, etc.

detritus: small particles of rock or other material worn or broken away from a mass, as by the action of water or glacial ice.

diaspore: a mineral (consisting of aluminum hydroxide, $HAlO_2$), occurring in crystals or in platelike or scaly masses.

dinoflagellate: any of chiefly marine, plantlike organisms of the order Dinoflagellata, which are important elements of plankton and the marine food chain.

downwarp: the bending downward of crustal formations.

drift: the component of the sea's movement that is due to the force of wind and currents.

Eastern Pacific High: an area of high atmospheric pressure prevailing seasonally in the central eastern Pacific region.

echograms: recordings of ocean soundings, produced by means of sound waves bounced off the bottom by surface devices.

ecosystem: a system formed by the interaction of a community of organisms with their environment.

endemic: restricted to or native to a particular locality, as in plant or animal life.

escarpment: a long, precipitous, clifflike ridge of land or rock, commonly formed by faulting or fracturing of the earth's crust; also *scarp.*

estuary: that part of the mouth or lower course of a river in which the river's current meets the sea's tide.

exoskeleton: a protective outer covering, often hard, as the shell of crustaceans, the scales and plates of fishes, etc.

fault: a break in the continuity of a body of rock, with dislocation along the plane of fracture.

faunal district: a region characterized by certain types or groups of animals, appreciably different from those of adjacent regions.

feldspar: any of several crystalline minerals (consisting mainly of aluminum silicates), usually glassy and moderately hard; one of the most important constituents of igneous rocks.

firn-basin: the place where a glacier starts forming.

fold: a portion of strata which is folded or bent, or which connects two horizontal portions of strata of different levels.

granite: a very hard igneous rock, usually gray or pink (consisting mainly of crystalline quartz, feldspar, and mica).

granodiorite: a granular igneous rock (consisting essentially of plagioclase feldspar and hornblende in combination with granite).

guyot: a flat-topped seamount, or submarine mountain, found chiefly in the Pacific Ocean (named after Arnold H. Guyot, Swiss-born American geologist and geographer).

gymnosperms: plants whose seeds are exposed or naked, not enclosed in an ovary; example: the conifers.

heartwood: the hard wood at the core of a tree trunk.

ice cap: a large permanent ice sheet, sloping in all directions from the center.

igneous: produced under conditions involving intense heat, as rocks of volcanic origin or rocks crystallized from molten magma.

igneous intrusion: the introduction of molten rock material between or among layers or masses of solid rock.

intrusive: having been forced, while molten or plastic, into openings between layers of rocks.

isostatic equilibrium: a state of equal weight or pressure in adjacent areas of the earth's crust.

kelp dock: a floating mass or "raft" of certain giant marine algae, which are anchored to the bottom by holdfasts at the ends of long tubular stems.

krummholz: the effect of strong winds in gnarling, twisting, and "pruning" trees and shrubs (German: "crooked wood").

lee side: the side that is sheltered, or turned away from, the wind.

lichen: any of a large group of mosslike plants, consisting of algae and fungi growing in close association in patches on rocks and tree trunks.

limestone: any stone consisting wholly or mainly of calcium carbonate.

live glacier; dead glacier: a glacier is said to be "alive" when it is still gaining new material or mass and moving outward from its point of origin; it is "dead" when it gains no increment and ceases to move outward or downslope.

loam: a rich soil containing a relatively equal mixture of sand and silt and a smaller proportion of clay.

magma: molten material beneath or within the earth's crust, from which igneous rock is formed.

mantle: the layer of rock material just below the outer layer or crust of the earth.

maritime: of or pertaining to the sea.

massif: a compact portion of a mountain range, containing one or more summits.

meltwater: water from melted snow or ice.

microclimates: locally differing climatic conditions within an area or region (e.g., a cool, moist climate on the north side, and a warm, dry climate on the south side, of the same mountain).

minus tide: a low tide below "tide zero" or the average level of low tide in an area.

mixed tides: characterized by unequal highs and lows in the two daily tides.

moraine: a ridge, mound, or irregular mass of boulders, gravel, sand, and clay, transported in or on a glacier.

mustelid: any of numerous carnivorous mammals of the family Mustelidae, such as weasels, martens, skunks, badgers, and otters.

Nevadan system: certain western mountain areas whose rock material, origin, and development apparently coincide with those of the Sierra Nevada. The overall event is called the Nevadan Revolution, or major mountain building period.

nudibranch: shell-less, marine snail of the suborder Nudibranchia, having external respiratory appendages on the back and sides.

nunatak: a hill or mountain that has been completely encircled by a glacier.

Pacific Flyway: a major route of migratory birds that follows the West Coast of North America.

peat: a highly organic soil, more than 50 percent combustible, composed of partially decayed vegetable matter found in marshy or damp regions, which is cut and then dried for use as fuel.

phytoplankton: the plant organisms in plankton.

pitch: the sap or crude turpentine which exudes from the bark of pines.

plankton: the minute animal and plant life found drifting in a body of water.

playa: the sandy, salty, or mud-caked flat floor of a desert basin having interior drainage, usually occupied by a shallow lake during or after prolonged, heavy rains.

pressure system: a temporary condition, but usually of some duration and thus affecting weather conditions during a period of time, characterized by a certain range of low or high atmospheric pressure.

ptarmigan: any of several grouses of the genus *Lagopus*, of mountainous and cold northern regions, having feathered feet.

quartz: one of the commonest minerals (silicon dioxide, SiO_2) having many varieties which differ in color, luster, etc., and occurring either in masses (as agate, bloodstone, chalcedony, jasper, etc.) or in crystals (as rock crystal, amethyst, citrine, etc.).

radiocarbon dating: a laboratory process that determines the approximate age of certain materials, based on the knowledge of the fixed rate of radioactive disintegration of the element carbon.

rain forest: a forest that owes its exceptional growth and density to extremely heavy rainfall (as on the Pacific Northwest Coast).

rain shadow: a region of reduced rainfall to the lee side of high mountains.

red tide: the discoloration of sea water (usually red or yellow) by a "population explosion" within one or another of certain groups of plankton organisms.

refugium (plural: *refugia*): area not denuded of life by some happening, such as glaciation, from which organisms later spread to repopulate adjacent denuded areas.

Roaring Forties: either of two areas in the ocean between 40° and 50°N or S latitude, noted for high winds and rough seas.

saltation: intermittent, leaping movement of particles of sand or gravel, as from the force of wind or running water.

salt pan: an undrained natural depression in which water gathers and leaves a deposit of salt upon evaporation.

seamount: a submarine mountain rising several hundred fathoms above the floor of the sea but having its summit well below the surface of the water.

seismograph: an instrument which measures and records the vibrations of earthquakes.

shoal: a place where a sea, river, or other body of water is shallow.

silt: earthy matter, fine sand, or the like, carried by moving or running water and deposited as a sediment.

slate: a fine-grained rock formed by the compression of clay, shale, etc.

slip face: the lee side of a dune where the slope approximates the angle of repose of loose sand, generally 32–35 degrees.

snout: the leading face or front of a glacier.

snowline: the line, as on mountains, above which there is perpetual snow.

snowpack: an upland field of naturally packed snow that melts slowly.

sounding: act or process of measuring depth, or examining the bottom of a body of water, with a lead and line; **soundings:** depths of water determined by a lead and line.

spindrift: spray swept by a violent wind along the surface of the sea.

spit: a narrow point of land projecting into the water; also *sandspit*.

stack: a column of rock isolated from a shore by the action of waves.

subcrustal convection current: a force below the surface of the earth which causes the flow or shift of material.

tannin: any of a group of astringent vegetable compounds (as the reddish compound which gives the tanning properties to oak bark) that are used chiefly in tanning, dyeing, and making ink, and in medicine as astringents.

taproot: a root having a prominent central portion growing vertically downward, and giving off small lateral roots in succession.

Teratorns: huge, condor-like flying birds, the remains of which are found in La Brea and other tar pits and fossil sites. They have been extinct since the Pleistocene epoch.

terrace: a nearly level strip of land with a

more or less abrupt descent along the margin of the sea, a lake, or a river.

tide zone: the vertical area of a shoreline between the lowest low tides and the highest high tides of an area.

tombolo: a sand bar connecting an island to the mainland or to another island.

troposphere: the inner layer of the atmosphere, varying in height between about six and twelve miles, within which there is a steady fall of temperature with increasing altitude and where nearly all cloud formations occur and weather conditions develop.

trough: any long depression or hollow, as between two ridges or waves.

tule fog: heavy inland ground fog, occurring during certain combinations of atmospheric conditions.

uplift: an upheaval that raises a part of the earth's surface above the surrounding area.

upwarp: a very broad arch of rock with gently dipping sides that results from uplift.

upwelling: the rise of colder sea water from near the offshore bottom, replacing the warmer upper layers.

water table: the depth below which the ground is saturated with water.

wave shock: the force or pressure exerted by heavy waves upon shoreline formations or organisms.

windward side: the side toward, or exposed to, the wind.

Wisconsin Ice Sheet: the glacial covering over the mid-continent during a certain period of glacial history (named for its central area).

xeric: adapted to a dry environment.

zone marker: an organism predominant in a certain tidal zone; an indicator of that zone.

zooplankton: the animal organisms in plankton.

PICTURE CREDITS

INDEX

Fairbanks

A L A S K A

Yukon River

Kuskokwim River

ALASKA RANGE

× Mt. McKinley
20,320

Wrangell Mts.

Chugach Mts.

•Anchorage

Cook Inlet

C O A S T   M O U N T A I N S

St. Elias Mts.

MIDDLETON I.

Mt. Fairweather ×
15,320

Juneau •

Sitka •

ARCHIPELAGO
ALEXANDER

Ketchikan •

Prince Rupert • Skeena R.

BRITISH CO

Bristol Bay

Alaska Peninsula

Alaska Peninsula

KODIAK I.

Gulf of Alaska

QUEEN
CHARLOTTE
ISLANDS

Queen
Charlotte Sound

P   A   C   I   F   I   C

VANCOUVER
ISLAND

CAPE

O

160°

50°

45°

40°

155°

150°

145°

140°

35°

135°